# Medieval Cultures in Contact

FORDHAM SERIES IN MEDIEVAL STUDIES
H. Wayne Storey, Series Editor

The Fordham Series in Medieval Studies (FSiMS) was founded to promote monographic studies, editions, and collections of essays devoted to a wide variety of medieval topics. The Series' primary interest is in methodological diversity and innovation in fields evermore under-represented in Anglophone academic presses. Its fields of inquiry include material, textual and manuscript culture, the linguistic and literary cultures of the medieval world, historical studies based particularly on new or newly-interpreted documentation, and editions of works that contribute to the re-evaluation of historical and literary documentation.

# Medieval Cultures in Contact

*Edited by*

RICHARD F. GYUG

FORDHAM UNIVERSITY PRESS
New York
2003

Copyright © 2003 by Fordham University Press
All rights reserved
LC 2003040868
ISBN 0-8232-2212-8 (hardcover)
ISBN 0-8232-2213-6 (paperback)
ISSN 1542-6378
Fordham Series in Medieval Studies, no. 1

Library of Congress Cataloging-in-Publication Data

Medieval cultures in contact / edited by Richard F. Gyug.
   p.  cm.—(Fordham series in medieval studies,
ISSN 1542-6378 ; no. 1)
Includes bibliographical references and index.
  ISBN 0-8232-2212-8 (hardcover : alk. paper)—
ISBN 0-8232-2213-6 (pbk. : alk. paper)
  1. Civilization, Medieval.  2. Europe, Western—Civilization.
3. Europe, Western—Social conditions.  4. Europe, Eastern—
Civilization.  5. Middle Ages—Historiography.  6. Christianity
and other religions.  7. Europe, Eastern—Social conditions.
8. Europe—Territorial expansion.  I. Gyug, Richard, 1954–
II. Series.
CB351.M3922   2003
909.07—dc21                                    2003040868

# Contents

Introduction     vii
    *Richard F. Gyug*

### PART 1: CULTURES IN CONTACT

1. Bilingual Philology in Bede's Exegesis
   *Carmela Vircillo Franklin*     3

2. Conversion or the Crown of Martyrdom: Conflicting Goals for Fourteenth-Century Missionaries in Central Asia?
   *James D. Ryan*     19

3. Speaking for Others: Imposing Solidarities on the Past. The Case of Venetian Crete
   *Sally McKee*     39

4. The Church of Dubrovnik and the *Panniculus* of Christ: Relics between East and West (and Men and Women) in Medieval Dalmatia
   *Richard F. Gyug*     59

5. Medieval Europe and its Encounter with the Foreign World: Late-Medieval German Witnesses
   *Albrecht Classen*     85

6. Dreams and Visions: A Comparative Analysis of Spiritual Gifts in Medieval Christian and Muslim Conversion Narratives
   *Linda G. Jones*     105

7. Venetian Commerce in the Later Middle Ages: Feast or Famine?
   *Alan M. Stahl*     139

8. *Quidam de Sinagoga*: The Jew of the *Jeu d'Adam*
   Jennifer R. Goodman — 161

9. Minstrel Meets Clerk in Early French Literature: Medieval Romance as the Meeting-Place Between Two Traditions of Verbal Eloquence and Performance Practice
   Evelyn Birge Vitz — 189

## Part 2: Teaching Cultures in Contact

10. Team Teaching the Literature of the European and Islamic Middle Ages: The European Perspective
    Kathryn L. Lynch — 213

11. Team Teaching the Literature of the European and Islamic Middle Ages: The Islamic Perspective
    Louise Marlow — 223

    Appendix. Sample Syllabus (English 315/Religion 365): Images of the Other in the European and Islamic Middle Ages
    Kathryn L. Lynch and Louise Marlow — 232

12. Center and Periphery in the Teaching of Medieval History
    Teofilo F. Ruiz — 247

    Appendix. Sample Syllabus (UCLA: History 121D): Crisis and Renewal: From Late Medieval to Early Modern, 1300-1525 — 257

Contributors — 273

Index — 275

# Introduction

## *Richard F. Gyug*

FOR MUCH OF THE TWENTIETH CENTURY, the study of medieval society was identified with the study of Europe in the high medieval period. It had a few themes known to all: courtly society, feudalism, manorialism, the age of faith, scholastic learning, Gothic art, the new romances, and the like. There were well established introductory and transitional topics, such as the end of Rome, the settlement of barbarians in the west, the beginnings of Europe under the Carolingians, or the disasters of the fourteenth century. Almost all these topics are concerned with western Europe and describe its society. Nonetheless, the western emphasis of Chaucer's *Canterbury Tales* or Henry Adams' *Mont Saint Michel and Chartres* (1904) has been balanced in the learned imagination by Marco Polo's *Il Milione* or Washington Irving's *Legends of the Alhambra* (1832). An interest in the world outside the west has been part of defining the bounds of medieval society, which has meant that as long as there have been medieval studies there have been debates about topics such as antagonism or exchange with the Islamic world, the west's debts to Byzantium, European expansion during the Crusades, or trans-Saharan bullion flows. The present essays grow out of such traditional themes of European identity and its relations with others, but they pose new questions about medieval cultures in contact and view the topic from different perspectives. First, the starting point is no longer exclusively European, but often begins with other cultures, or with European groups formerly considered peripheral. Secondly, the emphasis is now on the meeting of cultures as a source of change.

Considerations of the relations between medieval Europeans and other societies have taken several forms in the past. Some have treated the question as secondary. For instance, in the debate about whether feudal society was the product of internal structural developments in the tenth and eleventh centuries, or originated in local responses to the ninth- and tenth-century Viking, Arab and Magyar incursions, neither school attached much importance to the culture of the invaders. Nationalist concerns meant that any discussion of cultural influence was contentious. In Spanish historiography of the Franco era, for instance, Américo Castro's claim that Spanish identity was formed from the living-together, the *convivencia*, of Muslims, Christians and Jews was countered by the arguments of Claudio Sánchez Albornoz and others that Spain's essential character was evident before the Arab invasion and persisted in the Reconquest's drive for unity. In English history, the nineteenth-century debate between A. E. Freeman and J. H. Round over the relative influence of resident Saxons or invading Normans on modern England resonated in the works of their successors through much of the twentieth century.

Nationalism aside, medievalists have often been open to explaining European developments as the result of external influences. Lynn White's work on scientific innovation and its social effects is an example in which the adoption of particular inventions or techniques came together in unique western circumstances to become eventually the west as we know it. Étienne Gilson and the students of scholastic thought gave credit to Islamic learning for its preservation of Greek thought. More recently Peter Dronke and Thomas Binkley have argued for the influences of Arabic love poetry and music on western courtly literature and music. Nonetheless, in each case the topic has been the development of northwestern European society.

The problem is particularly marked in considering the Islamic world, the great antagonist in western medieval histories from the eleventh century to Henri Pirenne. Works such as Edward Said's *Orientalism* (1978) have alerted scholars to the divide between the religious concerns of Muslim scholars and the western secularism of an earlier generation of European orientalists. The latter saw the former as unscientific and insular, while Muslim scholars now consider the orientalists to have been apologists for imperialism. The critique of the orientalists was not that they sought external explanations for European events, as was the case with some of the medievalists noted above, but that they posed irrelevant western questions about non-western topics.

More recently, the study of non-western societies for their effects on the west has changed to consideration of societies as separate and worth studying on their own. Such an approach is basic to comparative literature or the social sciences, the latter often beginning with independent case studies in order to arrive at general conclusions applicable to several societies. A similar respect for the internal histories of groups peripheral to the traditional view of medieval society has created a view of the western medieval past with many aspects, dissolving in particular the notion of a single western European society. With the increased interest in non-western groups in the own right and the recognition of multiple European perspectives, the study of cultures in contact is no longer limited to European contact with one group or another, with Europeans the common ground in each encounter.

The approach to cultures in contact running through several essays in this volume is that the meeting of cultures promotes historical change in the original societies and creates new hybrid societies at the point of contact. Of course, change can occur without the influence of cultural contacts, but the present essays are concerned with cultures in contact. They argue by their example that medievalists can search for understanding through comparisons. This approach recognizes the intrinsic interest in the study of individual cultures and does not deny internal agency. Most of the essays go, however, beyond comparison, which need not be historical or reflect any causal association between the compared items. They demonstrate that meaningful change is often a product of cultural contacts, and that the medieval world was rich in the meeting of cultures. Although the idea has been treated in the past, as the examples above show, it has rarely been as central an approach as it now is. And it has rarely been allowed to stand on its own, as many of the present papers assume it must.

As a separate issue from the role of cultural influences on the societies of the medieval west, several papers study the cultures formed at the points of contact. It is a commonplace with its own traditions that border societies and cultures are different and interesting due to their position: frontier societies have meant self-reliance, independence, and virtue bred of conflict and necessity to scholars such as Charles Julian Bishko writing on the Iberian Christian peasants on the frontier with Islamic Spain. One of the lessons of the essays in this volume is that there are many other models, and many other ways to consider cultures in contact and the changes arising from such contacts.

In the first section of this volume, several essays consider the meeting of two cultures, or the reactions within one culture to many meetings. Several examine the effects on the imagination within a culture long after contact, and the contacts between disparate elements within a culture that thought itself undivided. Some analyze cultural contacts that give rise to new identities, or act as the formative influences on cultural development. The locales, periods and protagonists are as varied as the approaches. They include the origin of western Christian culture in Bede's England, the contact of east and west in the Islamic and Asian worlds, the western perceptions of the east in German literature, and Mediterranean studies, an area where the meeting of cultures was prominent. The relations between the Christian majority and the culture of the Jewish minority in northwestern Europe, and the interaction between the occupational cultures of minstrels and clerics are considered. The second section of the volume presents two models for teaching cultural contacts in the middle ages: one discusses the need to recognize such interactions as part of medieval history, and two linked essays show how literary diversity has been treated in practice.

The first essay in the first section, Carmela Vircillo Franklin's article, "Bilingual Philology in Bede's Exegesis," examines an aspect of the new culture formed from the meeting between classical and Christian Mediterranean cultures and those of the Germanic and Celtic north.

Most of the essays in the volume deal with the high and late medieval periods when travel, interchange and a sense of European identity were well established. In the later periods, European identity and its limits had forms with recognizable ties to early modern and modern attitudes. In the early medieval period, however, the world was different. The relations to a Roman past, the first thoughts of what Christian society implied, and the growth of local societies meant that thoughts about other cultures were cast in different forms.

Franklin's subject is one of the critical figures in this early period, the Venerable Bede. An Anglo-Saxon living a form of life, monasticism, developed in late-antique Egypt and sixth-century Italy, learned in Latin literature and Christian patristics far from the lands that had created both, Bede's formation and education repay consideration for what they can tell us about the adoption and adaptation of cultures. Bede's history of his people was an ecclesiastical history, which presents religious development in terms of the meeting of cultures and the triumph of Roman Christianity. The issue in the essay is Bede's reading of the Bible, and his careful commentaries on it. In 679-680, Ceolfrith, the abbot of Wearmouth-Jarrow, had brought from Italy to the monastery a great pandect, or one-volume Bible, containing the Vetus latina translation from Greek. As part of what Bede describes as a self-conscious creation of a Roman church in England, over the next generation the monks of Wearmouth-Jarrow prepared new pandects based on a different source, Jerome's Vulgate translated from Hebrew and Greek, but incorporating their own scholarship. Bede's philological exegesis, in the tradition of Augustine, found rich materials in comparing the Latin translations from the different sources, and in contrasting them with biblical quotations in patristic works. In his later work, Bede also compared the Latin text with Greek originals, but it is his inquiries through layers of sacred scripture that reveal his relation to distant cultures he sought to make his own.

The second theme in the volume, presented in essays by James Ryan, Sally McKee, Richard Gyug, Albrecht Classen and Linda Jones, are the relations between the medieval west, formed from the meeting of earlier cultures, and its neighbors. James Ryan's essay, "Conversion or the Crown of Martyrdom," examines missionary activity, an instance of a self-conscious meeting of cultures. Although several essays in the volume argue that cultures were complex and communities could be defined in many ways, religious allegiance was a principal form of communal identification for many groups throughout much of the medieval period. There were many separate linguistic or ethnic cultures in the Christian west, but Crusades and missions were two forms of cultural contact in which western Europeans presented themselves as Christian and one. This was a definition based on an evangelical imperative and fostered by legends of missionary zeal in preaching to pagans in northern and western Europe during the early medieval period. Ryan argues, however, that it was the rise of Islam and the expectation of conflict formed during the Crusades that shaped later attitudes of the west toward religious contact, even when the circumstances differed.

Ryan's topic is the relations between fourteenth-century Christian missionaries and the cultures they encountered in the Chaghatai Khanate of Central Asia. The failure of the mendicant missionaries to leave many traces either at home or in Asia was the result of the attitudes they brought to their vocation. The experience of the Crusade period and the long-standing Islamic prohibitions against Christian proselytizing had taught the missionaries to expect challenge and conflict. Thus, wherever missionaries went, they went prepared to die as martyrs. Despite their heroic efforts, they were ill-equipped for any other reception, and unable to adapt when faced with such. Convinced of their superiority and bracing to defend it at any cost, they appear to have learned little from the lands they visited, and neither the west nor the east shared in the exchanges typical of some of the cultural contacts considered in the other essays.

The mendicant missions to Asia were striking and unusual points of contact between cultures, as were the Crusades that formed their model. More universal, and applying to cultures beyond the medieval west, were contacts arising through conquest and colonization, a topic addressed in Sally McKee's essay, "Speaking for Others: Imposing

Solidarities on the Past. The Case of Venetian Crete." Although the issue is colonization, characterizations of the medieval west based on Crusades and missions has meant that religious allegiance is often taken as a defining element in such contacts. The relations between Venetians and Cretans have been discussed, therefore, in terms of religious-ethnic divisions, in which the preservation of ethnic identity was a cause of Cretan resistance. Contrasting the definitions presented in official records with the arrangements revealed in notarial instruments, McKee questions such analyses, and challenges one-dimensional notions of identity. Medieval polemicists, like their modern descendants, relied on relational terms to define ethnic identity: a group is defined by its boundaries with other groups. In official records and narrative travelogues, Cretans appear as hostile to the ruling Venetian minority. On the other hand, notaries recorded facts, or at least decisions, without the overt purpose of narratives or proclamations. In notarial registers, Cretan nobles, who in narrative sources lead the resistance and are always Greek, are seen in marriages with Venetians and in many acts of accommodation. Confrontation and tension were as likely to exist along the division between noble and peasant, or rural and urban dwellers, as between Cretan and Venetian. The root of the problem with modern descriptions of these complex relations lies in anachronistic applications of modern notions of identity and ethnicity to medieval culture. The hard and fast boundaries between groups familiar from simplified nationalist presentations are not to be assumed for medieval cultures.

A similar question of identity formation is posed in my essay, "The Church of Dubrovnik and the *Panniculus* of Christ: Relics between East and West (and Men and Women) in Medieval Dalmatia," which concerns internal problems of assimilation and solidarity in a city straddling several cultural boundaries. Societies and cultures existing in border zones were places for the meeting of cultures, and for the definition of cultures in both exclusionary and inclusive terms. Medieval Dubrovnik lay between the Slavic east and the Latin west, between Orthodoxy and Catholicism. The community was a polyglot entrepot for trade between the Balkans and Italy, and home to several linguistic and religious cultures, including two groups of Roman Catholics, one using the Latin liturgy and the other using the vernacular Glagolitic liturgy. Nonetheless, later Ragusans of the Renaissance stressed the medieval city's harmony and stasis under a patrician elite proud of its Latin roots and Roman Catholicism. We can see this harmony as a fiction covering tensions resolved out of the public eye, especially since the legends recorded by later Ragusans point to several public conflicts based on the problems of assimilating the city's diverse population. The conflict analyzed in the essay concerns the nuns of S. Simeon who were custodians of the cloth used by Simeon the Prophet to hold the infant Christ at the Presentation in the Temple. The cloth brought miracles to women suffering difficult births until it was used to help a Serbian princess visiting Dubrovnik. This breach of Catholic solidarity led to a decline in the relic's efficacy, and eventually its seizure by the commune and translation to the cathedral. In this episode we see a hegemonic response to the problems of assimilation, one perpetuated by Ragusans in an attempt to preserve their small republic lying between larger societies.

The question of whether and to what extent the medieval definition of culture was tied to religious identity is considered also in Albrecht Classen's essay, "Medieval Europe and its Encounter with the Foreign World: Late-Medieval German Witnesses," in which Classen examines late medieval German literature for its treatment of outsiders. A common assumption has been that the structures, beliefs and values of western medieval society were closed, intolerant and suspicious of others, both those without, and several groups within, such as Jews, heretics and women. Thirteenth-century authors and audiences could, however, be intrigued by, attracted to, or tolerant of the distant foreigner. Wolfram von Eschenbach is shown to have been a noteworthy idealist who ignored race and downplayed religious identity in favor of universal human virtues, especially the chivalric virtues. In the nearly-contemporary epic *Herzog Ernst* (ca. 1220), the anonymous author describes a traveler who sees the mythical east in positive terms, except during moments of conflict. Later in the thirteenth century, Ulrich von dem

Türlin continued Wolfram's emphasis on humanistic tolerance: although the Saracen princess in his tale ends up converted and there is no doubt about Christian superiority, the Saracens are courtly and virtuous. In other words, difference need not be negative in itself, and ignorance of Christianity is not a vice. Classen asks whether similar views were held after the fall of Acre in 1291, or whether the closure of the east led to changes in values. The answer is that tolerance remained common: about 1300, the anonymous author of the crusade epic *Reinfried von Braunschweig* was still influenced by Wolfram's tolerant treatment of non-Christians. Early works continued to be copied and revised. In the popular printed adaptation of *Herzog Ernst*, the east became a sensational element, a means of attracting an audience through an emphasis on difference and distant without religious connotations or any trace of crusader antagonism. Even where the rhetoric of crusade and conflict survives, as in the anonymous chapbook *Fortunatus*, the events of the work stress adventure amid exotic courts, not eternal hatred.

Conquest, colonization, crusade and exchanges in border regions are obvious topics in considering medieval cultures in contact. A different approach, taken in Linda Jones's essay, "Dreams and Visions: A Comparative Analysis of Spiritual Charisms in Medieval Christian and Muslim Conversion Narratives," is the comparison of genres in different cultures. Such comparisons have the potential to raise questions about the structural roots of common practices, the possibility of shared origins, and the rationales for divergent practices. It was such commonalities or differences that impressed those who encountered cultures other than their own. The autobiographical conversion narratives of Christians and Muslims considered by Jones are sources in which definitions of culture could play a large role, because the narratives are concerned explicitly with leaving the world of one culture and entering another. Conversion narratives are also striking for their immediacy and their concern with profound experience. Although the Muslim and Christian traditions of conversion narratives developed independently, in both traditions the intensity of such changes of conviction marked them as divine in origin, best expressed in dreams and visions. Despite the personal nature of conversion, the common goal of instruction means that both traditions use rhetorical devices and formulaic elements. The formulas differ, however, in each culture. Thus, Christian authors address the narratives to God or the Virgin Mary while Muslims address their co-religionists. More significantly, the Christian authors associated conversion with confession and redemption, whereas the Muslims list God's blessings and the parallels between their lives and the life of the Prophet Muhammad. Such differences highlight the different expectations of the narratives' audiences. Similarities in the accounts, such as the use of dreams and visions to signal and describe inspiration, suggest that although there are few indications of common origins or direct influence between Muslim and Christian narratives, they both stand within a post-classical tradition that assigned priority to a spiritual world.

Most of the essayists consider themes of identity and cultural formation in terms of religious identity, but economic rationales such as those considered by Alan Stahl in his essay, "Venetian Commerce in the Later Middle Ages: Feast or Famine?" often provided the context for contact. The missionaries described by Ryan were not merchants, but they were near contemporaries of merchants such as the Polos who traveled the same routes. The patricians of Dubrovnik in my essay used their religious identity in support of security and commerce. Venetian Crete analyzed by McKee was part of a trade empire. Even the monastic world of Bede had close ties to growing Anglo-Saxon kingdoms drawing wealth from a north-sea trading zone. That religious authors left more eloquent and self-conscious reflections on cultural identity is not to deny the importance of social and economic contacts. Indeed, the exchanges of traders, migrants and merchants were probably more influential in the long term than the cultural contacts of their religious contemporaries. With trade came circumstances that could affect cultures, including residency in foreign lands, legal accommodations between diverse systems, the recognition of common interests, and, of course, conflict. Economic relations are, therefore, the context for such issues as the revolutionary contacts made by Iberian voyagers of the fifteenth century and the contacts made during the European expansion of the high medieval period, of which the Crusades were only a part.

The reform of the Venetian mint in 1417 and the failure of the reforms are Stahl's starting point in demonstrating changes caused by changes in trade and its financing. In the early fifteenth century, Venetian trade was growing, but silver and gold imports for the Venetian mint were declining. The failed reform was an attempt to re-establish the supply of coins needed to pay for goods, especially spices, in the Levant. The shortfall in metal imports appears to have been made up by developing new trade in the west and carrying more goods, especially textiles, from Europe to the east. Contrary to Doge Mocenigo's famous deathbed oration, which is probably spurious (as Stahl has shown elsewhere), expansion in Europe was the basis for the ongoing success of Venetian trade in the east.

The essays described above examine contacts between cultures associated with ethnic, religious or linguistic groups from different regions, a definition of culture based on the nineteenth-century identification of a nation and its people. The divisions within western European society also provide grounds for the meeting of cultures, as is demonstrated in essays by Jennifer Goodman and Evelyn Birge Vitz. Goodman's essay, "*Quidam de Sinagoga*: the Jew of the *Jeu d'Adam*," considers the interplay between literary works and their audiences, and the tension between cultural divisions and demands for assimilation. Near the end of the twelfth-century Anglo-Norman *Jeu d'Adam*, the prophet Isaiah is challenged by an anonymous speaker coming out of the synagogue. The play has presented many problems, including difficulties in localizing it and analyzing its structure. The brief intervention of *quidam de sinagoga* has not hitherto received much attention, but Goodman argues that it is central to the play's purpose. The scene and the play make full sense only when an audience including Jews is posited. Casting aside the assumption of a uniform Christian audience, an assumption which lies behind the literary criticism of most works in the western vernaculars, opens new windows on the purpose and structure of the play. The Jew's resistance and hostility to Isaiah can now be seen as the true moment of catharsis. The vernacular could provide the means of communication suitable for a mixed audience with a common daily language but distinct learned languages, Latin and Hebrew. The possibility of a mixed audience resolves the question of the play's localization in favor of northern France, where there were suitable Jewish communities. It also fits the context of twelfth-century Christian proselytizing and disputations. The Christian author does not demonize the Jews, but considers them incomplete Christians in need of persuasion in order to make them repent. For the dramatist, a division in medieval culture is healed by defining away the history of the minority to make it part of the majority's religious viewpoint.

Within medieval society, classes, occupations or genders could also be divided into groups with distinct cultures and common experiences. Culture is, of course, a term broad enough to include group identities of many sorts. Confrontation, misunderstanding, exchange and interdependence are not confined to meetings between diverse ethnic groups, as Evelyn Birge Vitz makes clear in her essay "Minstrel Meets Clerk in Early French Literature: Medieval Romance as the Meeting-Place Between Two Traditions of Verbal Eloquence and Performance Practice," an analysis of the relations between two professions in medieval France. Minstrels and clerics had much in common: both were attached to courts, addressed the same courtly audience, and sought to entertain their patrons. They were, however, distinct in training and were considered distinct by themselves and others, with clerics claiming literacy and authorship, and the minstrels performance, as their branches of entertainment. Usually the creation of romance is ascribed to clerics, but Vitz argues that romance was a product of contact between the clerics and minstrels in the setting of twelfth-century courts. Clerics wrote the romances, and minstrels performed them before audiences. Romances were not intended for silent reading. Their clerical authors were guided, therefore, by the needs of minstrels, who collaborated in the work of art as performance. The case is supported by instances from French and Anglo-Norman court circles of literate minstrels reading clerical works of other genres and probably composing the works they performed. There were also clerics writing works in which oral sources are cited and the conventions of courtly performance are kept in mind. The collaboration between the cultures of cleric and minstrel united clerical learning and the skills of minstrels to create a hybrid work – romance – unlike what either culture had produced before.

The second section of the volume examines how the lessons of the many cultural contacts discussed in the earlier essays could be used in classrooms. The topic of cultural contacts is fundamental for medievalists, whose period of study includes, for instance, the origins of medieval societies in the post-classical world, the expansion of the new medieval religions, Islam and Christianity, the meeting of cultures around the Mediterranean, and the interplay of cultures within medieval society. Medievalists interested in teaching such topics are faced, however, with texts and curricula shaped by national histories, communal histories, and the traditional vision of a unified western European culture, all of which are likely to stress continuity, internal change or exclusionary definitions. National histories have further limited the possibilities for teaching cultures in contact by their neglect of other histories, thus leaving students and academics with unbalanced perspectives and gaps in their knowledge of the many parts of the medieval world.

Louise Marlow and Kathryn Lynch in their essays, "Team Teaching the Literature of the European and Islamic Middle Ages," reflect on the difficulties and rewards they have experienced at Wellesley College in teaching a course called "Images of the Other in the European and Islamic Middle Ages." Marlow, writing on "The Islamic Perspective," and Lynch on "The European Perspective" comment on practical concerns: the relation of such a course to their departments and the faculty, the need to demonstrate relevance, the lack of source materials in translation, especially for non-western topics, and the problem of providing students with basic historical and cultural contexts before addressing the literature. Even making comparisons could be challenging when genres differed. Lynch notes, however, that such a course provided fruitful educational opportunities for both students and professors. The latter have often been trained in disciplinary fields, and teach and conduct research in specialized sub-fields. For European medievalists, a term spent reading Islamic literature and travel narratives could shed fresh light on their own fields, as could consideration of the differing theoretical perspectives. One of the great organizational advantages of such a course was its multi-cultural content, which would address many colleges' needs. For the students, the questions of cultures in contact considered in many of the current essays found an ideal place for discussion in Lynch and Marlow's course on the literature of the larger medieval world.

The study of cultures in contact is one of several trends in medieval studies not reflected in an older curriculum, or in texts based on the older curriculum. One goal in teaching medieval subjects is, therefore, to assimilate the lessons learned from the study of cultural change into the curriculum. Teofilo Ruiz addresses this desire in his essay, "Center and Periphery in the Teaching of Medieval History." Ruiz notes that teaching surveys while doing justice to topical research now involves consideration of women's studies, minority cultures and the vast silent majority of medieval people outside the elite. The problem for teachers of surveys has been particularly acute in such practical concerns as the supply of texts and sources. In this case, the medium of instruction is too often at odds with the purposes of the instructors. Ruiz notes that source books, a student's first access to the thoughts and lives of the medieval period, emphasize political, institutional and intellectual history, not the new fields of cultural history. They are also concerned with the center, not the peripheries being considered in cultural contacts. Peripheries when treated at all are poorly integrated adjuncts to the main story. The problem is compounded by the economics of source-book publication, because most texts are reproduced from out-of-copyright nineteenth-century translations, thus ensuring a dated curriculum. Ruiz calls, therefore, for new texts to reflect topical concerns, the integration of the artifacts of medieval society into courses, and the relation of course content to extra-curricular concerns. A model of what can be done at a practical level is Paul Halsall's *Internet Medieval Sourcebook* (www.fordham.edu/halsall/sbook.html): it provides the older translations at no charge and supplements them with translations of works suited to contemporary interests.

The title "Medieval Cultures in Contact" covers a wide range of themes and topics, from the formation of the medieval west in the meeting of cultures, to the contacts between the exclusionary cultures of Christianity and Islam, the problems of identity formation and cultural distinction, and the meeting of diverse classes and groups within western medieval society. The essays share common ground in their emphasis on the creative results possible in the meeting of cultures, the intrinsic interest in studying the margins that define a culture's limits, and the diverse elements in a period often assumed to be unitary. Scholars have long recognized that the culture of western society did not stand alone in the medieval period, but the essays point to ways in which this recognition can be amplified and taught to others.

***

"Medieval Cultures in Contact" is the first publication in the series *Fordham Essays in Medieval Studies*. The general editor of the series, H. Wayne Storey, has been a constant source of encouragement and guidance. He was also the organizer of the Fordham medieval conference "Cultures in Contact" held on March 22, 1997, at which many of the authors presented earlier versions of the essays published here. The executive committee of Fordham's Center for Medieval Studies proposed the series and has provided assistance and advice for this volume. The Graduate School of Arts and Sciences at Fordham generously supported the conference. Of course, it is the enthusiasm of medievalists for their discipline and their commitment to new directions that lies behind the volume and the series. They are its inspiration.

# 1
# Cultures in Contact

1

# Bilingual Philology in Bede's Exegesis

*Carmela Vircillo Franklin*

DURING A VISIT TO ROME IN 679-80, the Anglo-Saxon monk Ceolfrith from Northumbria acquired a magnificent pandect, an entire Bible bound as one volume, and brought it back to England with him, to his monastery of Wearmouth-Jarrow. We now know that the book that Ceolfrith bought in Rome was the so-called Codex Grandior, a pandect written under the supervision of Cassiodorus, the scholar-monk founder of Vivarium, in Calabria in the sixth century.[1] Bibles circulated at this time largely in parts, either as individual books or as group of books – the Pentateuch, for example, or the Gospels generally were bound as independent codices –, and a pandect of this size and quality was certainly unique in all of England. Written in large uncials and comprising ninety-five *quaterniones* or 760 folios, it contained the text of the Latin Bible according to the Old Latin or Vetus latina version, the *antiqua translatio* as Bede who grew up as a monk under the shadow of this book tells us, a version, that is, most strikingly characterized by the Old Testament based not on the Hebrew but on the Greek Septuagint (Meyvaert 1996, 835-839). When, about ten years later, Ceolfrith became abbot of the twin communities of Wearmouth and Jarrow, he undertook a massive effort to prepare a new edition of the Bible. As a result of this endeavor, three complete pandects were copied at the

---

[1] The question of whether the pandect bought by Ceolfrith in Rome is to be identified with Cassiodorus' Codex Grandior has long been debated. Paul Meyvaert's study (1996) proves it conclusively.

scriptorium of Wearmouth-Jarrow. One of these survives intact to this day and is known as the Codex Amiatinus, certainly one of the most magnificent books to have survived from the early Middle Ages, as well as perhaps the largest, at 1030 folios (Marsden 1995, 107-139). The two sister pandects were still in existence at the time of the Reformation, but survive today only in some scraps that were used in bindings (Marsden 1995, 123-129).

The old pandect in the *antiqua translatio* brought from Rome by Ceolfrith served as the model for the format, pictures, script and layout of the new pandects (Meyvaert 1996, 835-839). This is exemplified by the famous illustration in the Codex Amiatinus of a scribe seated and engaged in copying a book, which, in the original picture in the Codex Grandior, was the Codex Grandior itself (Meyvaert 1996, 870-882). In the back there is an open cupboard containing on its shelves nine volumes, most likely one of the Bibles which Cassiodorus describes in the *Institutiones* as being prepared at Vivarium; scattered on the floor lies another much smaller book identified as the smaller pandect containing the Vulgate text and again described in the *Institutiones*, as well as the traditional instruments associated with the work of scribes and illuminators – pens, inks, a compass. In the older pandect the picture portrayed Cassiodorus at work on his bibles; in the Codex Amiatinus, this image has been transformed into a picture of Esdra who is here depicted as a high priest and scribe, responsible for the restoration of the canon of Jewish Scripture by his work as copyist and editor of the scriptural books destroyed during the Chaldaean devastation of Judaea.[2] Such a portrayal of Esdra as a restorer of the Scriptures goes back to the non-canonical 3 Esra, but is found also in patristic literature and must have been seen as an inspiring parallel to the activities at Wearmouth-Jarrow. As Richard Marsden has said, "the miniature makes a compel-

---

[2]This reflects the Septuagint version of the Codex Grandior which contained 3 Esra, the only place where Esra is referred to as *pontifex*. The canonical book of Esra, on the contrary, comprises only our 1 Esra and 2 Esra [=Nehemias] where Esra is referred to only as *sacerdos* and *scriba* (Meyvaert 1996, 873-877).

ling statement about the importance of textual scholarship in the propagation of divine law, an importance which Ceolfrith and Bede would have endorsed" (Marsden 1995, 139).

This picture underscores the landmark scholarly efforts expended at Wearmouth-Jarrow during Bede's lifetime toward the creation of a body of biblical authority. Such an enterprise entailed not only the copying of the Amiatinus, its sister pandects and other biblical codices, but also the textual and scholarly toil which both preceded and followed the copying of the new bibles. It is within this broader framework, this wholesale activity of creating biblical authority at Wearmouth-Jarrow that my remarks must be considered.

While the text in the Codex Grandior was, as Bede recognised, a pre-Vulgate version,[3] the new pandects, it was decided, would contain the biblical text in the "new translation," the version rendered afresh from the Hebrew and Greek originals by Jerome in the fifth century and commonly referred to as the Vulgate. The choice of Jerome's translation as the text to be copied into the three new pandects at Wearmouth-Jarrow has rightly been placed within the "Roman" ideology of the church of Northumbria, solidified after the Council of Whitby in 664. This "Romanitas" was manifested, for example, by the arrival of John the Archcantor of St Peter's Basilica in Rome to teach the Anglo-Saxons how to chant; by the decision by Benedict Biscop, the founder of the twin monasteries, to build the church at Wearmouth not in wood, the traditional building material of the Anglo-Saxons, but in stone "in the Roman manner," and to import glaziers to make window glass and glass vessels. Wearmouth-Jarrow, it was widely known, was a monastic community self-consciously Roman in its outlook, art, liturgy, and script – the codex Amiatinus and its sister pandects were written in "Roman" uncials (Blair 1990, 165-174). The Vulgate was part of this Roman

---

[3] Actually, from Cassiodorus' *Institutiones*, which were not available to Bede, we know that the Codex Grandior's Old Testament text was in Jerome's revision of the hexaplaric text, the Gospels in the Vulgate and the rest of the New Testament most likely in some sort of Old Latin version (Marsden 1995, 130-131).

outlook. Gregory the Great, for example, the most revered figure in the Romanized Anglo-Saxon Church, had chosen it for the *lemmata* of his great commentary on Job, and we know that many of the biblical books that served as models for the Ceolfrithian text were Italian.[4]

There was no single copy that served as the basis for the text of the new bible. Rather, the community of Wearmouth-Jarrow under the leadership of its abbot Ceolfrith undertook the revision and creation of a new biblical text according to a variety of manuscripts. The quality of the text in Amiatinus is not solely dependent on the models available. Richard Marsden has shown, for example, how scholarly efforts at Wearmouth-Jarrow were employed to deal with the very poor exemplars available for Psalms and Tobit. While the result for Psalms are disappointing, the book of Tobit in the Codex Amiatinus shows the hand of skilled textual critics. The three pandects commissioned by Ceofrith represent not a new copy of the Bible but in reality a new edition of the Bible, aptly called "the Ceolfrithian text."

Bede was still a young man when this monumental work on the text of the Bible was conceived in the last decade of the seventh century, for he was born in 672 or 673, and Ceolfrith had become abbot in 688-9. Bede's involvement in this enterprise as it progressed must, however, have been considerable, and is one which still remains to be fully disclosed. In addition, his large body of exegetical writings begun at the latest in the first decade of the eighth century must also be seen as part of the larger biblical program of Wearmouth-Jarrow.

Self-consciously following the model established by the Fathers – one of his recurring self-defining phrases was *patrum vestigia sequens* –, Bede's working methods reveal him as the natural heir of the Late Antique exegetical tradition (McClure 1985, 18). Bede's large exegetical output, addressed to monks, bishops, and one, on the Canticle of

---

[4]Out of eleven manuscripts surviving from England between the fourth and the first half of the eighth century, ten were written in Italy; the eleventh may be African. The importance of Roman uncials in the formation of English writing has also been recognized (Marsden 1995, 110-111).

Habbaccuc, to a nun, presented the patristic tradition in its many aspects. As he says in his letter to bishop Acca of Hexham to whom he dedicated his commentary on Genesis, he wishes to introduce the patristic materials to his Anglo-Saxon brethren.

For the Latin fathers Augustine, Ambrose, Jerome, and to a lesser degree Gregory, the Bible meant not the Vulgate of Jerome as it now very clearly meant at Wearmouth-Jarrow, but rather a version of the Old Latin translation. The many commentaries on the Bible by the fathers were based on biblical versions that in some cases could be very different from the Vulgate. Even the *lemmata* used in Jerome's exegetical treatises are taken from an Old Latin version, not his own Vulgate.

Furthermore, some of the Latin fathers, in particular Jerome and Augustine, certainly the most influential of the patristic commentators, employed a scholarly philological approach to the text of Scripture, not the more narrow, moralizing manner of Gregory and Cassian, for example. The words of Scripture themselves, not the general meaning, carried the weight of much of the patristic exegesis that was important to Bede. In his efforts, therefore, to make the patristic tradition available to his students, Bede placed his textual scholarship in the service of his exegesis. He studied the difference between the old and the new translations, between Latin text and Greek text in some cases (Laistner 1939, xxxix-xl), between different manuscripts of the new versions. He put his erudition in the variations of the language of the Bible to didactic advantage, as Jerome and Augustine had done before him. I would like to illustrate this point by several examples taken from Bede's commentary on Genesis, which, more than any other biblical book in this period, had a rich patristic tradition of exegesis.[5] Augustine alone had discussed this book in its entirety or in part in four major works. Jerome had also treated it, as had Ambrose and Isidore. The creation story in particular

---

[5]My study of Bede's exegetical *opus* is still at its beginning. I have used for the commentary on Genesis Charles W. Jones' 1967 edition (CCSL 118A) which includes an *apparatus fontium*. However, I soon discovered many inaccuracies in the *apparatus*, which therefore cannot be used as a reliable index of Bede's patristic sources.

provided the opportunity for the discussion of nature; the Hexaemeron – the "six days" – was the first and foremost book of science for the early Middle Ages.

PASSAGE I: Gen. 3: 14

VULGATE: super pectus tuum gradieris / et terram comedis cunctis diebus vitae tuae

VETUS LATINA: pectore et ventre repes et erit tibi terra cibus in omnibus diebus vitae tuae

Augustine, *De Genesi Contra Manichaeos* II, 26-27 (PL 34: col. 210): Dicitur ergo huic: *Pectore et ventre repes.* Quod quidem et in colubro animadvertitur, et ex illo animante visibili ad hunc invisibilem inimicum nostrum locutio figuratur. Nomine enim pectoris, significatur superbia, quia ibi dominatur impetus animi; nomine autem ventris, significatur carnale desiderium, quia haec pars mollior sentitur in corpore. Et quia his rebus ille serpit ad eos quos vult decipere; propterea dictum est, *Pectore et ventre repes.*

Ambrose, *De paradiso* xv, 74 (CSEL 32.1: 331-333): *Supra pectus* inquit *tuum et in utero tuo ambulabis.* qui sunt qui in utero suo ambulant nisi qui uentri et gulae uiuunt, quorum deus uenter et gloria in pudendis eorum, qui terrena sapiunt et cibo onerati ad terrena curuantur? ... pectore autem et uentre ait reptare serpentem non tam propter corporis figuram quam quia propter terrenas cogitationes de illa caelesti benedictione sit lapsus; pectus enim frequenter recessus quidam accipitur sapientiae.

Bede, *In Genesim* I, iii, 14 (CCSL 118A: 65): *Super pectus tuum gradieris, et terram comedes cunctis diebus uitae tuae. Super pectus* quippe *grad*itur serpens, quia omnes gressus diaboli nequitiae sunt et fraudes; nam in "pectore" calliditatem et uersutias cogitationum eius indicat, quibus *ad eos quos uult decipere serpit*, pro quo antiqua translatio habet, *Pectore et uentre repes.* Repit autem pectore cum terrenas hominibus, quos sua membra facere desiderat, cogitationes suggerit. Repit et uentre cum eos ingluuie superatos in aestum libidinis excitat. .... Deuorat autem terram cum errore peccantium pascitur ac delectatur, eosque seducens ad interitum rapit. Sicut enim sancti saepe caelorum, ita nomine terrae hi *qui terrena sapiunt*, indicantur, quomodo in sequentibus Adae dicitur, *Terra es et in terram ibis*, quod nostra translatio habet, *Quia puluis es et in puluerem reuerteris*.

This passage describes God's first curse after the Fall, the one uttered against the serpent, to be followed by those against Eve and Adam in the ensuing verses. The basic difference between the Vulgate and the Old Latin translation is that while in the Vulgate God tells the snake that he will "walk" (*gradieris*) on his chest, in the Old Latin he tells him "you will creep on your chest and belly." The textual history of this verse ilustrates the complexity of the Latin bible. The source of the difference in this instance is clear. The Hebrew text here uses a very precise but rare word to indicate the underside of a reptile (Remley 1988, 174). The Greek translation of the Old Testament, the Septuagint, reflects either the precision of the Hebrew or perhaps the ambiguity of the word by using two Greek terms (τῷ στήθει σου καὶ τῇ κοιλίᾳ), and this leads to the Old Latin version, which includes both *uenter* and *pectus*. The Old Latin *pectus et venter*, as is commonly the case, represents a literal translation of the Greek Old Testament, while the Vulgate attempts a direct translation of the Hebrew. As one can see from the passage in *De Genesi contra Manicheos*, the Old Latin text of the Bible provided an irresistible exegetical opportunity to Augustine to stress the duality of sin, originating in both the intellect and carnal desire. The heart or the mind, the *pectus*, is here presented as the spring of one kind of sin – pride, the sin of the intellect, – and the belly as the source of lust or the sins of the flesh. Ambrose, on the other hand, in his *De paradiso* (and one notes how different his Old Latin biblical text is) does not stress the doublet *pectus et venter* or *uterus* in his case; rather he emphasises the typological view of the serpent as *delectatio* or "corporeal pleasure" (just before Ambrose has said that the woman symbolizes our senses, and the man our mind or intellect). Ambrose's discussion further concentrates on the "creeping" to which the serpent is condemned. He introduces the word *reptare* to describe the serpent's crawling close to the ground, and allegorizes the serpent's food, the earth or ground, as "earthly thoughts or concerns." Ambrose pointedly refuses to allegorize the parts of the body. As we turn to Bede's discussion, we note how he, in a manner typical of his approach, integrates both Augustine's and Ambrose's exegesis. Bede retains the apposition highlighted by Augustine and symbolized by *pectus* and *venter*, but his allegorizing of *pectus* privileges Ambrose's accent on worldly thoughts or concerns rather than Augustine's image of the heart as the seat of pride. This is further developed by Bede through his discussion of the verb *repes* which is not singled out in Augustine's exegesis at all, but is found in Ambrose's discussion of *reptare*, as I pointed out. Bede uses this verb and the images it conjures up to relate the fate of fallen humanity with the double quotation of Genesis 3: 19 in both Vulgate and Old Latin. Again, it is the Old Latin translation's use of *terra* rather than the Vulgate's *pulvis* that conveys Bede's exegetical point.

This passage certainly illustrates the synthetic nature of Bede's exegesis; he integrates two interpretations of this verse that might even be described as contradictory. But it also shows the importance of the Old Latin version for Bede's didactic purposes. For the rich patristic exegesis of this verse was centered most starkly on the use of the contrast *pectus / venter* and the image of the snake "creeping" on the ground, all tersely expressed in the Old Latin curse *pectore et uentre repes*. The Vulgate's anemic – if you will allow me – *super pectus tuum gradieris* simply could not bear the weight of the rich and multilayered patristic inheritance that Bede wished to convey through his exegesis.[6]

PASSAGE II: Gen. 4: 25-26.

VULGATE: cognovit quoque adhuc Adam uxorem suam et peperit filium / vocavitque nomen eius Seth dicens / posuit mihi Deus semen aliud pro Abel quem occidit Cain / sed et Seth natus est filius quem vocavit Enos / iste coepit invocare nomen Domini

---

[6]Bede may have consulted an Old Latin version for this biblical verse, or perhaps he relied on Augustine's quotation of the biblical text in his exegesis, contrary to Remley (1988, 175), who was misled by Jones' inaccurate apparatus.

VETUS LATINA: et cognovit Adam Evam mulierem suam et concepit et peperit filium et vocavit nomen eius Seth dicens suscitavit enim mihi deus semen aliud pro Abel quem occidit Cain et Seth natus est filius et nominavit nomen eius Enos hic speravit invocare nomen domini dei.

Bede, *In Genesim.* II, iv, 26 (CCSL 118A: 91): *Sed et Seth natus est filius quem uocauit Enos. Iste coepit inuocare nomen Domini.* Enos interpretatur "homo" uel "uir." Vnde recte qui tale nomen ipse habet, *nomen Domini* incipit *inuocare.* ...Mystice autem sicut Abel occisus a Cain passum Dominum, ita natus pro eo Seth resuscitatum eum a morte designat. Vnde apte apud septuaginta translatores nato eo dixisse fertur pater siue mater eius, *Suscitauit enim mihi Deus semen aliud pro Abel, quem occidit Cain.* Quod ideo recte iuxta mysticos sensus "semen aliud" appellatur, cum idem Dominus qui occisus est, resurrexit, quia nimirum mortalis occisus est, resurrexit immortalis. Mortuus est ne nos mori timeremus; surrexit ut nobis resurgendi a morte spem fidemque tribueret.

The second passage presents Bede's exposition of Genesis 4: 26, that to Seth a son was born whom he called Enos, the first to invoke the name of God. The preceding verse in both the Vulgate and the Old Latin rendering is, however, also important in this discussion. Bede begins by providing the meaning or etymology of the name Enos, which is supplied to him by Jerome's *Hebrew Questions on Genesis.*[7] It is the significance of Enos' name as "man" in Hebrew that launches Bede's next point, namely that if Enos represents humankind as it first addresses God, then his father, Seth, is a *figura* or "type" of the resurrected Christ, the one who generates a saved humankind just as Seth generates Enos. It is in this context that Bede places the discussion of Seth's conception and birth. The Vulgate reads, "The Lord placed (*posuit*) another seed in me in the place of Abel whom Cain killed." But in the Vetus latina we

---

[7] 4, 25 (CCSL 72: 7-8): *Et uocauit nomen eius Seth: Suscitauit enim mihi deus semen aliud pro Abel, quem occidit Cain.* But Jerome cannot be Bede's exegetical source because in his commentary he is interested only in the fact that Seth means *thesis, id est positio. Quia igitur posuerit eum deus pro Abel, propterea Seth, id est positio, appellatur.* Nor does Augustine in *De Ciuitate Dei* XVI, xv which also discusses this passage, provide Bede's material. No other source is cited in Jones' edition.

are told, "The Lord arose/awoke (*suscitavit*) in me another seed in the place of Abel whom Cain killed." *Suscitavit* is the translation of the Greek ἐξανέστησεν, as one would expect for the Old Latin bible. While in patristic exegesis Abel is often portrayed as a type of Christ, the innocent victim who is murdered by his brother, the figuring of Seth as the resurrected Christ is not found in Augustine or Jerome nor in any of the other sources Bede appears to have relied on for this verse. This particular aspect of the exegesis seems original to Bede. As Bede explains further on in this discussion, according to the mystical sense of the Scripture, Abel killed by Cain represents the Lord in his passion, and Seth born in his place represents the resurrected Christ. Enos, the son of Seth, portrays figuratively the human race who is born daily by water and the Holy Spirit through faith and the sacrament of the Lord's passion *and* resurrection. Central to Bede's own interpretation of the biblical verse is the resurrection of Christ for which the conception of Seth becomes a *figura* or metaphor. Hence, the relevance of the word used in the biblical Old Latin *suscitavit*. For while the Vulgate uses the word *posuit* for God's action in the conception of Seth, the earlier translation, "aptly" as Bede says, employs the word *suscitavit* which insinuates the Resurrection. The use of the word *suscitavit* is exegetically more appropriate, for it makes the typology of Seth as the resurrected Christ and of the human race, typified by his son Enos, as the children born out of that Resurrection more philologically precise.

There is also another point that contributes to Bede's discussion, and illustrates his careful philological approach to exegesis. Bede recognizes that either Seth's father or mother, Adam or Eve, could have uttered the words *Suscitavit enim mihi Deus semen aliud pro Abel, quem occidit Cain*. This reading of Bede is clearly influenced by the Vetus latina where *et concepit et peperit* refer to Eve and *et vocavit ... dicens* therefore would also have to refer to her.[8] In the Vulgate, however, the absence of *concepit*, and the use of *-que* to break the parallel with *peperit* make it more likely that it is Adam who is speaking. Bede's

---

[8] This is confirmed by the Greek where *dicens* is in the feminine form – λέγουσα.

identification of the speaker with the woman may also be part of his exegetical interpretation here, for the figure of Eve as the mother of Seth might have been figured by him as Mary the mother of Christ, although nothing explicit is said about this. Augustine in his discussion of this passage in *De civitate Dei* (XVI, xv) assumed that it is Adam who is speaking even though he was commenting on the Old Latin text. Bede's attention to the nuances of the biblical translations and to exegetical concerns permits him on occasions to depart even from Augustine's authority.

PASSAGE III: Gen. 8: 7

VULGATE: (Noe ... dimisit corvum) qui egrediebatur et revertebatur donec siccarentur aquae super terram

VETUS LATINA: (Noe ... emisit corvum) ut videret utrum cessasset aqua et exiens non est reversus donec siccaret aqua a terra

Jerome, *Hebraicae quaestiones in libro Geneseos* 8, 6-7 (CCSL 72: 10): *Post quadraginta dies aperuit Noe ostium arcae, quod fecit, et emisit coruum, et egressus non rediit ad eum, donec siccaretur aqua de terra. Pro ostio fenestra scripta est in hebraeo. Et de coruo aliter dicitur emisit coruum et egressus est exiens et reuertens, donec siccarentur aquae de terra.*

Bede, *In Genesim.* II, viii, 7 (CCSL 118A: 123): *Qui egrediebatur et non reuertebatur donec siccarentur aquae super terram. Non ait egressus est et reuersus est in arcam, sed Egrediebatur,* inquit, *et non reuertebatur donec siccarentur aquae super terram,* quia uidelicet huc ullucque uolatu dubio uertebatur, modo abire incipiens, modo ad arcam uelut intraturus rediens, nec tamen fenestram unde egressus fuerat repetens, sed potius foris uagans usque dum remotis aquis requiem sibi ac sedem extra arcam repperiret. Cuius egressui atque itineri recte comparantur hi qui sacramentis quidem celestibus institui atque imbuti sunt, nec tamen nigredinem terrenae oblectationis exuentes, lata potius mundi itinera quam ecclesiasticae conuersationis claustra diligunt.

My third example is taken from the story of the flood. After forty days, the rain has stopped, and Noah dispatches the raven to see if the waters have subsided from the land. The original text of the Vulgate reads that the raven was sent out and returned while the waters were still drying up on the land. You will note, however, that in the Old Latin translation the raven went out and did not return. The lemma in Jerome's *Hebrew Questions on Genesis* as usual follows the Old Latin version – the raven does not return – but Jerome notes also that the Hebrew says that the raven left and did return. Bede clearly knew of the two contrasting readings and of their respective sources, one in the Hebrew and the other in the Septuagint. He was familiar with Jerome's *Hebrew Questions on Genesis*, which he cites constantly in his own commentary; furthermore, the evidence of the Codex Amiatinus, which originally followed the Vulgate text in the "positive" reading and was then corrected with the addition of *non*, as well as the evidence of other biblical manuscripts connected with the Ceolfrithian text, confirms that the standard Vulgate text available to Bede was in the positive (Marsden 1995, 204-205). In addition, Bede's own emphatic discussion of the unsatisfactory behavior of the raven in his exegesis of the biblical verse betrays his awareness of the textual variation between the Vulgate text and the Old Latin text even as he chooses for his *lemma* the "negative" reading of the old translation. Why does Bede choose the negative verb, following the reading of the Vetus latina, despite the authoritative evidence of the original Ceolfrithian text and Jerome's own note referring to the Hebrew version?[9] The key to understanding Bede's choice is again provided by his understanding and further development of the exegetical tradition. The allegorizing of the ark as the church occupies a central position in Bede's exposition of the story of the flood; it was also central to Augustine's discussion of the flood in his *Contra Faustum*. The window of the ark, Bede instructs his readers in the passage immediately preceding this one, "designates the sacraments of the divine mysteries,

---

[9]Although the fact that Jerome does not say specifically that this is the Hebrew reading, and the fact that his citation does not correspond *verbatim* to the Vulgate version known by Bede might have tempered the weight of the Hebrew authority in Bede's estimation.

by which those who are baptized are initiated.[10] But some use these sacraments for the illicit activities of the world, while some use them for works of piety; the former are figured in the raven; the latter in the dove" – the dove, that is, who is sent next out through the window of the Ark, and obediently returns both the first and the second time (*In Genesim* II, viii, 6 [CCSL 118A: 122]), and who is further allegorized in the discussion of Genesis 8-11.

It is clear that Augustine's *Contra Faustum* (XII, 20)[11] informed Bede's allegory, but the more monastic tinge of this exegesis appears to be entirely his own. While for Augustine the raven who does not return to the Ark after forty days represents those who are seduced by the *immunditia cupiditatis* or heretical Donatists, for Bede the raven who does not return to the Ark is like those who prefer "the wide paths of the world rather than the enclosures of ecclesial *conversatio*." The use of *mundus* here (which is the Vulgate equivalent to the Old Latin *saeculum*), of *claustra*, of *conuersatio* provide a monastic ring to Bede's discussion. This monastic interpretation appears to be original to Bede. For such exegesis to work out the raven could not return to the Ark. In this example, the Old Latin text of the Bible not only is used by Bede to prop up his commentary but even to emend the Vulgate text itself.

It is his understanding of the requirements of exegesis that informs Bede's textual criticism and in some cases, as illustrated by my example of the exposition on the raven, to question and revise the established Ceolfrithian text. Knowing no Hebrew and without, most likely, a Greek version of the Old Testament, Bede engaged in bilingual philology by consulting and comparing the two translations available to him, one from

---

[10]The flood of course is frequently allegorized as baptism by water; the wood of the ark is connected with the wood of the Cross.

[11]*Quod post dies quadraginta emissus coruus non est reuersus, aut aquis utique interceptus aut aliquo supernatante cadauere inlectus, significat homines inmunditia cupiditatis teterrimos et ob hoc ad ea, quae foris sunt in hoc mundo, nimis intentos aut rebaptizari aut ab his, quos praeter arcam, id est praeter ecclesiam baptismus occidit, seduci et teneri* (CSEL 25: 348). But Jones' edition fails to note this in the *apparatus fontium*.

the Greek and the other from the Hebrew. Later in his life, while writing his second commentary on Acts, Bede's exegesis will be further enriched by his close study of the original Greek text of this biblical book. My discussion of these passages does not mean to propose that Bede's exegesis subverts the Vulgate Ceolfrithian text. Rather, as illustrated by his notes on Genesis, Bede wished to transmit and build upon the patristic inheritance, to translate it for a generation whose Bible would have a different language.

## REFERENCES

Ambrose. *De Paradiso. Sancti Ambrosi Opera.* Pars prima. 1896. Ed. Karl Schenkl. Corpus scriptorum ecclesiasticorum latinorum 32: 263-336.

Augustine. *Contra Faustum.* 1891. Ed. Joseph Zycha. Corpus scriptorum ecclesiasticorum latinorum 25: 249-797.

Augustine. *De Genesi contra Manicheos.* 1865. Patrologiae Cursus Completus, Series Latina 34: cols. 172-220.

Augustine. *De Genesi ad litteram libri duodecim.* 1894. Ed. Joseph Zycha. Corpus scriptorum ecclesiasticorum latinorum 28: 1-435.

Bede. *Libri quatuor in principium Genesis.* 1967. Ed. Charles W. Jones. Corpus Christianorum, Series Latina 118A.

*Biblia sacra iuxta vulgatam versionem.* 1969. Ed. Robert Weber, O. S. B. Stuttgart: Württembergische Bibelanstalt.

Blair, P. H. 1990. *The World of Bede.* Cambridge: Cambridge University Press.

Jerome. *Hebraicae quaestiones in libro Geneseos.* 1958. Ed. Paul de Lagarde. Corpus Christianorum, Series Latina 72: 1-56.

Laistner, M. L. W. 1939. *Bedae Venerabilis. Expositio Actuum Apostolorum et Retractatio.* Cambridge: The Mediaeval Academy of America.

Marsden, R. 1995. *The Text of the Old Testament in Anglo-Saxon England.* Cambridge Studies in Anglo-Saxon England 15. Cambridge: Cambridge University Press.

McClure, J. 1985. Bede's *Notes on Genesis* and the training of the Anglo-Saxon Clergy. In *The Bible in the Medieval World. Essays in Memory of Beryl Smalley*, ed. K. Walsh and D. Wood, 17-30. Oxford: Basil Blackwell.

Meyvaert, P. 1996. Bede, Cassiodorus, and the Codex Amiatinus. *Speculum* 71: 827-883.

Remley, P. G. 1988. The Latin textual basis of *Genesis A. Anglo-Saxon England* 17: 163-189.

*Vetus latina.* 2: *Genesis.* 1951-54. Ed. Bonifatius Fischer. Freiburg: Herder.

# 2

# Conversion or the Crown of Martyrdom: Conflicting Goals for Fourteenth-Century Missionaries in Central Asia?[*]

*James D. Ryan*

THE ENTIRE HISTORY of the Middle Ages might be painted in terms of cultures in contact, communication, and conflict. In any such attempt, a central theme would be the spread of Christianity. Beginning in the Roman world, missionaries moved out on every frontier to bring strangers the good news of salvation and to bend them to the Christian ethic. Through missionaries civilization was reshaped as it was preserved; barbarians who threatened to destroy *Romanitas* were won over, through conversion, to the missionaries' altered vision of Roman world order. Few developments loomed as large to medieval commentators, who gloried in the triumph of the gospel over pagan gods. It is important to note, however, that they saw in these events a conflict between cultures, and proof of the superiority of their Christian ethos. Clearly, contact between cultures does not always enhance communication between them.

The special focus of this paper will be Christian missionaries of the fourteenth century and their contact with other cultures within Chaghatai Khanate, in Central Asia. This is but one episode in the story of

---

[*]Research, in the Vatican and other archives, was partially supported by a grant from The City University of New York PSC-CUNY Research Award Program.

evangelization in the High Middle Ages, but an illustrative one. The thirteenth- and fourteenth-century mission effort, which brought Franciscans and Dominicans, many of them erudite and keen observers, to Persia, India and China, as well as to the steppes of Asia, might have been a story of cross-cultural enrichment, of the infusion of new ideas into European and Asian lands, and the development of new cultural constructs. In fact it was not, and when the mission to Asia petered out in the second half of the fourteenth century it left little intellectual legacy. This paper, tracing the evolution of that mission effort, and focusing particularly on the abortive mission to Chaghatai Khanate, will attempt to suggest why the efforts of so many dedicated missionaries had such little result.

A main problem for missionaries arose from the fact that they perceived proselytization primarily in terms of challenge to and conflict with other cultures, and particularly with Islam. This had become an over-arching theme in the wake of Muslim expansion in the seventh century, when major parts of the Christian world were transformed into *dar al Islam*, territory subject to the will of Allah. Christians and other "peoples of the book" were not forced to abandon belief or cult, but they were absolutely forbidden to proselytize. No one could publicly challenge the Prophet, *Quran*, or law of Islam, and violators of that rule were put to death. This effectively stopped mission activity in the Mediterranean world from the eighth through the tenth centuries, but it also created a paradigm for the development of mission activity in Islamic regions. All those who followed the dictates of the gospel to "go ... and make all nations ... disciples: [and] baptize them" (Matt. 28: 19) were at risk, and any Christians who publicly affirmed their faith within Islamic lands might, like the dozens of ninth-century zealots killed by Muslim authorities in Cordoba, have faced martyrdom (Coope 1995). The Islamic prohibition against mission activity also helped shape the European response to Islam, and when Christian communities assumed the offensive at the beginning of the second millennium, their militancy culminated in the first crusade (Erdmann 1977; Fletcher 1997, chap. 9).

In the first century of the crusade movement evangelization was generally subordinated to military and secular considerations. Crusade leaders sometimes secured the surrender of territories by entering into treaties that guaranteed virtual freedom of worship to vanquished communities, causing clerics intent on spreading what they believed to be the true faith to raise complaints. In Germanic expansion against the Bohemians and Slavs, missionary clerics often complained about interference from lay warriors who sometimes made treaties which allowed paganism to be practiced (Erdmann 1977, chap. 3). From the eleventh century forward, as Christian forces occupied newly conquered lands in Sicily, Spain, the Levant, and northern Europe, non-Christians were frequently found in separate, self-administered enclaves, in which, as long as they paid the exactions of Christian overlords, they could practice their faith with little hindrance. Since conversions could not be forced, missionary activity among a captive population was always problematic, but it was impossible without the support of Crusader lords, who often discouraged missionaries because of perceived economic self-interest.[1] This was especially true in the Levant, where missionaries encountered active opposition from Christian lords with Muslim or other non-Christian slaves, because lords feared loss of control over them after conversion (Kedar 1984, 76-78, 146-151, 212-215). In general, mission activity played a subordinate role in the first centuries of crusade activity.

This situation began to change as the thirteenth century dawned, when several factors rekindled enthusiasm for evangelism and allowed the mission to become a distinct activity in its own right. These include the rise of the mendicant religious orders, millenarian expectations which influenced the friars and which they helped excite, and novel opportunities for mission activity created by the rise of the Mongol empire. The papacy did not play a major part in the mission movement,

---

[1]For Spain, see O'Callaghan (1990, 13-18) and Burns (1990, 61-63). For Sicily see Abulafia (1990, 107-111). For the Levant see Kedar (1990, 144-152). For the Baltic region, see Christiansen (1997, 43-49, 69-70).

but assumed a role as it unfolded by incorporating missionary activity into the evolving structure of the Roman church. Before focusing on mission activity in Central Asia in the fourteenth century, it will be necessary to briefly examine each of these elements.

The mendicant orders were chiefly responsible for creating the new mission effort. Living in the world, yet set apart from secular life by vows of poverty, chastity and obedience, friars preached and taught Christian life by example. To this pastoral work they soon added scholarship, joining teaching faculties at Paris and other universities. As they demonstrated dedication and ability, the papacy used them for such varied tasks as legates, ambassadors, inquisitors, and crusade preachers; and when papal attention was drawn to the mission, the mendicants became both generals and foot soldiers in campaigns of evangelization.[2] The Franciscans and Dominicans did not become involved in mission work on papal orders, however. Rather the mendicants' mission activity grew out of their own sense of purpose, as the beginning of the Franciscan mission illustrates.

St. Francis himself had attempted to preach to Muslims on three occasions, despite the risk of martyrdom, and during the Fifth Crusade actually made his way to the Egyptian court, where he preached a sermon to Sultan al-Kamil (Moorman 1968, 24-25, 48-49). In 1219 he dispatched Berard of Carbio and his companions to preach the gospel in the Iberian Peninsula.[3] With the support of Alfonso II, King of Portugal, they made their way to Seville, where their attempt to preach in the main mosque resulted in arrest. Because they railed against "Muhammad and his damnable law" even from their cell, they were sent to Morocco for judgment. There they demanded appointments as chaplains for the

---

[2]For overviews of medieval mission activity, see Fletcher (1997) and Latourette (1938). For Franciscan mission effort, see Simonut (1947), Daniel (1975), and (for their mission activity in Asia Minor and Greece) von Auw (1979). For the Dominicans, see Altaner (1924) and Loenertz (1937).

[3]Berard (also known as Otto Berard and Baraldus) was accompanied by Peter, Odo, Accursio and Adjutus. See *Annal. Fran.* (1897, 15-19 and 579-596), *Acta SS.* (January 16), and Thurston and Atwater (1956, 1: 103).

Sultan's Christian mercenaries, and refused to return to Europe. Their impertinence so infuriated the sultan that, on January 16, 1220, he personally split open their heads (*Acta SS.*, Jan. 16). These five earliest Franciscan martyrs became heroes to their confreres because of their zeal for souls and willingness to embrace martyrdom. St. Francis expressed delight when he learned that Berard and his companions had been martyred: "Now I can truly say I have five brothers" (*Annal. Fran.* 1897, 593). A longing for martyrdom became an essential part of Franciscan *religio*, and a recurring theme in Franciscan missionary activities through the fifteenth century.[4]

It was not until 1235, fifteen years after the deaths of the Franciscan protomartyrs, that the papacy assumed a direct role in the evolving mission. This began when Gregory IX (1227-41) issued *Cum hora undecima*, a mission bull addressed to friars in and on their way to mission fields in Africa and Asia (Fontes 1950, 286-287). The Bull was issued again by Innocent IV (1243-54) in 1245, with slight modifications, and thereafter became the standard bull of mission privilege, continuously reissued through the thirteenth and fourteenth centuries (Muldoon 1979, 36-37). By 1245 its salutation already listed twenty actual and proposed mission lands, including "the lands of the Saracens, ... the Bulgarians, the Cumans, the Ethiopians (*Ethyoporum*), ... the Alans, the Gazarians (*Gazarorum*), the Nubians, Nestorians, Georgians, [and] Armenians" (Fontes 1962, 36). This demonstrates how far afield missionaries had ventured before the papacy began sponsorship of mission activity. In succeeding decades, as the bull was periodically

---

[4]Daniel characterizes longing for martyrdom as "an external expression of ... spirituality encouraged by St. Francis' emphasis on example [and] the supreme example ... signify[ing] the friars' love for their persecutors" (1975, 45). This developed despite a clear awareness, attested to by tracts and treatises written by members of the order, that actively seeking a martyr's death raised significant theological problems. Daniel gives many examples of missionary zeal for martyrdom in Franciscan writings from the twelfth through the fifteenth centuries, including some in which theological problems associated with seeking a martyr's death were examined (1975, 101-127).

reissued, this gazetteer of mission fields was enlarged as missionaries made their way to new territories.[5]

The opening lines of *Cum hora undecima* testify to the importance of millenarian expectations in the mission. "Since the eleventh hour has come in the day given to mankind ... spiritual men [with] purity of life and the gift of intelligence must go forth again to all men and all peoples of every tongue and every kingdom to prophesy because ... the salvation of the remnant of Israel will not occur until ... the fullness of peoples enters first" into the kingdom of heaven (Fontes 1950, 286). Because these words echoed Joachim of Fiore's apocalyptic prophecy (Reeves 1969; Reeves and Hirsch-Reich 1972), the bull struck a particularly responsive chord with Franciscan missionaries (Reeves [1976] 1977, 32-47; Daniel 1975, 20-22; and Burr 1989). It solemnly reminded them of the impending apocalypse, and urged them to hasten it by uniting all Christian communities scattered across the world. Because the missionaries were preparing for the final days, the threat of martyrdom was not a deterrent to their activity, but an encouragement, and the most dedicated among them did not shrink from attempting anything, even the patently impossible.

*Cum hora undecima* was more than a mere rallying cry, however. As it was issued again and again, it gave friars entering new territories extraordinary spiritual powers, some withheld even from bishops in Europe, including reconciliation of heretics and schismatics, and removing irregularities (Muldoon 1979, 36-38). Other bulls complemented *Cum hora undecima* with additional powers. One such, for example, *In apostolicae servitutis*, issued by Nicholas IV (1288-92) gave Franciscans laboring in Tartar lands the authority to absolve any who laid violent hands on clerics, to dispense clerics from irregularities, and to reconcile heretics and schismatics (Fontes 1954, 134). These various

---

[5]In 1288, for example, when Nicholas IV addressed *Cum hora undecima* to Dominican missionaries, the salutation listed three additional peoples, and added the catch-all phrase "other foreign nations of the East not in communion with the Holy Roman Church" (Fontes 1954, 142).

papal bulls armed missionaries for their three related goals: confirming the faith of those already Christian, combating heretics and reconciling schismatics, and conversion of infidels. In this fashion, beginning in the middle of the thirteenth century, a framework was created for new mission initiatives, and by the early fourteenth century Franciscan and Dominican friars had reached the ends of the known world in their quest for converts.

This became possible only after Mongol rulers invited Christian missionaries to enter Asia and work there, in the late thirteenth century.[6] Early papal contact with the Mongols, initiated by Innocent IV (1243-54) on the eve of the First Council of Lyons, had discouraged mission activity.[7] The best known of Innocent's ambassadors, John of Plano Carpini, OFM, returned with haughty letters from Khan Güyük (1246-48), demanding the pope and western kings submit at once and send tribute (Dawson [1955] 1980, 85-86). Another Franciscan, William of Rubruck, entered Mongol territory as a missionary in 1253, but after almost two years spent in Asia concluded that it was "inadvisable for any friar to make any further journeys to the Tartars" (Jackson 1990, 278), both because of harsh conditions he had endured and because the khan refused him permission to function as a missionary (Ryan 1997, 148-149).

This situation changed dramatically less than two decades later, when various Mongol courts either encouraged or allowed friars to work as missionaries. The Mongol prince Hülegü (d. 1265) subdued both Persia and Mesopotamia, but his forces were defeated by the Mamluks at 'Ayn Jalut, Syria, in 1260. Thereafter the Ilkhanate, which governed the regions he conquered, opened diplomatic contact with the pope and

---

[6]For an outline of Mongol history (with an excellent bibliographical study) see Morgan (1986).

[7]For western diplomatic and missionary contact with the Mongols, see Schmieder (1994), Richard (1977), de Rachewiltz (1971), and Soranzo (1930). Good briefer surveys are provided by Bentley (1993, 155-164) and Phillips (1988, 57-140). Primary source collections for these diplomatic and missionary encounters include: Van den Wyngaert (1929), Golubovich (1906-1929), Dawson ([1955] 1980), and Yule and Cordier (1914).

western kings, and gave western missionaries a friendly welcome. In search of allies against Egypt, successive ilkhans dispatched at least eight embassies west between 1263 and 1291, offering military cooperation, subsidies, return of the Holy Land to the Franks, and, finally, pledging to be baptized in Jerusalem after its recovery.[8] The khans of Qipchaq, the Khanate of the Golden Horde, north of the Ilkhanate, routinely gave or renewed *yarliqs*, grants of privilege, to missionaries (Richard 1977, 187). Möngke-Temür (1267-80), for example, exempted "Latin priests which according to custom are called brothers" from military service, corvée, and all forms of tax, and took their churches and bell towers under his protection (Bihl and Moule 1924, 56-58). The Great Khan Qubilai (1260-94) went even further. According to Marco Polo, in 1271 Qubilai invited the papacy to send "a hundred men of learning, thoroughly acquainted with the principles of the Christian religion, as well as with the seven arts, and qualified to prove to the learned of his dominions by just and fair argument, that the faith possessed by Christians is superior to, and founded upon more evident truth than any other" (Komroff 1926, 9). On short notice newly elected Pope Gregory X (1271-76) could supply only two "men of letters and science, as well as profound theologians, ... friars of the Order of Preachers, who happened to be on the spot," whom he dispatched to the khan with valuable presents (Komroff 1926, 11-12). They turned back after arriving in Syria, however, and the call for wise men from the west went unanswered until the papacy of Nicholas IV (1289-92). His letter to the Great Khan, *Gaudemus in Domino* (Fontes 1954, 154-155), was carried to Cathay by John of Montecorvino, and presented, in 1294, to Timür Öljeitü (1294-1307), Qubilai's successor

---

[8]Grousset (1970, 353-371, 397-398) and de Rachewiltz (1971, 150-159). Hülegü proposed a joint Tartar-Christian campaign as early as 1263-64. Abaqa (1265-82) authored three embassies to the papal court, on one of which, during the Second Council of Lyons (1274), three Mongol envoys were solemnly baptized (Setton 1976, 1: 112-118). Arghun (1284-91) sent four embassies west, promising to receive baptism in 1288 (Moule 1926, 114). Hülegü, Abaqa, and Arghun all encouraged western missionaries in Persia-Mesopotamia.

(Dawson [1955] 1980, 226). By the last decade of the thirteenth century western missionaries were at work in all parts of the Mongol empire except Chaghatai Khanate, in Central Asia, where protracted civil wars and weak khans made the situation too dangerous for mission travelers.

Because the opening up of the Mongol world presented such an opportunity for evangelization, one might expect the popes to have engaged in prudent planning and attentive nurturing to foster the spread of the Roman Church in Asia. The fragmentary records that survive, however, demonstrate only intermittent, reactive papal involvement. In the thirteenth century, missionary expeditions to Asia were primarily in response to the arrival of political emissaries, as de Rachewiltz (1971) makes abundantly clear. Similarly, in the fourteenth century, papal action usually followed the arrival of missionary travelers at Avignon, reporting their exploits. At such times the mission and its needs were brought home to the popes, and, by fits and starts, papal responses created a hierarchical framework for the mission in Asia. News of Montecorvino's successes in China − more than 6,000 baptisms, the construction of churches in Khan-baliq, and the conversion of an important Tartar vassal (Dawson [1955] 1980, 224-225) − arrived in 1307. Clement V (1305-14) immediately instructed the Franciscans to select seven friars, who, after consecration as bishops, would carry a pallium to Montecorvino. They were instructed to anoint him archbishop of the newly created see of Khan-baliq, with authority to oversee and organize a hierarchy for the entire Tartar empire (Moule 1926, 182-189). Clement thereby laid the foundation for a new mission strategy for Asia, which subsequent popes built upon over the following decades (Richard 1977, 123-124 and 144 ff.; and Fedalto 1973, 375 ff.). There was no systematic follow-up, however.

Succeeding popes did expand the hierarchy, but only sporadically, through *ad hoc* measures in reaction to newly received reports from the Asian and other mission lands. This was the case in 1318, when John XXII (1316-34) created a second archbishopric, at Sultaniyya, recently designated as capital city of the Ilkhanate. This new see was not created in hope of advancing the conversion of the Mongols in Persia, however, because by 1318 there was no reason to hope the ilkhans might be baptized. Although they continued to show customary Mongol toleration toward missionary friars, they had professed Islam for more than twenty years.[9] The impetus for creating a new archbishopric at Sultaniyya seems to have been the arrival at Avignon of the Dominican William Adam, who had traveled as a missionary in various parts of Asia between 1312 and 1317, and who wrote *De modo Saracenos extirpandi* on his return. Describing various Christian communities in India, on Indian Ocean islands, and in Ethiopia, *De modo* suggested that alliances with Christian peoples east of Muslim dominated territory might set the stage for a renewal of crusading and success against the Mamluks (Richard 1977, 169-172). John XXII's fascination with this concept is clear from the prologue to the bull, *Redemptor noster*, which established the new archbishopric and appointed Franco of Perugia (*de Perusio*, the vicar of the Dominican missionary arm, the *Societas Peregrinantium*), its first archbishop (Loenertz 1937, 137-141). Where we have documentation, it shows a comparable story underlies the creation of other new sees, such as that erected in India in 1330.[10]

Perhaps it could not have been any other way. There was appalling ignorance in Europe concerning conditions in Asia. The distance, the time required for travel, and the utter foreignness of Persia, Qipchaq, India and Cathay were significant impediments to understanding Asia's peoples, politics and problems. The papal court evidenced interest in those lands, and reacted, only when a mission traveler returned from the east. The missions continued to grow, however, without papal oversight,

---

[9] Ghazan (1295-1304), a son of Arghun, had converted to Islam on his accession, and the ilkhans were Muslim thereafter. Ironically, Öljeitü (1304-16), his brother and successor, had been baptized and dubbed Nicholas (in honor of Pope Nicholas IV) about 1291. Öljeitü's son, Abu Sa'id (1316-35), was the last ilkhan (Morgan 1986, 160-162 and 170-173).

[10] When Jordan Catalan returned in 1329 from an extended mission in India he wrote a memoir, preserved as the *Mirabilia Descripta*. John XXII subsequently erected a new episcopal see for *Columbum* (Quilon, India), and appointed Jordan its first bishop on August 9, 1329 (Ryan 1993, 659-660).

through the efforts and enthusiasm of the friars, and by 1330 an anonymous compiler could list forty mendicant convents in the Middle East and Asia; in Qipchaq, Georgia, Greater Armenia, Persia, Mesopotamia, and China (Golubovich 1906-1929, 2: 72).

Part of that growth lay in Chaghatai Khanate, in Central Asia, through which the Silk Route passed. Because of its turbulent history Chaghatai became a mission venue later than other khanates, and had fewer mission outposts. Partly for these reasons, surviving records concerning Mongol politics and the mission are extremely sketchy. Nevertheless, unique documents have survived for Chaghatai which provide a vivid picture of the mission there, and illustrate the character of western contact with other cultures. A review of these documents against the political background of the khanate will illustrate why mission contact had so little impact on either European or Asian cultures in the period under discussion.

Few facts are known concerning the beginnings of mission work in Chaghatai and the ecclesiastical organization established there. Three episcopal sees were set up; at Urgench, where Qipchaq bordered Chaghatai; at Samarqand, in the west; and at Almalyq, generally considered the capital of Chaghatai, in the east. Almalyq was probably the earliest of the three. Although there is no record of when, why, or by whom a bishopric was established there, it was in existence prior to 1328, when Carlino of *"Grassis"* died in Europe, and was memorialized as "bishop of Almalyq" (Golubovich 1906-1929, 3: 343). As will be seen below, events in the khanate in that era may have forced him to flee his see. Before more is said of the see of Almalyq, its incumbents and its martyrs, however, brief outlines of the murky history of Chaghatai Khanate and of the importance of Almalyq are in order.

Chaghatai Khanate, termed the "Middle Kingdom" by some Europeans, included all the territory between the western reaches of the Mongolian desert and the Amu Dar'ya River. Chingiz Khan had conquered the area in the second decade of the thirteenth century and made it the *Ulus*, an appenage, for his son, Chaghatai.[11] The great Central Asian trading centers of Bukhara, Samarqand, and Tashkent lay in its western regions, but Chaghatai and his successors eschewed urban living, preferring the traditional nomadic life which their cousins, the Yüan in China and ilkhans of Persia, gradually abandoned. As a consequence the khanate lacked formal political structure and had no real capital. Almalyq, a way-station on the silk route, served as the major rallying point for the nomadic warriors who ruled there. Over time, as political and military power began to drift west, into the more densely populated areas, *Ulus* Chaghatai became little more than a loose confederation of Turks, Uighurs, Qara-Khitais and Persians (to mention only the chief groups), led by a Mongol minority (Manz 1989, 21-27; Kwanten 1979, 249-250).

Although Islam was the state religion in most of Central Asia before the Mongol conquests, and particularly strong in western Chaghatai, Mongol rule allowed Christianity to enjoy a renaissance throughout the khanate. Like other Mongol khans, Chaghatai's descendants generally endorsed the religious toleration enjoined by the *yasa* (Chingiz' law), which mandated that "the pure, the innocent, the just, the learned and the wise of every people shall be respected and honored."[12] Nestorianism enjoyed a resurgence in eastern Chaghatai, where there were significant Christian enclaves. Mongol toleration did not protect all religious practice, however. Chaghatai and some of his successors persecuted Muslims for following dictates of the *shari'a*, such as

---

[11]Some western documents call Chaghatai *Media imperio*, perhaps reflecting confusion between it and the long-gone empire of the Medes, which encompassed some of the same area (Yule and Cordier 1914, 85 n. 3). Boyle concisely summarizes the reigns of Chaghatai khans (1965, 2: 3-4), based on the genealogical tables in Hambis (1945), but the paucity of sources, brief tenures, and turbulent accessions make Chaghatai's dynastic tree problematic.

[12]No copy of the *yasa* survives, but its contents are reported in Persian and Arabic sources. The passage quoted is the second *yasa* as recorded by Bar Hebraeus, who continued: "Since the Mongols noted among the Christians sincerity and charity they held [them] in early stages of their rule in high esteem" (Bedjan 1890, 411-412).

slaughtering animals by cutting their throats or performing ritual ablutions in running water, because these practices were contrary to the *yasa* (Boyle 1965, 2: 2). Most of Chaghatai's successors were more accommodating to Islam, but toleration continued as the official policy, and when European missionaries entered the khanate in the fourteenth century, Mongol rule prevented Muslims from hindering their preaching or punishing attacks on Muhammad and the Quran. By the third decade of the fourteenth century, however, as religions and ethnic differences began to pull the khanate apart, this situation changed.

Tradition dictated that the khanate should be held by a descendent of Chaghatai, but since the khanate was very unstable politically, and because under Mongol custom inheritance passed not to the eldest son, but to a senior male in the direct line, there were plenty of possible candidates who might be raised to the khanate by disgruntled emirs. Du'a (1282-1306) had reestablished authority over the entire khanate before his death, but as his six sons succeeded one another, central authority in the realm waned. One of these, Eljigidai, favored Christianity during a brief reign (1326). Our chief source concerning Eljigidai is a 1329 letter of John XXII, acknowledging the Dominican envoy, Thomas Mancasola, whom he had sent to Avignon. Mancasola reported the khan's conversion, and subsequently John XXII created a new see at Samarqand on November 2, 1329, naming Mancasola its bishop (Ripoll and Bremond 1729, 1: 187; Richard 1977, 183, 187-188). Long before the new bishop could return with papal greetings and gifts, Eljigidai had been deposed. His successor, Tarmashirin (1326-34), embraced Islam, taking the name 'Ala al-Din, and ushered in a period of persecution. His successor, Buzan, restored toleration in 1334, and authorized Christians and Jews to rebuild their houses of worship, but his reign only lasted a few months. Buzan had received homage from Muslim emirs in Bukhara and Samarqand after he displaced Tarmashirin, but they would not be loyal to his pro-Christian successor, Cangshi (1334-37) who withdrew to the region around Almalyq, in the east. There he welcomed Nicholas, the papal-appointed successor to John of Montecorvino as archbishop of Khan-baliq, on route to Cathay, a destination he never reached. With Cangshi's encouragement, Nicholas tarried long enough to strengthen the mission at Almalyq, and may have installed a Franciscan, Richard of Burgundy, as bishop in that process.[13] We do know that Nicholas built or enlarged the Franciscan establishment there because Benedict XII addressed two letters to Almalyq. One, *Laeti rumores Deo*, thanked Cangshi for giving Nicholas permission "to construct and repair churches, as well as to preach freely"; the other, to nobles at Cangshi's court, thanked them for having donated land for a convent (Wadding 1931-1964, 7: 212-213).

The license to preach was particularly important because it allowed the Franciscans to confront Islam aggressively, without suffering the consequences of the outrage their words provoked. The experience of Pascal of Victoria, known to us only through a letter he sent west from Almalyq in 1338 (Yule and Cordier 1914, 81-88), amply illustrates the audacity of the missionaries. Pascal had entered the Mongol world at Tana in 1334, first spending a year in Sarai (in Qipchaq), where he learned Turkic. Leaving there with only a native servant as companion, Pascal traveled to Urgench in the company of Armenians and Muslims. There, because "the emperor of the Tartars had been slain by his natural brother, ... the caravan ... was detained for fear of war and plunder" (Yule and Cordier 1914, 86), stranding him in the Muslim quarter. Pascal took advantage of these circumstances to preach before the mosque for twenty-five days on the "cheats, falsehoods, and blunders of [the Muslim's] false prophet" (Yule and Cordier 1914, 87). The disorder of imminent civil war notwithstanding, he enjoyed license to preach, and although he was beaten he was not otherwise molested, and continued on to Almalyq, an arduous journey which, according to Pegolotti's *Description of Countries*, usually took three months (Yule and Cordier

---

[13] So Richard conjectures (1977, 163). As he notes (1977, 155), when Clement V created the see of Khan-baliq, he gave the holder of that see power to determine the distribution and appointment of bishops in the vast realm of the Tartars. Although that authority was somewhat curtailed by the creation of an Archbishopric at Sultaniyya in 1318, Almalyq remained in the province of Khan-baliq.

1914, 147-148). During that time, "constantly alone among the Saracens [he wrote], by word and act and dress, I publicly bore the name of the Lord Jesus Christ." Despite his conduct, he arrived at Almalyq safely (probably in 1336) to take up residence with friars already there.

Pascal's narrative vividly conveys his single-minded otherworldliness as a missionary. Asking his brethren at home for prayers, and vowing to stay in the East until his death, Pascal explained the importance of the mission: "For [Christ] hath said that when the Gospel shall have been preached throughout the whole world, then shall the end come, and it is for me to preach among divers nations ... to declare the way of salvation." Pascal fully expected "[for] the forgiveness of my sins, and that I may safely reach the kingdom of Heaven," "to suffer [for God's] name" (Yule and Cordier 1914, 88).[14] Friars like Pascal seem to have believed that their preaching was more liable to result in their own translation into paradise, as martyrs, than in the conversion of their auditors. As events at Almalyq demonstrated, martyrdom was a realistic prospect for missionaries in Asia.

A great deal is known about the fate of these missionaries because, after their deaths, their confreres compiled their *passio*, a record of their sufferings, and preserved it in their memory.[15] According to this *relatio*, the mission at Almalyq flourished briefly under Khan Cangshi. One of the friars, Francis of Alexandria, won the khan's gratitude by removing a cancer from him, "more by prayer than by physic," and was put in charge of the education of his seven-year-old son, whom the friars baptized Johannes (Yule and Cordier 1914, 32). But Cangshi was poisoned in 1337, and his four sons killed, events which led to the accession of Ali Sultan (1338-39), another convert to Islam, in the next

---

[14] The phrases quoted are out of order, but the meaning has not been changed.

[15] Various versions of the *relatio* of the martyrs' suffering exist, all apparently based on the reports circulated in Franciscan convents after their deaths. An authoritative text can be found in Van den Wyngaert (1929, 1: 510-511). Yule translates a version of the passio found in Bartholomew of Pisa (Yule and Cordier 1914, 31-33), that deviates only in small detail from that printed in Wadding (1931-64, 7: 255-256). It was also included in the Chronicle of the 24 Generals (*Annal. Fran.* 1897, 530-532).

year. Ali allowed a new wave of persecution, "order[ing] that all Christians should be made Saracens, and that whoever should disobey ... [would] be put to death" (Yule and Cordier 1914, 32). The convent was sacked and burned, and seven who refused Islam, including Bishop Richard, Pascal, and their companions, were slaughtered.

This was not the end of the story of this mission outpost, however. Ali Sultan was in turn deposed by Kazan (1339-46), whose rule was restricted to eastern Chaghatai (which thereafter became known as Mongholistan). There he restored some stability, and only one year later a papal embassy led by John of Marignolli, the last western witness to events in Almalyq, was warmly received there and allowed to preach freely.[16] "There we made a church [Marignolli wrote], bought a site, made fonts, sang masses and baptized many" (Yule and Cordier 1914, 225). When Marignolli's party left Almalyq for Cathay, they probably left some of their number to hold the ground in Chaghatai. Unfortunately, little else can be confidently stated concerning the mission at that site. There is no record of successor bishops for the see, and no firm evidence of a continuing Franciscan presence there (Richard 1977, 164; Rondelez 1951, 1-17).

*Summary*

This paper illustrates the scope, nature, and the limitations of mission interaction with Asian cultures in the High Middle Ages. It provides a snapshot of the extensive mission movement carried out by mendicant friars who toiled and died in foreign lands in the thirteenth and fourteenth century. They achieved few of their larger aims. They did not convert the Mongols or others to their faith, and the cultural evolution that attended such conversions in other times did not occur. Factors that made their efforts possible have been outlined, and the paper suggests

---

[16]Marignolli helped lead a papal delegation to China, dispatched in response to the arrival of ambassadors from the Yüan court who requested a successor for Archbishop Montecorvino. See Ryan and sources cited therein (1997, 158-160).

why they were frustrated. Such a brief account cannot create appreciation of the remoteness of the areas they traveled through, however, and their reports are so matter-of-fact that they mask the utter isolation missionaries must have felt. They were impelled to venture forth by their faith and their hope of achieving salvation. But that very expectation, and the methods they used to achieve their goals, seem to have negated chances for long-term success. Their eagerness to court martyrdom moved them to liminal regions and into contact with new and strange cultures, but they were neither receptive to nor appreciative of those other cultures, and blind to the fact that their methods prevented communication with peoples they were so eager to reach. In the final analysis, in Chaghatai Khanate as in other Asian mission lands, there was contact but little communication, and, perhaps tragically, neither Asia nor Europe was lastingly enriched or stimulated by the mission experience of this era.

REFERENCES

Abulafia, D. 1990. The End of Muslim Sicily. In *Muslims Under Latin Rule 1100-1300*, ed. J. W. Powell, 103-133. Princeton.
*Acta SS.* = *Acta Sanctorum quotquot toto urbe coluntur*. 67 vols. 1643-1940. There have been three editions, the most recent Paris, 1863-70. Entries to this work are cited herein by the date of the feast.
Altaner, B. 1924. *Die Dominikanermissionen des 13. Jahrhunderts*. Habelschwerdt.
*Annal. Fran.* 1897. *Annales Franciscorum*. Vol. 3: *Chronica XXIV Generalium Ordinis Minorum*. Quaracchi.
Bedjan, P., ed. 1890. *Gregorius Bar Hebraeus. Chronicon Syriacum*. Paris.
Bentley, J. 1993. *Old World Encounters*. New York and Oxford.
Bihl, M. and A. C. Moule. 1924. Tria nova documenta de missionibus F M Tartariae Aquilonaris. *Archivum franciscanum historicum* 17: 55-71.

Boyle, J. A. 1965. Caghatay Khanate. *The Encyclopaedia of Islam*. New Edition. Leiden. 2: 3-4.

Burns, R. I. 1990. Muslims in the thirteenth-century Realms of Aragon: Interaction and reaction. In *Muslims Under Latin Rule 1100-1300*, ed. J. W. Powell, 57-102. Princeton.

Burr, D. 1989. *Olivi and Franciscan Poverty: The Origins of the Usus Pauper Controversy*. Philadelphia.

Christiansen, E. 1997. *The Northern Crusades*. New edition. London and New York.

Coope, J. 1995. *Martyrs of Córdoba: Community and Family Conflict in an Age of Mass Conversion*. Lincoln, Nebraska.

Daniel, R. E. 1975. *The Franciscan Concept of Mission in the High Middle Ages*. Lexington, Kentucky.

Dawson, C. [1955] 1980. *Mission to Asia*. Originally published 1955 as *The Mongol Mission*. London. Reissued by Medieval Academy Reprints for Teaching. Toronto.

de Rachewiltz, I. 1971. *Papal Envoys to the Great Khans*. Stanford.

Erdmann, C. 1977. *The Origin of the Idea of Crusade*. Trans. M. W. Baldwin and W. Goffart. Princeton.

Fedalto, G. 1973. *La chiesa latina in Oriente*. Vol. 1. Verona.

Fletcher, R. 1997. *The Barbarian Conversion*. Berkeley and Los Angeles.

Fontes. 1950. Pontificia Commissio ad redigendum Codicem Iuris Canonici Orientalis (P.C.R.C.I.C.O.) Ser. 3, vol. 3: *Acta Honorii III (1216-1227) et Gregorii IX (1227-1241)*. Ed. A. Tautu. Vatican City.

———. 1954. P.C.R.C.I.C.O. Ser. 3, vol. 5, book 2: *Acta Romanorum Pontificum ab Innocentio V ad Benedictum XI (1276-1304)*. Ed. F. Delorme and A. Tautu. Rome.

———. 1963. P.CR.CiC.O. Ser. 3, vol. 4, part 1: *Acta Innocentii PP. IV*. Ed. M. M. Wojnar. Rome.

Golubovich, G., ed. 1906-1929. *Biblioteca Bio-Bibliografica della Terra Santa e dell'Oriente Francescano*. Vols. 1-5. Quaracchi.

Grousset, R. 1970. *The Empire of the Steppes*. Trans. N. Walford. New Brunswick, New Jersey.

Hambis, L. 1945. *Le chapitre CVII du Yuan che*. Leiden.
Jackson, P., trans. 1990. *The Mission of Friar William of Rubruck*. Introduction and notes by P. Jackson and D. Morgan. London.
Kedar, B. 1984. *Crusade and Mission: European Approaches toward the Muslims*. Princeton.
———. 1990. Subjected Muslims in the Frankish Levant. In *Muslims Under Latin Rule 1100-1300*, ed. J. W. Powell, 135-174. Princeton.
Komroff, M., ed. 1926. *The Travels of Marco Polo*. Revised from Marsden's Translation. New York.
Kwanten, L. 1979. *Imperial Nomad – A History of Central Asia 500-1500*. Philadelphia.
Latourette, K. S. 1938. *A History of the Expansion of Christianity*. 7 vols. Vol. 2: *The Thousand Years of Uncertainty*. New York.
Loenertz, R. 1937. *La Société des frères pérégrinants: étude sur l'orient dominicain*. Rome.
Manz, B. F. 1989. *The Rise and Rule of Tamerlane*. Cambridge.
Moorman, J. 1968. *A History of the Franciscan Order from its Origins to the Year 1517*. Oxford.
Morgan, D. 1986. *The Mongols*. London.
Moule, A. C. 1926. *Christians in China Before the Year 1500*. New York.
Muldoon, J. 1979. *Popes, Lawyers and Infidels*. Philadelphia.
O'Callaghan, J. 1990. Mudejars of Castile and Portugal in the twelfth and thirteenth centuries. In *Muslims Under Latin Rule 1100-1300*, ed. J. W. Powell, 11-56. Princeton.
Phillips, J. R. S. 1988. *The Medieval Expansion of Europe*. Oxford.
Richard, J. 1977. *La Papauté et les missions d'Orient au moyen âge (XIIIe-XVe siècles)*. Rome.
Ripoll, T. and A. Bremond. 1729. *Bullarium ordinis fratrum praedicatorum*. Vol. 1. Rome.
Reeves, M. 1969. *The Influence of Prophecy in the Late Middle Ages: A Study in Joachimism*. Oxford.
———. [1976] 1977. *Joachim of Fiore and the Prophetic Future*. New York.

Reeves, M., and B. Hirsch-Reich. 1972. *The Figura of Joachim of Fiore*. Oxford.

Rondelez, V. 1951. Un évêché en Asie centrale au XVIe siècle. *Neue Zeitschrift für Missionswissenchaft*. Schöneck-Beckenried. 6: 1-17.

Ryan, J. D. 1993. European Travelers Before Columbus – the Fourteenth Century's Discovery of India. *Catholic Historical Review* 79: 648-670.

———. 1997. Conversion *vs* Baptism? – European Missionaries in Asia in the Thirteenth and Fourteenth Centuries. In *Varieties of Religious Conversion in the Middle Ages*, ed. J. Muldoon, 146-167. Gainsville.

Schmieder, F. 1994. *Europa und die Fremden. Die Mongolen in Urteil des Abendlandes vom 13. bis in des 15. Jahrhundert*. Sigmaringen.

Simonut, N. 1947. *Il Metodo d'Evangelizzazione dei Francescani tra Musulmani e Mongoli nei secoli XIII-XIV*. Milan.

Soranzo, G. 1930. *Il Papato, l'Europa Christiana e i Tartari*. Milan.

Setton, K. M. 1976. *The Papacy and the Levant (1204-1571)*. Vol. 1. Philadelphia.

Thurston, H., S.J., and D. Atwater, eds. 1956. *Butler's Lives of the Saints* (edited, revised and supplemented). 4 vols. New York.

Yule, H., and H. Cordier. 1914. *Cathay and the Way Thither*. 2nd ed. Vol. 3. London.

Van den Wyngaert, A. 1929. *Sinica Franciscana*. Vol. 1: *Itinera et relationes fratrum Minorum saeculi XII et XIV*. Quaracchi.

von Auw, L. 1979. *Angelo Clareno et les Spirituels Italiens*. Rome.

Wadding, L. 1931-64. *Annales Minorum*. 3rd ed. 32 vols. Quaracchi.

# 3

# Speaking for Others: Imposing Solidarities on the Past. The Case of Venetian Crete*

## *Sally McKee*

IN THE LATE SUMMER of 1367, Tadeo Giustiniani, the Venetian representative in charge of pacifying the island of Crete after a prolonged rebellion begun in 1363, issued a series of proclamations involving insurgents not yet captured. Among the rebels he outlawed figure two Greek Cretans, Sifi Gavala and his mother-in-law Rovithi, both inhabitants of the countryside in the district of Rethimno. Sifi's crime is not specified, but Rovithi's inflammatory words are recorded in the proclamation. She is reported to have said to a fellow Greek Cretan, "Why did you flee from us and from your family? Why did you go with the Latins? Oh, how I wish I had in my hands the eyes of all those who joined the Latins and the eyes of all Latins!"[1] Throughout all the archival

---

*Portions of this article appear in my monograph, *Uncommon Dominion: Venetian Crete and the Myth of Ethnic Purity* (Philadelphia, Penn., 2000).

[1] "Item cum Papadia Rovithi, socrus Sifi Gavali, habitatrix casalis Orthea, districtu Rethimni, insule cretensis, tempore rebellionis et guerre proxime preterite pessima femina extiterit contra honorem ducalis dominationis et status insule cretensis cumque habita triumphali victoria per nostros predessores de grecis rebellibus et proditoribus facta fuerit gratia remissio dicte Papadie Rovithi et ceteris ad gratiam et obedienciam prefate dominationis reddire volentibus suis demeritis non inspectis cumque dicta Papadia Rovithi inmemor et ingrata talis et tante gratie maligno spiritu instigata in suo malo proposito perservans sua fuerit verbis turpibus et enormis in obprobrium danum preiudicium et detrimentum prefate dominationis et status insule cretensis et animo et intentione volendi subvertere mentes et animos aliorum et eos conmovere in rebellione

and literary sources surviving from Venetian Crete, there is perhaps no more eloquent and personal expression of Latin-Greek hostility than the words of this village woman, whom the Venetian authorities condemned *in absentia* to having her own eyes plucked out and placed in her hands, just to drive the lesson all the way home.

It would be very hard indeed to argue that Rovithi was evincing anything other than anti-Latin hostility. And it is hard to argue with all the historians who have subsequently cast the struggles of that island under Venetian rule in ethnic terms. But the resort to ethnic identity as a conclusive explanation for behavior is as unsatisfactory for the past as it is for the present. As scholars, we cannot help but be influenced by the concerns of our age, in which cultural preservation is understandably on

---

prefate dominationis et inter cetera dicere Leoni Calergi, filio quondam ser Georgii dicti Pilea, habitatoris casalis Orthea, qui fuit et est fidelis et obediens dominationi hac verba, videlicet, 'et quare fugiebas et a nobis et a domo tua et quare ibas tu cum latinis? Quod utinam haberem ego in meis manibus occullos erutos omnium illorum qui a nobis recesserunt et eciam latinis iverint et etiam occullos omnium latinorum,' prout de predictis omnibus et singulis et quolibet predictorum nobis constat plena fides ex fama publica precedente et clamosa insinuatione subsequente et ex publicis attestationibus et legittimis aprobationibus inde factis et secutis secundum quod de predictis omnibus et singulis et quolibet predictorum in actis nostre curie plenius continetur. Idcirco nos Tadeus Iustiniani, cretensis provisor, secuti formam iuris et ex vigore nostri arbitrii procedentes contram dictam Papadiam Rovithi nec ipsa nec alii de suis malis verbis et operibus [...] et ne eius demerita transeant inpunita et ut eius pena ceteris sit in exemplum attenta quod ex verbis mulierum ut plurimum omnia mala de mundo proveniunt quibus et hiis similibus ut remedium apponatur in hunc modum. Proferimus, pronunciamus, declaramus et in hiis scriptis solemnialiter condepnamus, videlicet, quod ambo occuli dicte Papadie Rovithi eruantur et erui debeant sibi de capite et quod sic eruti ponantur et poni debeant ei in manibus propriis ut sentiat et sciat quid sit habere in manibus occulos proprios sicut desiderabat et volebat habere in eius manibus occulos omnium fidelium subditorum dominationis tam grecorum quam latinorum ut premittatur et quod dicta Papadia Rovithi perpetuo sit et esse debeat forbannita de tota insula cretensis et de omnibus aliis insulis quod tunc et eo casu debeat igne conburi taliter quod penitus moriatur mandantes predicta omnia et singulis et quolibet predictorum publice proclamari debere in lobio Rethimni et ea inscriptis mitti rectoribus insule ut ea faciant scridari et in actis suarum curiarum ad futuram rei memoriam registrari" (ASV ADC *Banni*, Busta 14bis: 137v n. 48 [5 Sept. 1367]).

the minds of many peoples around the world. There is a wide-spread belief that individual cultural heritages deserve protection in the face of global assimilation to a few dominant cultures. Consequently, the emphasis in discussions of collective sentiments and solidarities of the past has been on the ways in which and to what extent peoples differentiate themselves from others. Few of us have stopped to consider why peoples persist in distinguishing themselves from others and distinguishing among other peoples, perhaps out of a fear that such a question implicitly challenges the desire for cultural survival and the right to self-determination.

Neither why nor how people distinguish among themselves is under discussion here. Rather, I intend to enter a space in between the two questions, in an effort to conceptualize the issue that I believe needs addressing. What concerns me is that the concept of identity is a one-dimensional word frequently employed to represent a three-dimensional reality, and Venetian Crete is a good example of that problem. The concept of identity itself is far too vague to accommodate the enormously complex set of social relationships in which human beings are enmeshed throughout their lifetimes.

Before I step into that middle ground, a few words about Venetian Crete are in order.[2] After the Fourth Crusade, which brought down the capital of the Byzantine Empire and placed it in the hands of western Europeans in 1204, Venice acquired rights to the island of Crete, which it held until the Ottoman Turks captured it in 1669, an occupation that lasted for nearly 460 years. Byzantine imperial authority had largely retreated from Crete by the time Venice took possession of it, and so the resistance met by the Venetian conquerors in making real their claim to the island came less from Byzantine forces than it did from the Genoese, who were also interested in acquiring the island, and from Crete's

---

[2]For a brief overview of the colony of Crete, see McKee 2000 and Maltezou 1991, 21-23. For a fuller, though badly-in-need-of-revision account of Venetian rule, see Thiriet 1959. See Jacoby 1989, 175-221, for Crete within the broader framework of Latin Greece.

indigenous population (Tsougarakis 1988; Borsari 1963, 27-66). In the process of establishing the first settlements, the authorities confiscated land that had once belonged to the Byzantine imperial fisc or was still in the possession of the local Greek-Cretan nobility. It granted the confiscated territory and property to Latin military settlers, known as feudatories, most of whom belonged to branches of Venetian patrician families. In spite of the economic advantages accorded the feudatories, the Latin population, which included artisans and other commoners, was a small minority throughout the colony's existence. The bulk of the island's population remained Greek-speakers, who worshiped according to the rite of the eastern church and who had customs and practices different from those of the Latin population – at least in the beginning of the occupation. In other words, they were Greek-Cretans.

After the conquest, the Greek-Cretan nobility, by then dispossessed of their estates by the new regime, retained little influence, and still less political power. To gain any bargaining power over the Venetian regime their only recourse was to arms. During the thirteenth century and the next, Greek-Cretan nobles, or *archontes*, one by one gained back some of their lands. Some of those families willingly became subjects of the Venetian government; others remained impoverished or left the island (Gerland 1903-4 and 1905-8). Below the status of the *archontes* came the great mass of the Greek-speaking, Orthodox peasantry, most of whom were of servile status under Venetian rule.

That, broadly speaking, is the setting. The best illustration of the limits of the word identity as it pertains to Venetian Crete is to range the sources at my disposal into two conventional groups. On the one hand, there are official and literary sources, in which category I include government deliberations, proclamations and court records, along with chronicles written by Venetian officials who were also members of the metropolis's burgeoning intellectual circles in the fourteenth and fifteenth centuries.³ On the other hand, there are notarial sources; specifically notarial registers into which were recorded formulaic transactions of mostly an economic nature, ranging from bills of sale, and contracts for employment and apprenticeships, to marriage contracts.⁴ The notarial document that is an exception to this arrangement is the will, which embodies both the impersonal formula of a transaction guided by law and the personal inclinations of its maker and, thus, spans both groups of sources. Notarial documents are not traditionally appealed to in discussions of identity in the past. Presumably, it is the intentionality of the first group of sources that gives them greater credibility when it comes to a people's identity. Governments say in their records what they mean to happen and occasionally why. Chronicles and other literary works are expressions of their authors' conscious and unconscious intentions. In contrast, notarial documents display a less obvious intentionality, in that they are witnesses to human actions – what they do, not what they say. They reflect the practice of human lives, as opposed to the theory that human beings are so fond of attributing to themselves and their actions. Notarial sources, moreover, have the unappreciated advantage that they can, through cautious study, display the material basis of the social and political changes appearing after the fact in official and literary texts, an advantage that comes from the tradition that actions speak louder than words. In this case, they present a picture of Cretan colonial society at odds with the one that emerges from the diplomatic and literary sources. This discrepancy is the area in between the question of why and how peoples differentiate amongst themselves that deserves attention.

The first group of sources, the official and literary, show that ethnic categories in Crete operated on two levels: the official and the popular.

---

³For descriptions of the contents of the Archives of the Duke of Candia (ADC), incorporated during the nineteenth century into the State Archives of Venice (ASV), see Gerland 1899, and Tiepolo 1973. For a list of chronicles, see Thiriet [1954] 1977.

⁴The protocols of the notaries working in Candia during three of the four centuries of Venetian rule have been incorporated into the Notarial Archive of the State Archives of Venice (Tiepolo 1973, 89).

The Venetian colonial authorities lent official status to the term "Latin" when it applied consistently in its courts the rule that a person of Latin descent was by definition free. This policy ran counter to the position of other powers around the Mediterranean and of Roman law, which directed that the juridical condition of a child follow that of the mother. But in Venetian Crete, until the 1340s, any villein or slave who was able to prove Latin paternity gained his freedom (McKee 2000, 124). In response to the number of cases involving claims to juridical Latinity that that rule provoked, thereafter the government arbitrarily closed off that avenue. The official categories of "Latin" and "Greek" appear to have been consistent with how the island's inhabitants, both colonizer and colonized, viewed themselves. Private documents, such as wills made by Latins and Greeks, reveal both nobles and commoners employing ethnic categories. The adjectives "Greek" and "Latin" appear frequently in connection to the church rite in which testators wished to be commemorated after death. One Greek testator wished to reward a female relative if she married a Greek man (McKee 1998a, 2: n. 399).Thus, there is no question at all that the public authorities and the population thought in terms of ethnic membership and used labels to designate themselves or others. To take them at their word, however, would be to miss the whole point about ethnicity and its unsatisfactory service as a definitive explanation for behavior. Furthermore, the subject of ethnicity is an example of how particular kinds of sources lend themselves to certain kinds of answers.

To illustrate this last point more concretely, an excerpt from a fifteenth-century travelogue about Crete shows how problematic it can be when a source is taken uncritically at face value. In the first quarter of the fifteenth century, Cristoforo Buondelmonti, a Franciscan priest from Florence, spent many years in the Aegean and wrote descriptions of his travels there, which were very popular in Italy and western Europe, to judge from the surviving manuscripts and the number of translations into other languages made of them in the fifteenth century (Van Der Vin 1980, 1: 133-135; Weiss 1960). The first, *Descriptio insulae Cretae*, was written in 1417, after at least two extended visits to the island. Buondelmonti's primary purpose in writing this work was to describe the classical sites in which he, as a man with humanist interests, took delight. Connected to those interests was his further intention to describe the geography of the island, and indeed, the earliest manuscripts were accompanied by a collection of maps, one of the earliest of its kind (Van Der Vin 1980, 1: 137).[5]

Unfortunately, a great deal of confusion obscures the scholarship on Buondelmonti's travelogues (Van Der Vin 1980, 1: 139-140). To begin with, two versions of the *Descriptio insulae Cretae*, one long and the other short, survive. The long version has been judged to be the earlier work, which the author composed not long after his second trip to Crete in 1417. He prepared the second and shorter version some years later. Each version contains substantially the same text, but in the second, he subtracted some information and added new material. Complications arise in the subsequent editions of his works. All editions of Buondelmonti's work since the eighteenth century are based on a small sample of the surviving manuscripts (Cornaro 1755, 1-18, 77-109; Legrand [1897] 1974; Van Spitael 1981). The most recent edition is the most unsatisfactory, since the redactor has chosen to collate from a small sample of manuscripts the long and the short version into one text, without taking into account that they are in effect two separate works.[6] It is impossible, therefore, to tell which material Buondelmonti inserted into his text at what point in time, information which might have bearing on the reliability of his reporting of those he met while in Crete.

In the following excerpt, taken from the least problematic edition of the *Descriptio*, an Orthodox monk is guiding Buondelmonti around a region to the west of Candia, the capital city, at a time when the island had been in Venice's possession for 200 years.

---

[5]Buondelmonti was also responsible for a collection of drawings of Constantinople (Thomov 1996).

[6]An indispensible guide to the pitfalls of Buondelmonti's work, particularly in the Van Spitael edition, is Tsougarakis 1985.

After a difficult road from the other part of Mt Ida, we reached the village of Merona, which was built on the mountain. While I was gazing at an infinity of nut trees and cultivated orchards under the high mountains, a certain monk said: "When our most holy emperor of the world and of the City left your divided and stained church to its errors and confirmed us in the holy orthodox faith, with the support of our highest patriarch, he sent to us Captain Calerghi to protect us against the treachery of your men. This man governed us with such great love and attention to the faith that even today his descendants are considered not just human beings but almost as gods in this land. The whole island is sustained by the expectations we place in them, and so whatever the least of them commands, we are with him as one in spirit and flesh. And so that my lords be not seized by your Franks, they never live in the same place together, but upon the saddle of the mountains of Dicte and Leucos they grow strong together with the greater part of them who reside there. Do you see the plain ornamented with great villages? It is entered through harsh and dangerous passes: exiles of whatever condition seek refuge here. They are led under the protection of Matheo Calerghi and well treated. […]" When he had finished his description of things lying eastward, the monk led me to the house of his lord, who received me graciously on account of our city; and while we spoke of many things in Latin and Greek, we slowly climbed the mountain with his retinue. At the roots of the mountain one hundred springs flow with fresh water, and in this area people now inhabit the vast country properties of the Romans. Hearing this, I eagerly asked the protopapas to explain, and he did so with carefully chosen words: "After Chir Foca subjugated the whole island on behalf of the emperor, the son of the emperor came to this island with twelve of the most important nobles and long-standing residents of the City of the Romans. He granted dominion and land to all these nobles. Then after a long time, now weary on account of continual warfare, they removed to those mountains and today bearing arms and names they have reached such great numbers that if they were all to unite, they could easily take possession of the island. First there are the Ghortazi, or the Saturi, five hundred in number; the Mellisini, or Vespasiani, who are three hundred; Lighni, or Suctiles, who are 1,600; Vlasti, or Painiali, who are two hundred; Cladi, or Ramuli, who are one hundred and eighty; Scodili, or Agliati, who are eight hundred. After a long time two other families came, who were graciously received by those nobles. They are the Arculeades, or Ursini, who are one hundred, and the Colonni, or Colonnenses, of whom about thirty remain and, not being in agreement with the others, they choose to settle near Sithia."[7]

There is a whole host of textual problems here, not least of which is the possibility that Buondelmonti learned from other sources a good deal

---

[7]"Capimus post gravem iter ab alia parte montis Yde rus Meronam, quod in monte erat hedificatum: ubi sic prospiciebam infinitas nucum arbores domesticaque arbusta sub altis videbam montibus, calogerus quidam talia dixit: 'Dum noster sanctissimusque totius mundi atque Polis imperator divisam atque maculatam vestram ecclesiam in suis dimisit erroribus et in sanctam hortodocxamque fidem, mediante nostro summo patriarcha, nos confirmavit, capitaneum Calerghi, ut ab insidiis vestrorum hominum defenderet, ad nos misit, qui in tanto amore atque fidelitate nos gubernavit, quod in hodiernum diem sui descendentes non tanquam homines sed tanquam divinos in terra ista tenentur. Insula tota sub spe ipsorum substentatur et quidquid minimus illorum precipit, presto in anima cum corpore sumus. Et, ut a vestris Franchis mei domini non decipiantur, nunquam in eodem loco insimul habitant, sed supra iuga montis Dicteique Leuci, cum maiore ipsorum qui hic resedit, concorditer convalescunt. Videsne planum cum magnis ruribus ornatum? In eum cum asperisque periculosis vallibus intratur: exules, cuiuscumque condictionis sint, huc convolant et coram domino Matheo Calerghi ducuntur et bene tractantur.[...]' Caloerus, postquam versus orientem omnia dixit, ad domum eius domini me conduxit, qui propter nostram civitatem in sui gratiam me reponit; et dum in latinoque greco multa dicemus, in montem ipse cum suis satrapis lentis gradimur passis, cuius in radicibus centum fontes recentem fluunt aquam, in quibus rura amplissima Romanorum habitant. Ubi talia audivi, avidissimus ut protopapa narraret exoravi, qui libratis verbis sic est orsus: 'Postquam chir Foca ex parte nostri imperatoris insulam totam subiugaverat, filius dicti imperatoris cum nobilibus duodecim principalioribus Romanorum Polis diuque civibus in hanc insulam venit, qui omnibus istis nobilibus dominium et loca concessit; deinde, magno tempore peratto, ex continuis preliis iam fessi in istis montibus conduxere, qui hodie arma et nomen portantes in tanta devenerunt quantitate, quod, si essent concordes, leve eis foret insulam possidere. Et primo sunt Ghortazi, id est Saturi, quingenti in numero; Mellissini, id est Vespasiani, qui sunt trecenti: Lighni, id est Suctiles, qui sunt mille sexcenti; Ulasti, id est Papiniali, qui sunt ducenti; Cladi, id est Ramuli, qui sunt centum octuaginta; Scordili, id est Agliati, qui sunt octingenti. Venerunt denique post longum tempus due alie generationes, qui ab istis nobilibus gratiose recetti fuerunt, scilicet Arculeades, id est Ursini, qui sunt centum, et Colonni, id est Colonnenses, qui fere treginta remanserunt et versus Settiam non cum aliis concordes locum eligere'" (Legrand [1897] 1974, 133-134).

of what he purports to have learned from the locals. His text is littered with Latin tags, specifically and most suspiciously from Book III of the *Aeneid*, where the refugees from Troy mistakenly wind up on the shores of Crete. In spite of problems such as these, more than one historian has argued that Buondelmonti's report is evidence of the survival of Byzantium in the memories of the island's Greek population and constitutes an example of nascent national sentiment among them.[8] This argument rests in part on the premise that with few exceptions the Greek-Cretan nobility was excluded from the economic and social benefits enjoyed by the Latin feudatories, on the grounds that they were Greek. Therefore, the story goes, the Greeks were hostile to Venetian authority and looked with nostalgia to a time when they lived under their true and original leaders.

If all we had were travelogues such as Buondelmonti's, it would be understandable to believe that all Greek-Cretans viewed the Latin-Cretans and the Venetian government as usurpers and oppressors and that a permanent state of tension between Latin and Greek Cretans existed. Indeed the language and terminology of the diplomatic sources encourages that view. For instance, chronicles of Venice's history, written by Venetian patricians who had served the colonial regime in Crete, cast the tensions in the colony almost exclusively in ethnic terms, despite ample evidence of feudatory resentment against the Venetian government. Petrarch, who lived in Venice for a number of years in the

---

[8] E.g., "And so, it is evident that the resentments of archontic as well as ecclesiastic power against the Franks' usurpations are grafted onto the jealously-preserved memory of Byzantium. In conclusion, it is possible to affirm that Buondelmonti served the sentiments of a nobility that had known how to shape the Cretan collective memory for their own political needs, making it an instrument of self-interested defense in the face of the colonial power, but also evidently an instrument of ideological pressure and hegemony over the population in the name of a common 'national' sentiment"(Luganà 1988, 420); and "The Byzantine idea, which the *archon* [that is, the Greek noble] class promoted and disseminated in order to further its own political claims, appealed to the popular imagination and strengthened the client relationship of the masses with the archontes" (Maltezou 1995, 278-279).

1360s, colludes in this depiction, as can be seen in his correspondence, where he castigates the Cretans for being ungrateful subjects of a beneficent power (e.g., Petrarca 1978, lib. 3 and 9). Even a few testators of wills resort to an ethnic paradigm when they dispose of their property in certain ways contingent on the possibility of war between the Greeks and the Latins. It is precisely at this point that notarial sources balance the view of Cretan society.

Some of what Buondelmonti reports undoubtedly came from his talks with local people. The details concerning the Calergi family in particular must certainly have come from locals and from Matteo Calergi himself. Without a doubt, the prestige of the Calergi family as reported in the *Descriptio* had a basis in reality. They were indeed one of the most powerful, if not the most powerful, Greek-Cretan noble family on the island. That family led one of the most formidable revolts against the Venetian rulers at the end of the thirteenth century, nearly one hundred years after the conquest. The leader of the family at that time, Alexis Calergi, entered into a treaty with Venice in 1299, on the basis of which he was given back much land and a considerable degree of autonomy on those lands (Mertzios 1948). However, as other historians have pointed out, the war led by Alexis Calergi against the Venetians was not in defense of all Greek-Cretan noble families, much less the Greek peasantry. Alexis Calergi cut a deal with the conquerors for himself, his family and his followers. Calergi's revolt was not a coalition of Greek nobles, a point which Buondelmonti's monk makes himself: if the Greek noble families united, they would easily gain control of the island. Even if it is generally understood that the Greek nobility did not unite around the idea of Byzantium or a common Greek identity, the question has still to be asked: why did they not unite?

But Buondelmonti's reporting is in some ways contradicted by the information to be found in notarial documents. It is known that the Calergi family in the fourteenth century was divided into several different branches. Some branches maintained hostile relations with the colonial regime; some maintained very close ties to the regime. One expression of those close ties was the Calergi family's policy, the extent of which has not been understood until very recently, of marriage alliances with the Venetian feudatory families of Crete in every generation since the end of the thirteenth century, right up to and beyond the revolt that the Greek woman Rovithi was accused of supporting in 1367. The result of the intermarriages was, however, apparently not the uniform Latinizing of those branches of the Calergi family. As long as they were on the island, they apparently perceived themselves and were perceived by others as Greek-Cretans, even though most branches of the family renewed kinship with the Latin feudatory families in every generation.

Furthermore, senior male members of the most prestigious branch of the Calergi, very likely the father or uncle of the Matteo Calergi whom we have met, were inducted in the 1380s into the Great Council of Venice, making them legally if not socially members of the Venetian patriciate (Thiriet 1959, 178 n 2). Forty years earlier, the notarial registers reveal that two Calergi brothers were residents of Venice already in the 1340s, while their sisters still lived in Crete (VMC PD 676, C/II, fragment). To go back to the proclamation outlawing Rovithi and her son-in-law, in it we learn that Rovithi had flung her threatening words at Leo Calergi, son of Georgios. Giustiniani's text makes it seem that she was merely castigating a fellow Greek and threatening Latins. Actually, it was probably more significant to the Venetian authorities that she was castigating, first, a nobleman, and second, an ally of Venice. Seen in this new light, Rovithi herself points to a way of understanding the divisions in Cretan life along lines other than ethnic.

Below the surface of the Greek revolt that Tadeo Giustiniani had come to Crete to subdue lies a peasants' revolt characterized by social and class concerns, though expressed in ethnic terms. Moreover, the evidence for unrest in the colony ranged against the notarial evidence of economic life in Candia suggests that the antagonistic divisions in the colony might more usefully be described as being between the countryside and the towns. Greek-Cretans, along with Latin-Cretans, appear everywhere in the Candiote notarial protocols, engaged in a wide variety of commercial activities. As disadvantageous as Venetian rule was for the majority of Greek-Cretans, it is very clear that those who lived in Candia had a better chance of prospering. We find there wealthy Greek-Cretans engaged in long-distance trade. At least five Greek noble families held seats in the island's advisory councils. As I have shown elsewhere, the best testimony in the notarial records that Greek-Cretans living within the vicinity of Candia had more opportunities to benefit in society is the number of Greek women, the poorest and least juridically capable section of the population, engaged in their own right and capacity in a variety of economic ventures (McKee 1998b). Out in the countryside, servitude characterized the lives of the majority of peasantry, the majority of whom were Greek. If the experience of Greek-Cretans in the city differed somewhat from that of the Greek peasantry, which, then, is the better description of those who rebelled in the villages and rural areas: peasant or Greek? That the population and the government described the revolt in ethnic terms is not consequently irrelevant so much as it is insufficient and misleading for purpose of understanding why the peasants revolted.

At the same time, the sources reveal that many Latin-Cretans and Greek-Cretans living in Candia shared cultural attributes. The Latin population, both feudatories and commoners, had absorbed aspects of Greek culture, such as given names, language and a tolerance of the eastern church that is often difficult to distinguish from promotion. Marriage between the Latin feudatories and the Greek noble families was not uncommon, as we saw in the case of the Calergi family. Marriages on the lower levels of society were even more common, although at times officially discouraged by the government.

The problem thus becomes one of reconciling the two pictures presented by the different sets of sources, because both are to different degrees valid, and of explaining them in light of the population's continued use of the terms "Latin" and "Greek" when it is obvious that the criteria for what defined "Latin" and "Greek" had evolved considerably over the first two centuries of Venetian rule. Evidently, the defining features of "Latin" and "Greek" were less important, since they changed, than the uses to which the ethnic terms were put and the situations in which they were employed. No doubt the nobility and clergy of Crete were able at times to rally the Cretan peasantry with appeals to a common past. But the Greek-Cretan peasantry could and did just as easily revolt against the Greek nobility as it did against Venetian rule. Once again, framing explanations around the concept of a Greek identity only goes so far in the effort to understand the historical actions of individuals.

One might argue that the incomplete, one-sided picture that characterizes much of the scholarship on Venetian Crete can be explained by the failure of scholars to consider all the surviving sources and not just a part or sampling of them. There is some truth to that argument, but it does not go far enough into the problem. The problem is conceptual, but not only in regard to a faulty methodology, whereby samplings of sources carry an unwarranted burden of representing the whole. More complicated assumptions are also in play. Attributing solidarities to peoples of the past, as scholars in many fields are so quick to do, reflects a lack of understanding of identity in the present.

A certain amount of confusion about identity underlies every discussion of communities in the past. It is particularly difficult when languages of the past come into play, because of the problem of false cognates. A recent collection of essays entitled *Concepts of National Identity in the Middle Ages* reveals that there is no consensus among the contributors about what the concept of national identity means (hence, the plural in the title), much less whether it existed in the past (Forde, Johnson and Murray 1995). The author of each article sets out the theoretical presuppositions for his or her discussion, with the result that a wide range of differing suppositions can be found throughout the volume. In an even more recent volume the author feels the same need to put forth initially in the work the presuppositions that she uses when using the words ethnicity, ethnic group and ethnic identity (Jones 1997).

Semantic problems plague every field, but rarely do we encounter a field of inquiry so burdened by *a priori* definitional problems as the topic of ethnicity, nations and national identity in the pre-modern world. There are perhaps more overviews and assessments of the debates over those terms than there are monographs exploring their meanings in a local setting. In a sense, that the cart is put before the horse is unavoidable, because it is difficult if not impossible to proceed without employing terminology. Literate individuals of the past used words to signify a conception of themselves or others as groups. But we are hobbled by the lack of agreement as to what our modern words mean to us and so we have a very hard time using them to translate and interpret the words employed in the past.

Almost every investigation into ethnicity, ethnic terminology, and ethnic sentiment winds up in the orbit of the debate described by Anthony Smith about the existence of nations in pre-modern times (Smith 1995). On one side can be found the "perennialists,", those who think that nations have always existed, at least as long as there have been written records. Those who believe that nations have existed as long as there have been people who believe that nations have existed are a subset of the perennialists. That, of course, raises the question: how do we know that they mean what we mean by the word "nation"? And, are we all agreed on what we mean by nation? On the other side Smith ranges the modernists. Modernists hold that nations could not have existed before the modern era, for the ideology necessary to unite a nation can only exist in a period when the ideology can be widely disseminated. The most popular subset of the modernists are those who follow the line of thought advanced by Benedict Anderson in his *Imagined Communities* (1983), in which he argues that print media is necessary to the formation of nations.

Smith's review of the debate (1995) has prompted me to wonder why we are arguing at all about whether or not nations existed in the past. Both sides of the debate seem to impose contemporary constructs on the past by debating the meaning of words like *natio*, *gens*, *ethnikos*, etc. I see the debate in other terms. How individuals in the past described themselves or others is less pertinent, or less historically significant, than the circumstance in which they described themselves or others and to what ends, an approach that has benefited from reading Patrick Geary on ethnic identity as a situational construct (1983).

Furthermore, to return to the two kinds of sources I have at hand, the problem in part is a confusion in methodology. In contrast to Smith's description of the debate, I would divide the investigators into national sentiment and ethnicity into different groups. In the first group are the generalists, whose primary concern extends beyond the limits of any one region, any one candidate for nation and any one historical period.[9] They are interested in themes that span epochs, and topics such as "the emergence of the modern nation in western Europe or eastern Europe." They seek universal instances and applications of "nation." Because their subject extends broadly over time and geographic space, they almost all rely on secondary works of the second group. The second group interested in nations and ethnicity of the past are those specialists in the history or literature of specific regions, countries or periods in history, such as Patrick Amory, who has written on ethnic terminology in Burgundian law codes from early medieval Europe (1994). They exploit primary sources to investigate collective sentiment and alliances in the past. A basic problem immediately presents itself. The members of the first group, who specialize in the theoretical framework of nations and nationalism, but who cannot be masters of all that is needed to study the question in both universal and local terms, depend on the monographs and studies of the second group of local specialists, who in turn rely on the first group for conceptual approaches to the problem of the "nation" and ethnicity.

Because their work has been the fodder for the generalists' cannons, the second group, the localists, must develop greater methodological precision than they have thus far demonstrated. Most of the work by specialists of the second group has thus far been based on narrative sources of various kinds, such as Buondelmonti's travelogue or Gregory of Tours' *History of the Franks*. To my knowledge, there has been insufficient attention paid to the questionable utility of literary narrative for determining collective sentiments of any kind, attributable to whole

---

[9] Of these historians, I appreciate most the views of Bartlett (1993) and Hobsbawm (1990).

populations, in periods when the majority of the population was illiterate. For too long we have studied past collective cultural identities, as Smith calls them, without sufficient awareness of writers as filters. Do the sources reflect the sentiments of the ruling elites, or do they apply to common people as well and how do we know that to be the case? Can we corroborate through other sources the claims made on the basis of narrative sources, and, if not, is more caution called for in our claims?

We scholars have not moved so far beyond the overt nationalism of nineteenth-century historiography that resurgent nationalism and the many claims to group identity in the twentieth century do not influence the concepts that we use in our work. We live in a time that concerns itself more with protecting or extending a people's right to be distinct than with why peoples ought to have that right, a historical condition that may be as it should be. Yet the constant questioning of our premises with the intention of testing rather than jettisoning them is one of the healthiest intellectual exercises human beings can do. Academics can do no less. When it comes to ethnicity in past times, historians tend to accept the official and literary sources at face value, because they have not thought to question what lies behind any people's assertion of itself as a group. Once ethnic identity is seen to exist only in relation to another ethnicity, then the traditional understanding of how peoples organize themselves mentally and are organized by political agencies becomes strained. If the understanding and consistent application of the understanding that identity is relational, situational, even fluid, and consists of various aspects, are hard to come by in the modern world, it seems, then, a little unreasonable to expect peoples in the past to have had any better grasp of their identities than we have of our own.

Ethnic identity is real, not because it exists always and always to the same degree and embodies universal rights to self-determination, but precisely because it is a tool, the merits of which are judged by people according to the historical conditions in which they live. Whether we are talking about the ethnic groups in the former Yugoslavia, the national aspirations of the Kurds, the distinction between a Roman and a Goth in Late Antiquity, or the difference between a Latin and a Greek in

Venetian Crete, the attribution to and activation of ethnic identity in a people are functions of human kind's political impulses, most frequently with devastating results.

## REFERENCES

Amory, Patrick. 1994. Names, Ethnic Identity and Community in Fifth- and Sixth-Century Burgundy. *Viator* 25: 1-30.

Anderson, Benedict. 1983. *Imagined Communities*. London and New York.

ASV ADC = Archivio di Stato di Venezia, Archivio del Duca Candia.

Bartlett, Robert. 1993. *The Making of Europe: Conquest, Colonization and Cultural change, 950-1350*. Princeton.

Borsari, Silvano. 1963. *Il dominio veneziano a Creta nel XIII secolo*. Naples.

Buondelmonti, Christophe/Cristoforo; see Legrand 1974, and Van Spitael 1981.

Cornaro, Flaminio. 1755. *Creta Sacra*. Venice.

Forde, Simon, Lesley Johnson and Alan V. Murray, eds. 1995. *Concepts of National Identity in the Middle Ages*. Leeds Texts and Monographs, New Series 14. Leeds, U.K.

Hobsbawm, Eric. 1990. *Nations and Nationalism Since 1780*. Cambridge.

Geary, Patrick. 1983. Ethnic Identity as a Situational Construct in the Early Middle Ages. *Mitteilungen der Anthropologischen Gesellschaft in Wien* 113: 15-26.

Gerland, Ernst. 1899. *Das Archiv des Herzogs von Kandia in Könige - Staatsarchiv zu Venedig*. Strasburg.

———. 1903-4. Histoire de la noblesse crétoise au moyen-âge. 1ère partie. *Revue de l'Orient latin* 10: 172-247.

———. 1905-8. Histoire de la noblesse crétoise au moyen-âge. 2ième partie. *Revue de l'Orient latin* 11: 7-144.

Jacoby, David. 1989. Social Evolution in Latin Greece. In *A History of the Crusades*, ed. K.M. Setton, 6: 175-221. Madison, WI.

Jones, Siân. 1997. *The Archaeology of Ethnicity*. London and New York.

Legrand, Émile, ed. [1897] 1974. *Description des îles de l'Archipel, par Christophe Buondelmonti, Version grecque par un Anonyme, Première partie ...*. Publications de l'École des Langues Orientales Vivantes, 4$^{th}$ series, vol. 15. [Paris] reprint Amsterdam.

Luganà, Francesca Luzzatti. 1988. La funzione politica della memoria di Bisanzio nella Descriptio Cretae (1417-1422) di Cristoforo Buondelmonti. *Bulletino dell'istituto storico italiano per il medio evo e archivio muratoriano* 94: 395-420.

Maltezou, Chryssa. 1991. The historical and social context. In *Literature and society in Renaissance Crete*, ed. David Holton, 21-23. Cambridge.

———. 1995. Byzantine "consuetudines" in Venetian Crete. *Dumbarton Oaks Papers* 49: 269-280.

McKee, Sally. 1998a. *Wills from late medieval Venetian Crete, 1312-1450*. 3 vols. Washington, D.C.

———. 1998b. Women Under Venetian Colonial Rule: Some Observations on their Economic Activities. *Renaissance Quarterly* 51/1: 34-67.

———. 2000. *Uncommon Dominion: Venetian Crete and the Myth of Ethnic Purity*. Philadelphia.

Mertzios, Konstantinos D. 1949. H sunthiki eneton-kallergi kai oi sunodeuontes autin katalogoi. *Kritika Kronika* 3: 262-292.

Petrarca, Francesco. 1978. *Epistole de rebus senilibus*. Ed. U. Dotti. Torino.

Borsari, Silvano. 1963. *Il dominio veneziano a Creta nel XIII secolo*. Naples.

Smith, Anthony D. 1995. National Identities: Modern and Medieval? In *Concepts of National Identity in the Middle Ages*, ed. Simon Forde, Lesley Johnson and Alan V. Murray, 21-46. Leeds Texts and Monographs, New Series 14. Leeds, U.K.

Thiriet, Freddy. [1954] 1977. Les chroniques vénitiennes de la Marcienne et leur importance pour l'histoire de la Romanie gréco-vénitienne. In *Études sur la Romanie gréco-vénitienne (Xe-XVe siècles)*, 3: 241-292. [orig. ed. *Mélanges de l'École française de Rome* 66] London.

———. 1959. *La Romanie vénitienne au moyen âge*. Paris.

Thomov, Thomas. 1996. New Information about Cristoforo Buondelmonti's Drawings of Constantinople. *Byzantion* 66/2: 431-453.

Tiepolo, Maria Francesca. 1973. Note sul riordino degli archivi del Duca e dei notai di Candia nell'Archivio di Stato di Venezia. *Thesaurismata* 10: 88-100.

Tsougarakis, Dimitris. 1985. Some Remarks on the "Cretica" of Cristoforo Buondelmonti. *Ariadne* 3: 88-108.

———. 1988. *Byzantine Crete: From the Fifth Century to the Venetian Conquest*. Athens.

Van Der Vin, J.P.A. 1980. *Travellers to Greece and Constantinople*. 2 vols. Nederl. Hist-Arch. Inst. Te Istanbul. Louvain.

Van Spitael, Marie-Anne, ed. 1981. *Cristoforo Buondelmonti, Descriptio Insule Crete et Liber Insularum, Cap. XI: Creta*. Herakleion.

Venice, Archivio di Stato di Venezia; see Archivio di Stato di Venezia.

VMC, PD 676, C/II, fragment = Venice, Museo Correr, Ms PD 676, C/II, fragment.

Weiss, R. 1960. Buondelmonti, Cristoforo. *Dizionario biografico degli italiani*. Rome.

# 4

# The Church of Dubrovnik and the *Panniculus* of Christ: Relics between East and West (and Men and Women) in Medieval Dalmatia*

*Richard F. Gyug*

MEDIEVAL DUBROVNIK ("Ragusa" It./Lat.) was a thriving city on the south-eastern shore of the Adriatic and a center for regional and Mediterranean trade. In its early history the city was often a dependent of more powerful states, such as Venice, which controlled Dubrovnik from 1204 to 1358, but in the later middle ages and early modern centuries it was an independent Republic governed by patrician councils. Despite the resemblance of its institutions and structures to those of contemporary Italian cities, Ragusan historians writing in the fifteenth, sixteenth and seventeenth centuries stressed that its medieval centuries had not been marked by the disorder and factionalism of Italian cities. In part, this is a golden-age simplification of a more complex past, but it does reveal the importance of historiography in Ragusan affairs, and raises questions about how the patrician elite controlled other groups, managed disputes within its own ranks and maintained the unity of the

---

*Research for this paper was conducted with the aid of a grant provided by the Social Sciences and Research Council of Canada to the *Monumenta liturgica beneventana*, a collaborative research project.

city, or at least how Renaissance historians thought such things had been done or should be done.¹

The historiography and patrician politics of Dubrovnik meet in the cult of the *Panniculus* of Christ, which in Ragusan legends is either Christ's swaddling clothes or the cloth with which Simeon received Christ during the Presentation in the Temple. The legends reveal that the cult of the relic, though less popular than the cult of Blaise, the city's patron, was a particularly female concern linked to the female monastery of S. Simeon, where it united women from both sides of the regional divide between the Roman and eastern churches. In describing the city's successful attempt to seize the relic and deposit it in the cathedral in 1379 (or 1424 according to some accounts), the legends provide telling glosses on the gender politics of later medieval Dubrovnik and the role of religion in communal life. The incident also tests the Renaissance chroniclers' myth of the harmonious Republic, and the city's oppressive reaction to the nuns' independent control of the cult confirms Susan Mosher Stuard's hypothesis on the importance of women to patrician society and the patriciate's expectation of solidarity among its members.²

---

¹For Renaissance historians of Dubrovnik and their utopian vision of their city, see Stuard (1992, 2-3); Stuard's study of the Ragusan elite notes the emphasis in late medieval and early modern Ragusan histories and literature on the harmony, stability and right order of the Republic, and asks whether such legends masked adaptations that occurred behind the closed doors with which the Republican elite hid their private lives and decisions (1992, 2-3, 8-9, 41-42, and passim). For general histories of Dubrovnik and topical articles, see Lučić 1991; and Krekić 1972 and 1980. For the regional context, see Fine 1983 and 1987. For a summary of the schools of Dalmatian historiography on communal history, see Dusa 1991, 2-7.

²Stuard's presentation of the problem was tentative: "perhaps the extent of women's power will remain an unanswered question figuring among the best kept secrets of old Ragusa" (1992, 108). To the extent the legends of the *Panniculus* corroborate Stuard's hypothesis they may also point to a means of supplementing the abundant documentary records of medieval Dubrovnik, which is poorly represented by contemporary narrative sources. The method has been proposed by Stuard (e.g., 1992, 18-19, on Renaissance legends of the city's Greek and Latin origins, which confirm Romance and Slavic bilingualism in the sixteenth-century city). For an exemplary study of a Ragusan legend,

The context for discussion of the Ragusan legends about the *Panniculus* is the medieval cult of Simeon the Prophet and the forms taken by the cult along the Dalmatian coast. The story of Simeon the Prophet, or Simeon the Just, is told in the Gospel of Luke (2: 21-35). When Mary brought the infant Jesus to the Temple in order to present him to the Lord, she encountered Simeon, a just old man who had been promised by the Holy Spirit to live until he had seen the messiah. Simeon took the child in his arms, and proclaimed the fulfilment of the promise.[3] The Presentation was a popular subject for depictions and commentary in the middle ages, in part due to wide-spread familiarity with Simeon's prayer of proclamation, the *Nunc dimittis*. In the various forms of its iconography, Simeon is often shown with covered hands as he receives the infant Christ from Mary.[4]

The cult of Simeon was widespread, and usually concentrated on relics of his arms, which were a sort of secondary relic of Christ whom they had held. Aachen and Saint-Denis both claimed arms of the saint, and both claimed the relics to have been gifts from Charlemagne, who had acquired them on pilgrimage to Jerusalem (Fondra 1855, 316; Reau 1957, 265; Reau 1959, 1221). The cult was well developed in the Adriatic region. Venice claimed an arm (Fondra 1855, 309-326; Reau

---

see Josip Lučić (1992) on the legend in which Richard I of England was shipwrecked near Dubrovnik in 1192; Lučić has shown that the event has at least a verifiable core, even if the details will never be known.

[3]The Gospel story circulated with embellishments in several non-canonical works, especially the works of James the Proto-Evangelist, the Gospel of Nicodemus and the Gospel of pseudo-Matthew. For the story and the legends, see Spadafora 1969, 1160-1161; and Acta sanctorum, Oct. 4: 2-24.

[4]Some later medieval representations show Simeon with his hands uncovered; e.g., the illustration of the scene in a fourteenth-century copy of the *Meditations on the Life of Christ* (Raguse and Green 1961, 58). The covered hands were a feature that originated in Byzantine iconography and spread widely in the west (Lucchesi Palli and Hoffscholte 1968; Reau 1957, 263; Reau 1959, 1221; Shorr 1946, 21, 26). Since the passage from Luke refers only to Simeon's arms ("in ulnas suas"), the covered hands may be based on the reference in some recensions of pseudo-Matthew to Simeon receiving Christ "in pallium suum" (Shorr 1946, 21 n 21).

1957, 265), but Zadar claimed the entire body, in defiance of every other claim, especially that of its rival, Venice.[5]

Important themes in Zadar legends about the cult related to child bearing and the inability of women to care for relics of the saint, issues repeated in Dubrovnik, as we shall see. In the 1370s, Elizabeth Kotromanić, queen of Hungary, visited Zadar. Since she had been praying for a male heir after bearing four daughters, she was attracted to the cult of Simeon, who was often invoked by couples seeking to have children (Reau 1959, 1221). In her anxiety, she stole a finger from the body of S. Simeon in Zadar and hid it in the breast of her dress. When she attempted to leave the church, she was wounded on her chest and unable to find her way out, but the condition vanished when she returned the finger to the body (Petricioli 1983, 19; Fondra 1855, 102-103). Impressed by the miracle, in 1377 she commissioned a silver chest as a gift for the church (Petricioli 1983, 7; Fondra 1855, 100). Female irresponsibility became an issue again after 1571, when most of the church holding the body of S. Simeon was demolished for new fortifications. The relic was moved to the sacristy, and the silver chest commissioned by Queen Elizabeth was moved to the female monastery of S. Maria. Several decades later, after new quarters had been prepared for the relic and the silver chest, which still survives in Zadar, inspectors found the chest neglected and darkened by humidity in a damp corner of the convent's chapter house (Petricioli 1983, 25-26; Fondra 1855, 178-212).

An early, much questioned source puts Dubrovnik in direct competition with Zadar for the body of Simeon. The twelfth-century verse-chronicle of Miletius claimed that the body was translated from Palestine and placed in the cathedral of Dubrovnik in 1159 (Coleti 1800,

---

[5]Legends related that the body of Simeon was brought to Zadar from Jerusalem in 1213 or 1273 (Fondra 1855, 65-66), or 1243 (Reau 1959, 1221; Weigert 1976, 360-361).

13; Fondra 1855, 306), but later Ragusans made few claims to Simeon's body.[6]

Simeon was, however, important in Dubrovnik for other reasons. Ragusans had a long association with Simeon as the titular saint of a female monastery located within the walls in the southwest quarter of the city. The first record of the monastery of S. Simeon dates to 1108, when Archbishop Dominicus, having heard that the monastery was threatened by the heirs of its founders, confirmed its independence from archiepiscopal and lay control (Smičiklas 1904, 20-21; Ostojić 1964, 474). The monastery appears frequently in records of the thirteenth and fourteenth centuries.[7] In the records of the minor council from 1301 to 1356, the monastery of S. Simeon is a recipient with other monasteries of communal alms on important feasts (Gelcich 1897, 304, 311, 339, 373, 393). Documents of various sorts use the monastery as a boundary or site identifier (e.g., Lučić 1993, 115). The abbess and monastery played a role in landholding and transactions involving land (Lučić 1993, 52-53, 139; Smičiklas 1907, 95-96). The monastery received bequests in 1234, 1281 and 1284 (Smičiklas 1905, 402; 1908, 464, 500; Stuard 1992, 88, citing Čremošnik 1951, 144-146), several times from 1295 to 1300 (Lučić 1993, 256, 260-261, 267-269, 274-275, etc.), and in 1352 and 1356/8 (Smičiklas 1914, 86, 659-662). In some bequests, individual nuns, perhaps family members, were the recipients (Lučić 1993, 297-298, 317-318).

---

[6]For doubts about the verse-chronicle, see Gozzi 1981, 33. The revisers of Fondra (1855, 307-309) repeat the legend that on 7 January 1159, a noble German crusader returning from Jerusalem brought the body of S. Simeon to Dubrovnik. The crusader left the body at the church of S. Vitus, from which it was translated fifty years later to S. Maria, the site of the cult. Many points in the legend appear in the following legends about the *Panniculus*. Since the monastery of S. Simeon existed already by 1108, as noted below, and the cult of S. Simeon's body does not develop elsewhere until the thirteenth century, it is likely that later narrators confused Simeon's body and the secondary relic of the *Panniculus* (see also Fondra 1855, 309).

[7]During the period there were seven female monasteries and at least eighteen recluses in the city; each of the houses held less than a dozen women (Stuard 1992, 88, 95 n 48).

The monastery continued to appear in records of the fifteenth and sixteenth centuries. In a will dated 1470/98, Georgius de Croxis, a Ragusan patrician and bishop of Trebinje and Makaraska, made pious bequests to several churches and monasteries of the city, including ten *hyperperi* to S. Simeon's; on his death in 1513, he was buried in the monastery (Coleti 1800, 302; Ostojić 1964, 476). In 1517, Leo X commanded the convents of Dubrovnik, including S. Simeon's, to admit as many girls as could be sustained by the monastic endowments, and to charge them no more than ninety ducats, unlike the former fee of 200 ducats, which had seemed unjust to the Ragusan councillors who asked for the decree (Coleti 1800, 214; Ostojić 1964, 476-477). In a visitation of 1573-1574, seven altars were recorded at S. Simeon's (Badurina 1991, 281). When the city was struck by a devastating earthquake in 1667, the monastery was severely damaged by the subsequent fire. With papal permission, the nuns of S. Simeon and three other female monasteries were united with the convent of S. Maria (Coleti 1800, 265; Ostojić 1964, 477). Parts of the monastery church's apse and the monastic houses still survive (Ostojić 1964, 477).

The monastery of S. Simeon was closely linked to a secondary relic of the saint; i.e., not his body, but the cloth with which he received Christ during the Presentation in the Temple. Several later medieval and early modern eye-witness accounts, which will be analyzed below for their evidence on the medieval history of the cult, report that there were annual processions of the relic. In the mid fifteenth century, Philippus de Diversis, a Luccan teaching in Dubrovnik, described a procession on 8 October, the feast of Simeon. In the procession, the rector and nobles carried the *Panniculus* used by Simeon to hold Christ from the cathedral to the monastery of S. Simeon (Coleti 1800, 52, citing Philippus de Diversis). According to the sixteenth-century annalist Nicolò di Ragnina the procession took place on 7 January, the feast of Simeon. He wrote that the rector and council, dressed in suitable robes ("maniche aperte et acomie") and bearing lamps paid for by the commune, carried the relic in procession with all the archbishop's clergy (Ragnina 199).

The late-eighteenth-century historian Jacopo Coleti reported that the procession was later transferred to the Sunday after Epiphany. By the eighteenth century, it had been moved again to the Second Sunday after Easter; and it no longer went to S. Simeon's, but to S. Maria de Castello, which had received the sisters of S. Simeon after the destruction of their convent. According to Coleti, the modern procession was marked not by pomp, but by dignity and reverence. In it, the clergy and sodalities marched with their flags and symbols. They were followed by the archbishop, Rector and Senate with the nobles and citizens in their train. Between the archbishop and the laity, four priests carried the reliquary on their shoulders. At the church of S. Maria de Castello, the holy cloth was used as the altar cloth for a solemn mass, then carried in procession back to the cathedral (Coleti 1800, 52). In the nineteenth century, the cloth, measuring 1.53 x .51 meters, was kept in a silver chest in the chapel of the cathedral dedicated to the church's relics; a piece of the treasured relic was given by Archbishop Jederlinić to Pius IX in 1844 (Škurla 1876, 98).[8] The relic and its sixteenth-century reliquary remain in the cathedral today (Dračevac 1988, 50 [plate]).

The documentary record shows that S. Simeon's existed as one of several female monasteries in Dubrovnik from before 1108 until 1667. Eye-witness accounts attest to its association with a relic of S. Simeon, the *Panniculus*. The monastery and relic clearly had prominent places in the city, but the record tells us little about what all this meant to the people of Dubrovnik and how they understood the monastery's role in the history of the city. The problem is similar to that faced for many questions concerning medieval Dubrovnik, so well served by its archives but short of narrative sources. In this case, however, the documentary record can be supplemented by later medieval and early modern legends.

The first account considered for this paper is in the *Annales Ragusini anonymi*, the oldest annals of the city, edited by Natko Nodilo from

---

[8]Škurla claims that the relic was brought to Dubrovnik from Jerusalem by an Albanian priest in 1050 (1876, 98); this variant on the *Panniculus* legend is not considered below, though it contains several of the standard elements.

several early modern manuscripts (Nodilo 1883, v-vii). Of the five or six annalists responsible for the work, only the first refers to S. Simeon. This annalist, likely a Ragusan friar writing in the second half of the fifteenth century, was responsible for about half the finished work; his last entry dates to 1485 (Nodilo 1883, viii).

The second account is in the annals of Nicolò di Ragnina, a Ragusan writing late in the sixteenth century, whose annals have been edited by Nodilo from later witnesses (Nodilo 1883, x-xii). In general, the legend of the *Panniculus* in the annals of Nicolò di Ragnina is closely dependent on that in the *Annales Ragusini anonymi*, with only a few differences of detail.

The third account was written over a century later by Junius Restić ("Restii"; d. 1735; ed. Nodilo 1893), a Ragusan senator and diplomat, who used his history of Dubrovnik to present a Republican view of his city's past. The differences in his account are striking for their emphasis on civic authority and their lack of interest in either the monastery of S. Simeon or the church of Dubrovnik.

The fourth account is reported in volume six of *Illyrici sacri*, a compendious history and fundamental collection of sources for the region. *Illyrici sacri* was published in eight volumes between 1751 and 1819 by the Venetian Jesuits Daniele Farlati and Jacopo Coleti. Farlati and his collaborator Filippo Riceputi were responsible for volumes one to five (1741-1775); Coleti for volumes six to eight (1800-1819). The church of Dubrovnik is the subject of volume six, published in 1800 by Coleti and based on information supplied by Ragusan correspondents. The treatment of documents in *Illyrici sacri* is often uncritical and credulous, but it remains the only source for many records and accounts now lost (Dusa 1991, 3; Fine 1975, 98 n 40; 1983, 248-249).[9] Coleti, an outsider and polemicist for the Roman church, was often at odds with

---

[9]Given Farlati and Coleti's record, historians have hesitated to rely on items without external corroboration, but I have found some of the uncorroborated documentary references to be accurate; see my forthcoming edition and study of the Lectionary and Pontifical of Kotor contained in the MS St. Petersburg, B.A.N., F. no. 200.

the earlier Ragusan accounts in his interpretation of the legend, as we shall see.

Each of the four accounts presents the legend with variants revealing the author's purpose and milieu, although the basic account is similar. First, in each account the *Panniculus* was brought in a sealed chest from Jerusalem to Dubrovnik in 843; it remained there unidentified in the church of S. Vitus. Next, in the eleventh century when the church of S. Vitus was demolished to make way for a new archiepiscopal palace, the distant successor of the priest who had been entrusted with the chest revealed its location to the archbishop. The archbishop and the priest unearthed the chest and discovered the identity of the relic. They kept it secret for the life of the archbishop. As the archbishop was dying, he bequeathed the relic to his sister, the abbess of S. Simeon's. The relic remained with the nuns, and a cult developed around it. Finally, after the nuns' guardianship of the relic was cast into doubt by careless treatment, the city seized the cloth and translated it to the cathedral. Thereafter, it was brought in procession once a year to the convent.

*The Arrival of the Relic, as yet unrecognized*

In the *Annales Ragusini anonymi*, under the entry for 842, the annalist noted that a large Venetian galley arrived that year in Ragusa. It was carrying lords from Ponente and Tramontana to the sepulcher of Christ. In Ragusa the lords gave alms to the churches and the poor, and many stayed to live in the city (*Annales* 19). Ragnina added that the Venetian galley had five banks of oars and was coming from Soria, two points not mentioned in the annals, written a century earlier. Ragnina did not note that some of the foreign pilgrims stayed on as permanent residents.

In 843, the galley returned from the sepulcher of Christ carrying Gioni, an Albanian priest ("Albanese prete"). He brought with him a sealed chest ("chascetella pizula, serata"), which he gave to Sargio, the priest ("plovano") of S. Vitus, for safekeeping. It was passed down secretly in the line of Sargio's successors to await the return of Gioni, whom they would know by certain marks on his left hand. But he did not return, and the chest remained hidden, buried in the church. At night many claimed to see lamps shining at the site, a marvelous thing, though no one knew why the light shone (*Annales* 19).

Ragnina told much the same story with minor orthographic variants (Giovanni for Gioni, "Arbanese" for "Albanese," "una casseta piccola serrata" for "chascetella pizula serata," etc.), although there are some differences in effect: the Albanian priest is "don" Giovanni; the chest is said to be closed and the light shines above it. It is only in the next passage that it becomes clear it had been buried (Ragnina 197-198).

Restić's account begins with general comments on the civic significance of the relic and its place in a wider context. He noted that such a treasure made the city the envy of nations, and its translation occurred in 843, at a time when Venice dominated the trade with Egypt and Syria, since Christians were still present in those regions. The first stage in the legend is otherwise similar to the earlier accounts, except that Restić wrote that the closed chest was given to Sergio, who is called a parish priest ("parroco e pievano").[10] Restić stressed that Sergius's successors knew where the chest was buried but not what it contained. There is no mention of the miracle of the lights (Restić 21).

The account in Coleti's *Illyrici sacri* adds several details, and some new interpretations. Coleti's source is described as "fame and a tradition accepted by most." The date, 843, Joannes, the Albanian priest, and the Venetian ship are the same as in the earlier accounts. Sergius, the priest of S. Vitus, is here called the host and fellow countryman of Joannes, the Albanian priest. Sergius's successors were still to identify Joannes by certain marks, but it is not specified that they were on his left hand (Coleti 1800, 51).[11]

---

[10]The point is anachronistic. Dubrovnik was not divided into parishes until the Republic did so in 1555 at the request of archbishop Ludovicus Beccatelli (Coleti 1800, 233-234).

[11]Coleti's account makes clear a number of additional points that could be deduced from the earlier accounts. Thus, for instance, he notes that the next stage in the story occurs two-hundred years later. Such additions are not described in the present summary.

## The Discovery of the Relic

At this point, the fifteenth-century annalist broke with the yearly structure of the annals and presented a series of later events, undated but dependent on the mystery presented in 843. The annalist reported that when a new archiepiscopal palace was begun and the church of S. Vitus was removed to make room for the palace, the chest remained undiscovered since the priest of S. Vitus was on pilgrimage to the sepulcher of Christ. When he returned after two years, the palace had already been built. Since he realized he no longer had access to the chest without the archbishop's knowledge, he went to the archbishop and told him the story supported with documents ("per scritture ordenate et autentiche"). The archbishop, thinking that the chest might contain money, agreed with the priest to reveal the secret to no one. He then went at night to the place and unearthed the box. When he had carried it back to his room and broken it open, since it could not be opened in any other way, he found it contained the *Panizelo* of Christ and a letter ("zetuleta") explaining everything. The archbishop, a Ragusan noble ("gentilhuomo"), decided to keep the relic secret, and instructed the priest to do the same (*Annales* 19-20).

Nicolò di Ragnina has a similar extension to the 843 entry in his chronicle. He added only that the priest of S. Vitus had gone to Jerusalem, and that the construction of the archiepiscopal palace took place 1040 years after Christ, although the date is confused in the manuscripts.[12] In Ragnina's account, the priest and archbishop went together to unearth the chest, and the chest was opened, but not broken open. More significant is the identification of the relic: in Ragnina, the *Pannicello* was the cloth with which Christ had been wrapped at his birth, his swaddling clothes. The anonymous annals had not specified which cloth it was. Ragnina also added that the archbishop placed the

---

[12] 1040 is the editor's conjecture. The manuscripts read "questo fo nelli anni 100 davanti vita di Cristo" (Ragnina 198 n. 3).

cloth in a crystal chest, and venerated it for the rest of his life (Ragnina 198).

Restić has a comparable tale, but was clear on the date, 1040, and added the name of the archbishop, Vitalis. He related that the new archiepiscopal palace was built by the Republic at the request of the archbishop. The archbishop's secretive greed is noted, and emphasized even more than it had been in the earlier accounts. When the chest is forced open, it is seen to contain the *Pannicello* in which Christ had been wrapped by the Blessed Virgin. Although the archbishop venerated the relic, there is no mention of the crystal reliquary (Restić 21).

Coleti's account is similar in outline, but different in detail. In order to make the pilgrimage to Jerusalem, the priest of S. Vitus first asked the permission of the archbishop. There is no mention of the archbishop seeking the Republic's support to build the new palace, unlike the reference in Restić. Coleti does not refer to the archbishop's venality in digging up the relic, a factor in each of the earlier accounts. When the archbishop and the priest of S. Vitus unearthed the relic, it was labeled as the cloth in which the infant Christ had been wrapped. In itself, this is not contrary to the identification in the earlier legends, but Coleti quoted the fifteenth-century account of Philippus de Diversis identifying the *Panniculus* as the cloth used by Simeon (Coleti 1800, 52; see below for comments on this discrepancy).

## The Relic in the Hands of the Nuns of S. Simeon

According to the *Annales Ragusini anonymi*, on the archbishop's deathbed, he summoned his sister, the abbess of S. Simeon, and gave her the relic secretly. For pious reasons, the abbess cut pieces from the *Panicello*, but it grew back each time (*Annales* 20).

In Ragnina's version of the gift, the sister of the archbishop is said to have kept the relic secret, as did her successors, until a later abbess began the practice of distributing portions of the cloth to those who asked (Ragnina 198).

Restić's account of the gift of the relic is brief, though generally in agreement with the earlier accounts. The monastery is identified, however, as dedicated to SS. Simeon and Jude, the apostles. The cult is not described, except to note that the relic became well known, to the joy of the city (Restić 21).

Coleti's account of the nuns' receipt of the relic is very full and differs from the earlier versions at several points. The archbishop made the gift to his sister, the abbess of S. Simeon, as in the earliest accounts. Coleti's informants supply, however, a deathbed dialogue: when the archbishop called his sister to his deathbed, he said he had nothing to give her as a sign of his fraternal love except something of inestimable value and manifest holiness. When she asked what it was and stood waiting attentively, he showed her the holy cloth, and told her the full story of its origins, how he had come by it, and how he had venerated it. The abbess, minding the command of her brother, honored and venerated the relic and offered prayers before it. Dying she passed the holy gift on to her virgin sisters, with an order to place it in their church and expose it for public veneration. The citizens were astonished at the relic, and their piety grew when they considered that the fame of such a worthy treasure had been hidden for over two-hundred years. They gathered from all parts intent on seeing and venerating the relic. All sought to compensate for the long period of neglect with offices and honors, and the faith and piety of Ragusans were increased by the miracles and healing that followed, although Coleti remarks that the miracles were undocumented. In describing the practice of giving particles of the cloth, Coleti is the first to note that they were given to women recovering from difficult births. The gifts were more generous than prudent, according to Coleti, but the cloth remained whole (Coleti 1800, 51-52). Although Coleti has doubts about the care of the relic, he is describing a cult commanded by an archbishop, fed by popular demand, and fostered by cloistered nuns in their church, features familiar to him from his own eighteenth-century church.

*The Relic's Mistreatment and Translation to the Cathedral*

In the account of the anonymous annalist, the abbess who had received the *Panicello* from her brother, the archbishop, cut pieces from the cloth, but it remained whole, as noted above. Once, however, she cut a piece for a schismatic queen of Bosnia. Since the piece had been given to an "infidel," the cloth did not return to its former size. When the Ragusan community learned this, they took the relic from the abbess, but promised to bring it back to the monastery each year on the feast of S. Simeon, and to give to the monastery ten *hyperperi* as alms for as long as the republic remained free (*Annales* 20). The full account, from the arrival of the relic to its translation to the cathedral, was included under the year 843 by the anonymous annalist, without dates for the later events described in it, but the annalist repeated the seizure of the relic later as the entry for 1424. In the 1424 entry, the Bosnian queen was specifically a heretic who did not revere the relic. Instead of the community of Ragusa, it is now the Signori who seize the relic to place it in their depository. The feast of S. Simeon is dated to January, and the closing comment about Ragusan freedom is omitted (*Annales* 54-55).

In Ragnina's account, the abbess who began distributing pieces of the relic was a successor of the sister of the archbishop.[13] This later abbess was also responsible for giving the piece to the schismatic queen of Bosnia, not called a heretic. The rectors made the decision to seize the relic, which they placed in the cathedral, a point not specified by the anonymous annalist. The feast of S. Simeon is dated to 7 January, and the contemporary procession described in detail (see above). The annual alms were five *hyperperi*, not ten as in the earlier account. There is no reference to Ragusan freedom (Ragnina 198-199). Ragnina's entry for 1424 repeats the description of the seizure of the relic, including the identification of the Bosnian queen as a schismatic but not a heretic, its placement in the cathedral, and the alms of five *hyperperi* (Ragnina 249).

---

[13]Since Ragnina had dated the archbishop to the eleventh century, and the seizure of the relic was dated to 1424, Ragnina filled the long interval with the successors of the archbishop's sister. The anonymous annalist, who had not given a date for the archbishop, made the archbishop's sister responsible for the mistreatment of the relic and a contemporary of its seizure by the city.

Restić was as laconic about the translation as he had been about the cult. He noted only that the relic remained with the nuns for some time, until, "per alcun disordine," as he discreetly puts it, the relic was taken by the Republic and placed in the public treasury where other relics were kept (Restić 21). The translation is undated, the cathedral is not mentioned, and the cause of the translation, perhaps too medieval for Restić and unbefitting the discretion, prudence and calm the outside world expected of Ragusan nobles, is passed over.

Restić added a more political story not attested in the earlier accounts. In 1396, after the emperor Sigismond's defeat at the Battle of Nicopolis, he visited Ragusa, and on 21 December entered the city, where he was presented with the key to the city. For nine days he stayed in the rector's palace. There he received the census owed the king of Hungary for the following two years, and was given, albeit with great difficulty, a piece of the *Pannicello* (Restić 182).

Coleti's account is the fullest, and the most influenced by Catholic Reformation notions on the role of religious women. He wrote that it was not fitting that the relic would remain forever with the nuns of S. Simeon. The irresponsible gift that prompted the city's seizure of the relic was not to a Bosnian queen, as in the earliest accounts, but to a princess from the royal house of Serbia. After the gift, not only was the piece not restored as in the earlier accounts, but Coleti states that the virgins were no more thrifty than they had been, and the cloth diminished with each subsequent gift. Due to popular outcry, the Senate decided to translate the relic to the cathedral. The virgins were granted the annual procession to compensate for their loss and make the relic available to them for venerating, kissing and fulfilling pious wishes. The rector and senate were to pay ten *hyperperi* annually to the convent. Unlike the other accounts, Coleti placed the translation on 8 October 1379 (Coleti 1800, 52, citing Philippus de Diversis).

There are several variants and much common ground in the accounts. Some variants are minor, but others are more telling and shed light on the early history of the city. The first problem is the identity of the relic. One of Coleti's sources, the commentator Philippus de Diversis, who wrote in 1440, called it the cloth used by Simeon to hold Christ (Coleti 1800, 52). The late-fifteenth-century anonymous annalist did not identify the relic except as the *Panizelo* (*Annales* 19-20). Although such reticence seems unusual, it is possible that the identity of the relic was common knowledge. In the next century, however, Nicolò di Ragnina called it the swaddling clothes of Christ (Ragnina 128), and he was followed by Junius Restić in the late seventeenth or early eighteenth century (Restić 21). In the late eighteenth century, Coleti's informants knew the relic once again as Simeon's cloth, and nineteenth-century commentators have the same identification (Coleti 1800, 51; Škurla 1876, 98; Fondra 1855, 309). Why did the Renaissance annalists differ in their identification of the relic, especially since the earlier and later identifications of the relic suit the name of the monastery that held it? The answer may lie in the politics surrounding the seizure of the relic and a desire to sever its connection with the nuns of S. Simeon.

The translation of the relic must be understood within the context of the role of women in Dubrovnik's political system, and in relation to the Ragusan elite's attempts to distinguish itself from its neighbors and subjects. The city was dominated by its patriciate, a circle of about fifty cognate groups that controlled the city's wealth, public and private, served in public office and sat on the councils that decided public policy. Within such a circle, questions of family, inheritance, marriage, dowry and recruiting or controlling new members were crucial (Stuard 1992, 59-89 and passim; Janeković-Romer 1994; Rheubottom 1988 and 1994). A feature of the patriciate emphasized by later chroniclers was its unusual harmony and seeming stasis over several centuries and through many external crises. Elsewhere such crises were catalysts, or even causes, for changes of other sorts, political and social: why not in Dubrovnik? Stuard has suggested that political accommodations were made to the changed circumstances, but at a private level, most notably in the households of the ruling elite where women retained a role they lost in contemporary Italy when power shifted to public assemblies (Stuard 1992, 108). Women also remained important as those who could maintain the noble circle as marriage partners and as the distributors of wealth through their dowries. It is remarkable, for instance, that in the late fourteenth century, after the population crisis of the Black Death, Ragusan women gained decisive powers as tutors of orphaned children and were able to show their jewelry in public display. In contemporary Italy, sumptuary laws were directed particularly at limiting female display, and new men were recruited from other classes to fill the gaps left by the plague (Stuard 1992, 100-111).

At first glance, the cult of the *Panniculus* in the years before 1379/1424 confirms the thesis that the women of Dubrovnik enjoyed considerable independent power, but the seizure and translation of the *Panniculus* indicates that such authority was conditional and limited. In the legend, the nuns of S. Simeon go from being the guardians of a popular relic to being dispossessed of their treasure. The period for the change, between 1379 and 1424 according to the chroniclers, covers the generations after the Black Death when Stuard's evidence places noble women at the peak of their authority (1992, 83-87), but women who attempted to exercise the authority that circumstance and Ragusan society had given them found themselves at odds with the expectation that patrician women should exert their power only in private and in support of patrician values, not in public or in contradiction of patrician policies.[14] Since the nuns of S. Simeon used their relic to create a public circle independent of patrician circles, they were pushing the limits of the authority allowed them.

By treating with a Bosnian schismatic, the nuns also acted contrary to patrician expectations of class identity. Ragusan patricians used

---

[14]See Stuard's analysis of the successful court challenge to Nicoletta de Goce's independence in testamentary matters during the last decades of the fourteenth century (1992, 85-87), and references to the imposition of dotal limits in 1423 (1992, 106). Could the coincidence of such measures with the seizure of the *Panniculus* indicate a patrician reaction to the post-plague independence of Ragusan women? Since much of the evidence presented by Stuard dates to the fifteenth century, the authority of Ragusan woman probably endured, but the incidences noted above and the attitudes of the anonymous annalist in the late fifteenth century and Nicolò di Ragnina in the next century suggest that the public power of Ragusan women was often under attack.

culture and religion as political tools. To emphasize the gulf between citizens and others in the city, patricians stressed their classical learning and their command of Old Ragusan for deliberations in council (Stuard 1992, 39). Ragusan chroniclers of the golden age were emphatic about the city's catholicity and defense of the faith throughout its history (Stuard 1992, 30; Krekić 1972, 138-143), perhaps to distinguish themselves from heterodox Bosnians, Orthodox Serbs, and Catholics who followed the Slavic Glagolitic liturgy. When the nuns of S. Simeon went beyond the noble circle in ways that contradicted patrician goals, they were dispossessed of the source of their independent power. In this instance, the tensions usually hidden within noble families are on display because religious women were outside the family, and thus political in public ways.

The Ragusan annalists and chroniclers who downplay or change the identity of the relic were unsure whether to stress the example of the case, or hide its unseemly break with the harmony they otherwise promoted. None of the Ragusans comment on the role of the relic in healing women after difficult births. Coleti was probably correct in reporting this cult: it fit the pattern of veneration for S. Simeon seen elsewhere, particularly in Zadar (see above), but would have been secondary to the question of family politics in the Ragusan accounts. For the fifteenth-century anonymous annalist, living soon after the events, the case was perhaps too public to be overlooked. Furthermore, his probably mendicant and clerical background encouraged him to describe the negative consequences of tolerating heresy or schism. Nicolò di Ragnina in the late sixteenth century was faced with a more difficult task. He included the incident because the earlier annalist had and the annual procession needed explanation, but he identified the relic as the swaddling clothes of Christ, thus distancing it from the nuns of S. Simeon and providing further justification for civic guardianship. Junius Restić, who was least explicit and referred to the incident only as a "certain disorder," made clear by his omission how embarrassed he was by the independent actions of the nuns, whom he further distanced from the relic by calling their house the monastery of SS. Simeon and Jude, the apostles (Restić 21).

The preceding analysis accounts for the reactions of the Ragusan chroniclers, but cannot explain everything about Coleti's account. On one level, he reported a Ragusan story with all the elements of female power and noble reaction described above, whether or not he understood their import in later medieval Dubrovnik. On a second level, he interpreted the story in light of the Tridentine church with which he was familiar. Thus, Coleti is the only account to report the female aspects of the cult – a sign of fidelity to a local tradition suppressed in the other accounts because of its implications –, but he describes women with public responsibility as careless, imprudent and even a little irreligious. The issue for Coleti's sources and the earlier annalists may have been civic virtue and patrician solidarity as argued above, but for Coleti himself the assumption was that religious women should lead regular lives, which for the post-Tridentine church often meant obedient and cloistered lives under clerical direction (McKelvie 1997, 4 and passim). Coleti's account makes clear that the purpose of the procession to the monastery in later years was to allow the nuns to venerate the relic without leaving the cloister.[15]

The gift of the relic to the abbess of S. Simeon by her brother the archbishop touches on a second question related to religious women. It is noteworthy that in none of the accounts does the relic become public until it was held by the nuns. The archbishop's secret gift is likely, therefore, to have been a patriarchal fiction. A public cult associated the relic with the nuns, and the very name of their house makes it likely that the nuns possessed, or claimed to possess, the relic from the beginning. But for the annalists, the relic's obscure early history and the archbishop's gift would have been means of transferring ownership to the archbishop, and thus ultimately justifying the relic's return to the rector

---

[15] A similar stress on enclosure is evident in the accounts from Zadar of the procession with the relics of S. Simeon to their new church in 1632; the procession visited several houses of cloistered women so that they could venerate the relic (Fondra 1855, 211).

and council, the archbishop's heirs as guardians of public religion. The need to justify the translation to the cathedral beyond the accusations of irresponsible stewardship is a hint that in the fifteenth century and thereafter the nuns were still seen by some as the rightful custodians of the relic, and had always seemed so. It is possible that the legend of the archbishop's secret gift to the abbess, his sister, is a creation of the period in which the relic was seized by the city.

The transfer of the relic from the archbishop to the abbess and finally to the rector and council also raises questions about the role of the city in religious matters. In the early middle ages, the city's prelates were active in civic government, but by the thirteenth century, the archbishop's role as chief magistrate had been taken over by lay authorities (Dusa 1991, 1). Historians have argued that in the later medieval centuries Ragusan affairs were clearly divided between church and state, and civic priorities were often placed above religious interests (Krekić 1972, 139-143). Ragusan chroniclers presented this shift from episcopal to lay government as unexceptional and untroubled, in contrast with the experience of high medieval Italian communes (Stuard 1992, 30-32). The legend of the *Panniculus* suggests, however, that the chroniclers were perhaps downplaying tensions that were part of the transition.

Each of the four accounts reflects these issues in different ways. By describing the archbishop's invention of the relic (no matter how fictitious, as suggested above), all pointed out the primary role of the archbishop in the early history of the city, but the three Ragusan authors were agreed in criticizing archiepiscopal power. In the Ragusan accounts, when the archbishop learned about the buried chest, he was moved by greed and venality in seeking to unearth it (*Annales* 20; Ragnina 198; Restić 21). The anonymous annalist and Nicolò di Ragnina did not name the archbishop. Junius Restić, the most Republican of the authors, though identifying the archbishop, attempted to undermine his authority even in the early period: he had the eleventh-century archbishop Vitalis ask for the senate's approval before beginning the new archiepiscopal palace (Restić 21).

All the authors agreed that popular religious control had passed to the rectors and council by the fifteenth century when the civil authorities seized the relic from the nuns of S. Simeon. Junius Restić is again the most emphatic since his account of 1396 shows how the Rector, Senate and nobles not only control the cloth, but cut it up to give to a visiting emperor (Restić 182).

Coleti is another matter. Despite what his Ragusan sources probably said, he made no mention of the archbishop's venal motives.[16] He also identified the archbishop as Vitalis. For Coleti this was more than simply respecting his sources. In common with other Catholic historians of the period, beginning with Ughelli (Ditchfield 328-360), Coleti was writing sacred history as the history of bishops. Vitalis was for him among the first archbishops of the city, an ecclesiastical hero credited with building the archiepiscopal palace, bringing the relics of S. Blaise to the city, and perhaps discovering the *Panniculus*. His name deserved mention.

This comparison of the legends of the *Panniculus* has pointed to several ways in which the legendary account may be read. Some aspects of the legend are embellishments, interesting as reflections of the chroniclers' values but irrelevant for earlier issues. The Republican values of Junius Restić and the Catholic-Reformation religiosity of Jacopo Coleti are both distorting: Restić's statement (21) that an eleventh-century archbishop sought civic approval for a new palace seems as anachronistic as Coleti's comment (1800, 51) that the priest of S. Vitus sought archiepiscopal approval before going on pilgrimage. Other aspects of the legends may also be embellishments, but they are telling reflections of what later chroniclers thought their own history meant. Thus, all the later chroniclers repeat the unlikely story of the archbishop's secret gift of the

---

[16]Indeed, Coleti shifted the charge of venality to the archbishop's sister, the abbess, by having the archbishop promise her riches on his deathbed; the language of the passage plays up the greed and acquisitiveness in her response (Coleti 1800, 51).

relic to his sister, the abbess of S. Simeon, because they wish to preserve contemporary authority.

Some aspects of the tradition make sense in light of issues determined from other sources. The civic seizure of the relic is plausible, for instance, as a sign of patriarchy, but more plausible when the role of Ragusan women in maintaining the civic elite is considered. The treatment of the nuns of S. Simeon confirms Stuard's hypothesis that Ragusan women were important supports of the patrician elite to the extent that they provided means to consolidate holdings, distribute wealth and secure alliances through their marriages. The nuns were humiliated because they were women who would not marry, gave gifts to those the patriciate disdained, and maintained a public cult in defiance of patrician discretion.

The result is a rehabilitation of legend as an historical source. Many difficulties remain in using such legends, but at the least the tales from late medieval and Renaissance Dubrovnik show us how the chroniclers of the period used their past. They took patrician family politics, the Latin Catholicism of their class, and civic control of the church, features they knew well, and found historical precedents for them in the history of the relic, or used them as devices to explain the history of the relic. To the extent the relic could not be fit into any contemporary motive or the Ragusan myth of a harmonious past, its story was simply repeated, at which points we can argue that critical moments in Ragusan society are emphasized in ways its copyists did not intend.

## References

Acta sanctorum = *Acta sanctorum quotquot toto orbe coluntur: vel a catholicis scriptoribus celebrantur*. 1863. Rev. ed. Jean Carnandet. 65 vols. Paris.

Annales = *Annales Ragusini anonymi; item Nicolai de Ragnina*. 1883. Ed. Speratus [=Natko] Nodilo. Monumenta spectantia historiam Slavorum meridionalium 14, Scriptores 1. Zagreb: Academia scientiarum et artium Slavorum meridionalium/Jugoslavenske akademije znanosti i umjetnosti (JAZU).

Badurina, Anđelko. 1991. *Likovnost Dubronika u vizitaciji biskupa Sormana 1573-4. godine*. In *Likovna kultura Dubrovnika 15. i 16. stoljeća*, ed. Igor Fisković, 280-281. Zagreb: Institut za povijest umjetnosti Sveučilišta.

Coleti, Jacopo. 1800. *Illyrici sacri tomus sextus. Ecclesia ragusina cum suffraganeis, et ecclesia rhiziniensis et catharensis*. Venice: apud Sebastianum Coleti.

Čremošnik, Gregor. 1951. *Spisi dubrovačke kancelarije*. Book 1: *Zapisi notara Thomasina de Savere*. Monumenta historica Ragusina. Zagreb: JAZU.

Ditchfield, Simon. 1995. *Liturgy, Sanctity and History in Tridentine Italy*. Cambridge: Cambridge University Press.

Dračevac, Ante. 1988. *La Cathédrale de Dubrovnik*. Trans. Françoise Kveder. Zagreb: Privredni Vjesnik,

Dusa, Joan. 1991. *The Medieval Dalmatian Episcopal Cities*. American University Studies, Series 9: History, vol. 94. New York: Peter Lang.

Farlati, Daniele; see Coleti 1800.

Fine, John V. A., Jr. 1975. *The Bosnian Church: A New Interpretation*. Boulder; New York and London: East European Quarterly, Columbia University Press.

———. 1983. *The Early Medieval Balkans*. Ann Arbor: The University of Michigan Press.

———. 1987. *The Late Medieval Balkans: A Critical Survey from the Late Twelfth Century to the Ottoman Conquest*. Ann Arbor: The University of Michigan Press.

Fondra, Lorenzo (d. 1709). 1855. *Istoria della insigne reliquia di San Simeone profeta chi se venera in Zara*. 2nd rev. ed. Zara: Fratelli Battara.

Gelcich, Josip. 1897. *Liber reformationum. 5: A. 1301-1356*. Monumenta spectantia historiam Slavorum meridionalium 29. Zagreb: JAZU.

Gozzi, Giorgio. 1981. *La Libera e sovrana repubblica di Ragusa, 634-1814*. Rome: Volpe.

Janeković-Romer, Zdenka, 1994. *Rod i grad: Dubrovačka obitelj od XIII do XV stoljeća*. Dubrovnik: HAZU.

Krekić, Bariša. 1972. *Dubrovnik in the Fourteenth and Fifteenth Centuries*. Norman: University of Oklahoma Press.

———. 1980. *Dubrovnik, Italy, and the Balkans in the Late Middle Ages*. London: Variorum.

*Liber reformationum*, see Gelcich 1897.

Lucchesi Palli, Elizabeth, and Lidwina Maria Margreta Hoffscholte. 1968. Darbringung Jesu im Tempel. In *Lexikon der Christlichen Ikonographie*, vol. 1: *Allgemeine Ikonographie A-Ezechiel*, ed. Engelbert Kirschbaum, 473-477. Rome: Herder.

Lučić, Josip. 1960. Dubrovnik. In *Dictionnaire d'histoire et de géographie ecclésiastiques* 14: 951-961. Paris: Letouzey et Ané.

———. 1991. *Dubrovačke Teme*. Zagreb: Nakladni Zarod Matice Hrvatske.

———. 1992. On the earliest contacts between Dubrovnik and England. *Journal of Medieval History* 18: 373-389.

———. 1993. *Spisi Dubrovačke Kancelarije: Zapisi notara Andrije Beneše, 1295-1301, Praecepta rectoris I (1299-1301), Testamenta II (1295-1301)*. Monumenta historica ragusina 4. Zagreb: HAZU.

McKelvie, Roberta Agnes. 1997. *Retrieving a Living Tradition : Angelina of Montegiove, Franciscan, Tertiary, Beguine*. St. Bonaventure, NY: Franciscan Institute.

Nodilo 1883 and 1893; see *Annales*; Ragnina, and Restić.

Ostojić, Ivan. 1964. *Benediktinci u Hrvatskoj i ostalim našim krajevima*. Vol. 2: *Benediktinci u Dalmaciji*. Split: [Benediktinski priorat- –TKON].

Petricioli, Ivo. 1983. *St. Simeon's Shrine in Zadar*. Trans. Nikolina Jovanović (from Croatian). Monumenta artis croatiae, Series 1, vol. 3. Zagreb: JAZU.

Ragnina = *Annales Ragusini anonymi; item Nicolai de Ragnina*. 1883. Ed. Speratus [=Natko] Nodilo. Monumenta spectantia historiam Slavorum meridionalium 14, Scriptores 1. Zagreb: JAZU.

Raguse, Isa, and Rosalie B. Green. 1961. *Meditations on the Life of Christ (Paris, BN ms. ital. 115)*. Princeton: Princeton University Press.

Reau, Louis. 1957. *Iconographie de l'art chrétien*. 2: *Iconographie de la Bible*: 2: *Noveau Testament*. Paris: Presses universitaires de France.

———. 1959. *Iconographie de l'art chrétien*. 3: *Iconographie des saints*: 3: *P-Z, Répertoires*. Paris: Presses universitaires de France.

Restić = *Chronica Ragusina Junii Restii (ab origine urbis usque ad annum 1451); item Joannis Gundulae (1451-1484)*. 1893. Ed. Speratus [=Natko] Nodilo. Monumenta spectantia historiam Slavorum meridionalium 25, Scriptores 2. Zagreb: JAZU.

Rheubottom, David B. 1988. "Sisters First": Betrothal Order and Age at Marriage in Fifteenth-Century Ragusa. *Journal of Family History* 13/4: 359-376.

———. 1994. Genealogical Skewing and Political Support: Patrician Politics in Fifteenth-Century Ragusa (Dubrovnik). *Continuity and Change* 9/3: 369-390.

Shorr, D. C. 1946. The Iconographic Development of the Presentation in the Temple. *The Art Bulletin* 28: 17-32.

Smičiklas, Tadeo, et al. 1904. *Codex diplomaticus regni Croatiae, Dalmatiae et Slavoniae*. Vol. 2: *Diplomata saeculi XII. continens (1101-1200) / Listine XII. vijeka*. Zagreb: JAZU.

———. 1905. Vol. 3: *Diplomata annorum 1201-1235. continens / Listine Godina 1201-1235*. Zagreb: JAZU.

———. 1907. Vol. 5: *Diplomata annorum 1256-1272. continens / Listine Godina 1256-1272*. Zagreb: JAZU.

———. 1908. Vol. 6: *Diplomata annorum 1272-1290 continens / Listine Godina 1272-1290*. Zagreb: JAZU.

———. 1914. Vol. 12: *Diplomata annorum 1351-1359. continens / Listine Godina 1351-1359*. Zagreb: JAZU.

Spadafora, Francesco. 1968. Simeone, il Vecchio. In *Bibliotheca sanctorum* 11: 1160-1161. Rome: Istituto Giovanni XXIII della Pontificia Università Lateranense.

Stuard, Susan Mosher. 1992. *A State of Deference: Ragusa/Dubrovnik in the Medieval Centuries*. Philadelphia: University of Pennsylvania Press.

Škurla, Stjepan (Stefano Skurla). 1876. *Ragusa: Cenni Storici*. Zagreb.

Weigert, C. 1976. Simeon der Gotträger. In *Lexikon der Christlichen Ikonographie*, vol. 8: *Ikonographie der Heiligen: Meletius bis zweiundvierzig Martyrer*, ed. Wolfgang Braunfels, 360-361. Rome: Herder.

# 5

# Medieval Europe and its Encounter with the Foreign World: Late-Medieval German Witnesses

## *Albrecht Classen*

THERE IS NO QUESTION that medieval Europe entertained a highly problematic relationship with outsiders, marginal figures, heretics, Jews, Moslems, and others. The paradigmatic structure of feudalism coupled with the ideologically rigid framework of the Christian church made it extremely difficult, if not impossible, for medieval people to confront foreigners in an open-minded, perhaps even tolerant fashion, although certain traces of "enlightened" thinking and behavior are detectable here and there after the late twelfth and early thirteenth centuries. We might point out such thinkers as Rabbi Moses ben Rabbi Maimon (1135-1204), Ramon Lull (1235-1315), John Buridan (ca. 1300-ca. 1366), Giovanni Boccaccio (1313-1375), and Nicholas of Cusa (1401-1464) who definitely harbored viewpoints different than those of the dominant church and the populace (Flasch and Jeck 1997). As Friedrich Heer observes: "This silence is no accident: for although during the 'open' Middle Ages Jews and women made a positive contribution to culture and society, both were later relegated to the life of the Ghetto, and it was they who suffered most when society closed its ranks during the later Middle Ages" (1961, 309). The history of the Crusades serves as a painful reminder of the terrible consequences of this narrow mind-set during the tenth through thirteenth centuries, although recent investigations have demonstrated that despite the apparently brutal conflict with its scores of killed and wounded, with its many burned and looted cities, and destroyed countryside, a number of individual contacts existed, and a few, probably highly educated people tried to meet representatives of the other culture and understand their peculiar characteristics (Goss 1986).

A pessimist might argue that the majority always tend to be ignorant and xenophobic, whereas only the few harbor different ideas, search for outside contacts, and embrace new concepts developed by people from other cultures. Nonetheless, taking a different approach, we would need to remember that even in a stereotypically "dark age" those who traveled in Asia included many European merchants, missionaries, perhaps some spies, and officials representing the French king or the German Emperor, the best known among them all probably being Marco Polo (Classen 1996b; Larner 1999). A number of witnesses can be heard who spent many years in Turkish, Arabic, or even Persian prisons and who later reported about their experiences (Beckingham 1983). Such reports did not always, if at all, open the minds or instill ideas of tolerance in those who heard or read them. Nevertheless these witnesses refute the traditional concept that medieval Europe was an enclosed fortress with no contacts to the outside world (Reichert 1992).

One of the most interesting medieval observers of the foreign and foreigners was Wolfram von Eschenbach (died ca. 1220/30), who presents startling because idealizing images of black people forming part of an international universe in which religion is irrelevant to human interaction, and skin color has no bearing on chivalry and virtue (Mielke 1992). Both in his grail romance *Parzival* and in his crusade epic *Willehalm* the narrator refers to the problem of how to integrate people of other races and religions, and emphasizes that tolerance and acceptance of differences constitute essential features of a harmoniously functioning world (Bertau 1983). Other authors, such as the anonymous author of the goliardic epic *Herzog Ernst* (ca.1220; King 1959), deal also with the foreign in a surprisingly unorthodox manner. The protagonist travels through many countries in the mythical East and encounters monsters of all kinds. Negative judgments, however, emerge only when there are moral and ethical conflicts between the Europeans and the peoples of monstrous races, whereas in all other cases the narrator presents a largely positive image of them, indicating that tolerant relations, or we could even claim multiculturalism, were a possibility (Classen 1996a, 214).

Whereas I have on a previous occasion examined at greater length these twelve- and thirteenth-century texts, Wolfram von Eschenbach's narratives and *Herzog Ernst* with respect to their approach to the motif of the Saracen princess (Classen 1997), here I would like to turn to the late Middle Ages and consider several literary documents for their reflection of the foreign world which increasingly made its presence felt even in the heartlands of Europe. In particular, I want to investigate how the cultural situation changed after the last crusades had been crushed and Acre, the last Christian bastion in Palestine, had been taken by the Arabs in 1291. The focal point, in other words, will be the period when European dominance began to shrink but a number of personal contacts established significant cultural bridges, such as the conversion to Christianity of the Mongol prince Öngut Körguz and his baptism as "Prince George" (Heer 1961, 155-156). It was a time when the "attraction of Muslim learning, Muslim culture, and Muslim sophistication was extremely strong" (Tolan 1996, xx; Rodinson 1988).

Admittedly, we would be hard pressed to find direct reflections of the changed situation on the southeastern borders of Europe and of the new balance of power between Orient and Occident in thirteenth- and fourteenth-century German secular literature. We can, however, observe significant transformations in the way in which certain literary motifs were incorporated and the protagonists operate not only on the traditional Arthurian stage, but instead increasingly explore new worlds, both of fictional and factual origin. Indeed, the Celtic background of Arthurian literature was rapidly losing its attractiveness for the contemporary audience and gave way to new exotic adventures, which take the heroes into the world of the Orient where they have to cope with entirely new experiences and people (Stanesco 1992).

The anonymous author of the goliardic epic *Herzog Ernst* (ms. A ca. 1190; ms. B ca. 1220; King 1959) and Wolfram von Eschenbach paved the way for their successors to explore avenues for Christian heroes to meet and accept non-Christians on an equal footing, either as warriors or as lovers. In particular, one of Wolfram's greatest achievements was to outline profound and entirely unorthodox erotic relationships between a Christian knight, Gahmuret, and a black queen, Belakane, in *Parzival* (ca. 1200), and between a Provençal count, Willehalm, and his originally Moslem wife, Gyburg, in *Willehalm* (ca. 1218; Heinzle 1994). In a subtle but powerful fashion the poet outlines certain forms of tolerance which would find few parallels in contemporary European literature (Schwinges 1977).

Only about eighty years later, i.e., about 1300, an anonymous Swiss writer who was obviously influenced by Wolfram's attitude toward non-Christians, formulates in the crusade epic *Reinfried von Braunschweig* the significant statement: "sit man nieman sol twingen / ze kristenlichen dingen" (since nobody should be forced to accept the Christian belief ...) and outlines a curious episode in which the protagonist defeats a young Persian king but does not kill him for humanitarian reasons (Bartsch 1871). In return for having spared his life the defeated king turns over to the Christians the city of Jerusalem and the Holy Grave. At the same time Reinfried strikes a friendship with his former opponent and accepts his invitation to visit Persia to satisfy his curiosity (Müller 1996, 326-27). Together the two young men tour the vast empire and observe a wide range of strange monsters, beasts, and plants. When Reinfried learns from messengers that his wife back in Europe has delivered a baby boy, he parts from his new-found friend and returns home, but not without having been lavishly honored by the king who gives him many valuable gifts.

In other words, the narrator, who must have been aware of the fall of Acre to the Arabs in 1291, did not hesitate to outline such personal, tolerant relations free of any religious prejudice, though he still believed, considering the reference to the successful crusade which provides the narrative framework, in the possibility of a Christian victory over the heathens. His romance turns into a truly medieval manifesto advocating religious tolerance as Reinfried refrains from baptizing the Persian king and accepts in him the fellow human being irrespective of the religious difference. The king himself points out that such a forced conversion would only result in hypocrisy and pretense, and would deeply hurt his own honor (Bartsch 1871, vv. 17876-95). Reinfried acknowledges that baptism cannot occur unless the person involved is truly convinced of the new belief (vv. 17920-21) and points out that "ze mînem gote kêre / muoz mit frîgem willen sîn" (vv. 17904-05; he who turns to my God must do so out of his free will). The idea of the crusade is basically lost and replaced by a rudimentary form of tolerance and curiosity about the exotic world in the East (Wentzlaff-Eggebert 1960, 289-290).

The situation in French literature seems to have been quite different, especially if we consider the genre of the *chanson de geste*. Here the topos of the "Saracen Princess" primarily served, as Sharon Kinoshita has argued recently, as an erotic justification for imperialistic attitudes toward the foreigners: "The violence of the military conquest of the religious and cultural Other must be erased in the Saracen's woman's willing embrace of the conqueror and all he represents ... . By casting the epic crusade in the form of an amorous intrigue, tropes of 'courtly love' ... may be mobilized in the service of an ideology of expansion and conquest" (1995, 286). Of course, a very similar conclusion could be drawn for Priest Conrad's Middle High German *Rolandslied* (ca. 1170), but both Wolfram and his successors counterbalanced this racially myopic ideology with their attempts to describe non-Europeans and non-Christians as members of Creation, as people of potentially very high cultural standards. In other words, strong medieval xenophobia was quickly balanced by a profoundly humanistic approach to other cultures at least in a few, though significant, cases.

One of the representatives of such a humanistic approach was Ulrich von dem Türlin, who flourished in the second half of the thirteenth century. Like Wolfram he composed a *Willehalm* epos (Singer 1968) in which he elaborated on those passages where Wolfram had deliberately left huge gaps. Apparently he relied heavily on Wolfram's text as a narrative framework without consulting any French source. From an acrostic we know that Ulrich dedicated his work to the Bohemian King

Ottokar II (1253-1278). Although most manuscripts only contain a fragment, the work itself is consistent and leads the reader to the point where Wolfram begins with his battle descriptions. This text can also serve us to explore further how the "Saracen-Princess" topos was applied in medieval German literature and whether the image of the converted princess is in agreement with the impression conveyed in the French and the early German tradition. The major aspect of this *Willehalm* epic consists of the long description of how the eponymous hero spends many years in a Moslem prison and how he wins Arabel's heart and hand, and returns with her to his home lands. The text concludes with an extensive description of her final conversion and baptism. Hans-Joachim Behr interpreted this romance as testimony to the absolute significance of courtly joy; i.e., the communal effort to create joy at court to a point at which the individual becomes subservient to society's well-being (1989, 134-138). Neither he nor other scholars, however, have paid any attention to the curious situation of the heathen world depicted in highly positive terms. Here I will focus on Arabel only and examine her as an intriguing example of how the "Saracen-Princess" topos was dealt with in late-medieval German literature.

As in all other crusade epics, Ulrich's narrative idealizes Christianity and presents it as the ultimate goal for his audience. In this sense neither the earlier Wolfram von Eschenbach nor the later author of *Reinfried von Braunschweig* would have contradicted him. Arabel's eventual conversion serves to confirm the superiority of the Christian religion and as such does not need any particular reexamination. The description of the heathen court and the characterization of Arabel and her husband Tybalt deserve, however, closer analysis. The author does not hide the fact that the prisoner has been taken to a heathen country as Arabel is said to rule over "heidentuomes" (Singer 1968, 77 l. 25; heathendom) and the members of the court are called "heidenriter" (78 l. 1; heathen knights). But he does not display any particularly negative feelings toward those people and their court. On the contrary, we notice that he portrays Arabel as a beautiful lady whose appearance dazzles Willehalm and who commands all the skills required of the wife of a renowned courtly ruler. Willehalm falls in love irrespective of the religious difference, which functions only as a hindrance which he has to overcome to prove his inner strength and true feelings for Arabel. Moreover, we quickly begin to learn how much the prisoner commands respect and how courtly Tybalt treats him as the most powerful representative of Christian knighthood (Singer 1968, 80-81).

Arabel clearly emerges as an ideal character despite her heathen religion. The narrator emphasizes: "Nu hoert von der minneholden, / der süez ich hôhe prüeven solde" (Singer 1968, 82 ll. 32-33; Now hear of the lovely lady whose sweetness I must doubtless confirm). Similarly, her women friends, widow queens whose husbands had been killed by Willehalm in battle, shine through their nobility and beauty. Even the deceased rulers earn epithets such as "edel[ ] môr" (94 l. 22; the noble black), and the only difference between the nobles of this world and the Christians lies in their adherence to "heathen" gods. After a while Willehalm is allowed to come out of his prison because one of the queens, Tussangulê, wishes to see him whom she describes as the most noble knight she has ever heard of (102). Nevertheless, the narrator also puts the following words of praise of Tussangulê's late husband in her mouth: "wie sich der göte helf vergaz / an dem edeln künege Tûzamanz / des tât ie was in prîse ganz!" (102 ll. 24-26; how deplorable that the gods denied their help for the noble King Tûzamanz whose deeds were highly praised).

Arabel, although she will soon fall in love with Willehalm, is an admirable wife and has an endearing relationship with Tybalt (Singer 1968, 104 l. 6) which finds its only parallel in that of her black friend's previous marriage (105). When Tybalt has to leave for war against his enemy, he communicates with her in the same way as any Christian ruler would: "… 'frowe, ich wil / urlop hân von dîner güete / und bit dich, daz dîn triuwe behüete / den helt, der hie gevangen lît" (112 ll. 18-21; Lady, I beg you to let me go and ask you that your loyalty will be the guard for the hero who is imprisoned here). Curiously, he even places her in the protection of their gods who here seem to be powerful and effectual. Mohammed is called "süeze[ ] Mahmet" (113 l. 6; the dear Mohammed), as the gods' help has often been proven. Ironically, Tybalt also appeals to the goddess Venus (113 ll. 16-17), not knowing that Venus will eventually take Arabel away from him and turn her love to Willehalm.

The narrator does not shy away from presenting the marital relationship as ideal and harmonious, filled with strong emotions and commitment. Arabel hugs and kisses Tybalt before he has to depart, which prompts the narrator to comment: "man muoste der minne kunst hie jehen / und minneklîcher liebe tuon" (Singer 1968, 115 ll. 10-11; you could here witness the art of love and its effects). The moment of separation is filled with love and pain, and Ulrich freely employs all his literary skills in conveying to his audience the depth of the emotions displayed by both persons, the one departing, the other staying behind, and thus conceived a literary image of profound and loyal love (119). Tragically for Tybalt, as the text insinuates indirectly, this love will not last, and Willehalm will soon replace the husband who is involved in warfare far from home. This does not mean, however, that the subsequent affair sheds a negative light on the marriage. The groundwork for the love between Willehalm and Arabel is laid from the very moment when the prisoner arrives at court and sees her (78), but it is not the male hero's Christianity, instead only his heroic figure and physical beauty which prepare her heart for loving him. Arabel later receives an introduction to his religion and accepts his teachings (132 ff.); from then on the Western concept of its own absolute dominance is borne out, as the two lovers escape on a ship, and despite Tybalt's pursuit, successfully make the voyage back to France. From here on Wolfram von Eschenbach's narrative continues, whereas Ulrich's lengthy literary interpolations end.

Several conclusions can be drawn from these few observations. Ulrich never speaks badly about Tybalt or Arabel, or, for that matter, any other heathen. They are simply the Christians' opponents and do not know anything about the true God. Nevertheless, here as well as in Wolfram's narrative, the heathens follow closely the ideal of a courtly lifestyle and emerge as respected, even admirable characters. Their only fault is not to accept Christ as their god and thus to stay in heathendom.

The "Saracen Princess" Arabel does not advocate tolerance and humanitarian ideas as in Wolfram's text, but she is nevertheless a positive character. The same applies to her former husband, his knights and servants, and Arabel's women friends and relatives. Werner Schröder correctly points out that the epic's true message rests in the love between Arabel and Willehalm, not in religious conflict or any possible effort to demonstrate the superiority of Christianity. Although their love is conditioned by this conflict, and to some extent even aggravates it militarily, from a human point of view, Ulrich offers a model case of how cultural differences could be overcome and new relationships created if love serves as the intermediary (Schröder 1984, 4).

Arabel becomes guilty of adultery, but as long as she is officially married to Tybalt and lives with him, she demonstrates that "heathens" can be praiseworthy people who are strong in their feelings, powerful in their actions, and noble in their behavior. Ulrich does not pursue the same agenda as Wolfram: whereas the latter has Gyburg proclaim that the heathens are her relatives and people worthy of the Christians' pity and mercy, Arabel simply abandons her former belief and follows her new lover, Willehalm. Yet, as a heathen queen and wife of Tybalt, Arabel illustrates that for the poet religious differences have no bearing on the evaluation of a person. Tybalt's court is as ideal as Willehalm's, and both men perform heroic deeds in warfare. In parallel to this, Ulrich's pre-conversion Arabel is as attractive in character and physical beauty as Wolfram's post-conversion Gyburg, as her conversion does not strengthen her personality, intellect, or renown. In this sense Ulrich's text contradicts Kinoshita's claims derived from her interpretation of the Old French *chansons de geste* as far as the first part of this epic is concerned in which Willehalm meets his future wife and both fall in love with each other. At the end of the epic, though, when the crusade theme gains in preponderance, Ulrich's relatively positive attitude toward the heathens gives way to traditionally hostile and confrontational perceptions. Willehalm, for instance, announces that Tybalt will be compensated for his love pains with deadly wounds on the battle field (Singer

1968, 395 ll. 10-12). This cannot, however, make us forget how the narrator introduced the world of the oriental court and how positively he painted the love between Arabel and her husband (Höcke 1996; Schröder 1989, 484).

It would be easily possible to find other, mostly negative examples in Middle High German literature of how Christians viewed Moslems, but the cases discussed here provide enough evidence that the topos of the "Saracen Princess" could be structured on the basis of different ideological agendas and might actually turn the traditional paradigm upside down, idealizing the heathens and singing a praise of their beauty, strength, and courtly behavior. Perhaps the modern labels "tolerant" or "humanitarian" are anachronistic (Heinzle 1994, 301-308), but the literary examples indicate that, at least conceptually, personal contacts based on friendship and love could have existed between Moslems and Christians. Some circles within the Christian church advocated fairly similar ideas at the end of the twelfth century, and it is likely that Wolfram knew their work (Schwinges 1977, 276; Bertau 1983, 245).

Ulrich von Türheim was less attached to theological questions and sources, and simply portrayed a world of heathen court life that was more or less the same as in Europe. The heathens are, according to his views, the losers not because he perceives them as the Christians' deadly enemies but because Willehalm needs to prove himself against a superior force and justify Arabel's decision for him over her heathen husband Tybalt. The "Saracen Princess" makes a deliberate choice for a new husband out of love for Willehalm, not, however, necessarily against Tybalt because he is a heathen and would not convert to Christianity. It could be that as the end of the Crusades appeared inevitable the religious motif lost its attractiveness in literary discourse and gave way to more open relations between different peoples (Höcke 1996, 310).

The "Saracen-Princess" topos is treated rather naively in *Herzog Ernst* and in Ulrich von dem Türlin's *Willehalm*, whereas Wolfram made a deliberate attempt to explore the cultural, religious, and ideological implications of marriage between a woman of Moslem and a man of Christian faith, both being of different races. The anonymous author of the later *Reinfried von Braunschweig* does not allow Eros to intervene in the course of his travel account, and hence dispenses with the "Princess" topos. Nevertheless his romance unequivocally determines that the time of religious conflicts is over, and so also is the destructive one-sided Christian claim on global superiority. Johann von Würzburg, in his crusade epic *Wilhelm von Österreich* (1314; Regel [1906] 1970), still resorted to this topic but not for religious reasons. Wilhelm and the Heathen princess Aglye meet as children and fall in love. Her father tries to prevent their union and sends Wilhelm away, but eventually, after Wilhelm has proven his chivalric prowess and Aglye her courtly ideals, the father is defeated and the young people are allowed to marry once she has converted to his religion. Tolerance in the modern sense cannot be detected in any of these texts, but certainly they show tolerant attitudes and enough interest in foreign peoples to make their voices heard and force the reader or listener to modify his/her epistemological paradigm. Two texts, one from the fifteenth, the other from the early sixteenth century, will illustrate this point even further.

The exploration of the East continued to exert a strong fascination for late-medieval audiences, and hence the goliardic epic *Herzog Ernst* experienced great popularity far into the sixteenth century (Gerhardt 1973). In the oldest print version of *Herzog Ernst*, the so-called *Das Lied von Herzog Ernst* printed in Bamberg in 1493 by Hannsen Spörer (King 1959), we even learn that the protagonist successfully rescues the Indian Princess from the crane people and returns with her to India where her parents, who this time have not been killed by the Grippians, welcome the former Crusader as their son-in-law. The Emperor is so happy about his daughter's safe return that he promises Ernst: "Vnd solt nach meinem tode sein / Gewaltig über indian" (King 1959, 66 ll. 11-12; you will wield all power over India after my death). Ernst stays in India for many years and experiences a joyful life filled with love and happiness. It is a life in which he does not appear to observe any significant cultural and religious difference with his former environment. Courtly festivals resemble those back in Europe (67 ll. 5-7) as the courtiers are also called "ritter( ) vnd ... knechte( )" (73 l. 10; knights and squires). Hunting and tournaments are the usual forms of entertainment also in India (77) where Ernst is greatly honored and given many valuable gifts.

One day he writes to his mother back in Germany "Wie wol es im ergangen wer" (King 1959, 82 l. 2; how fortunate his life had been), indicating that the foreign world represents a viable alternative to his former existence. Eventually, though, after the Emperor has died, Ernst returns to Germany and assumes the throne because "jm gefiel baß teütsche land / Dann in der haydenschaffte" (86 ll. 5-6; he liked it better in Germany than in the heathen country). Obviously it was not possible for the composer of this song to completely ignore religious differences between both worlds; yet the traditional crusader mentality has given way to an early-modern curiosity and interest in the exotic Orient that offers a comfortable alternative to conflict-ridden Europe. The "Saracen-Princess" topos lost much of its ideological edge and simply satisfied the interest in the mysterious East. Significantly, therefore, the early-modern narrator indicates that a Christian ruler could easily marry a heathen princess without any religious qualms about his spiritual well-being and without being criticized for it by the Church.

In other words, the sixteenth-century German audience was no longer interested in the Crusader ideology and instead was primarily concerned with sensational accounts such as contained in this balladic folk epic. The issue of tolerance of foreign cultures had become defused, probably because internal problems concerned the Europe reading audience much more than missionary tasks, and the "Saracen" Princess had turned into an erotic cultural icon simply representing the difference of the East, though certainly without (!) the imperialistic approach characterizing the modern age (Said [1978] 1995). Ernst's encounter with the princess in the *Lied* version (King 1959) is void of any religious connotation, and instead she serves to prove his chivalric abilities and success as a leader of his people. Moreover, she illustrates that the exotic foreigners must not be categorized according to the same ethnic and moral standards. Whereas the narrator characterizes the crane people as murderers and thieves, the Indians are admirable, honorable, and grateful. This form of differentiation, however, was already noticeable in the twelfth- and thirteenth-century versions. Nevertheless, in the *Lied* version we not only learn that the princess is a beautiful and noble young lady, but also that she is a member of a people who share by and large the same social and ethical value system as the Christian Europeans. Consequently Herzog Ernst's sojourn of ten years turns out to be most pleasurable and comfortable for him and his servant: "Es was keinem fürsten nye baß / Dann weil er zů india was" (King 1959, 77 ll. 4-5; No lord ever had a better life than he while he stayed in India).

Even before the composition of this popular song, other authors vivaciously expressed their disagreement with the traditionally narrow European viewpoint and argued for a tolerant treatment of other people. In 1432/33 the southern French Bertrandon de la Brocquière, who had traveled throughout Arabic and Turkish lands, observed in his travel account that the Moslems (here the Turks) were highly peaceful people and exercised a particular form of tolerance with respect to the people in the territories that they had conquered (Kühnel 1993, 422).

Finally, the anonymous author of the chapbook *Fortunatus* (1509; Müller 1990) indicates that Christian travelers face more dangers and criminal injustice in Christian lands than in Turkish territories. The protagonist was nearly killed in London for being in the service of a Florentine merchant who had been falsely accused of having stolen jewels and having killed another man (Müller 1990, 408-422). He must fear the same destiny in Constantinople again because his servant Lüpoldus killed their inn-keeper when he tried to burglarize them (458). He and all his men are only safe from unfair prosecution once they have crossed the border into the Turkish empire where they receive, in return for some money they have to pay per person, a safe conduct through the land ("glaitt," 462). Nevertheless, once Fortunatus has arrived at the Turkish emperor's court and discovered that "souil der verlogneten cristen vnder dem volck was" (463; so many of the lying Christians were in the throng) he quickly leaves again and continues with his grand Tour d'Europe through the Northern countries.

Religion is no longer the decisive criterion to determine the ethical and moral standards of a people. The anonymous author harbors highly negative views about his contemporaries but does not distinguish among Christians and non-Christians as such. At a later time, when Fortunatus has embarked on his second world travel which takes him through the eastern Mediterranean and as far as India, danger arises for him again from his competitors, the Italian merchants who envy his wealth and personal contacts with the Sultan and his political advisors (Müller 1990, 486-488). Nevertheless, Fortunatus succeeds in securing a pass from the Sultan to travel to the East accompanied by guides and translators (489-492) because they have become his friends ("was ym lieb," 488; "gûten freünd," 492). Before Fortunatus returns home to Cyprus, the Sultan invites him to an honorable dinner to find out about his experiences. Again the protagonist emphasizes the great help he had received from the Sultan in the form of the pass: "sagt ym wie das er durch seiner brieff willen gar eerlich vnd schon von allen herren entpfangen wâr worden / vnd wie ym all ander herren für vnnd für so grosse fürdernus hetten gethon" (493; told him how he had been welcomed in a friendly and very honorable fashion by all lords and how these lords had provided him with great help).

Eventually, however, even Fortunatus betrays his own value system and steals a magical cap from the Sultan with which he can transport himself wherever he wants at a moment's notice (Müller 1990, 497). The Sultan is deeply distraught over the loss of his most valuable treasure and tries to retrieve the cap with the help of an emissary, Marcholando (500-502). Yet, Fortunatus does not accept any offer to sell the cap either, although he asks the emissary not to begrudge his unwillingness in this matter. Since the King of Cyprus does not help Marcholando in retrieving the cap, it stays in the possession of Fortunatus, who argues: "Angesehenn / das kayn haydenn kainen Christen liebhaben mag / noch auch kayn gûtes günnen Vnnd wo künig Soldan das hûtlin hett vnd mein wâr / er sandte es mir warlicher sachen auch nit wider" (503; considering that no heathen can like a Christian, nor let him have any good, and considering that if King Soldan had the cap in his possession although it belonged to me, he certainly would also not return it to me).

Fortunatus' theft does not have any significant consequences for him, but both his treasures, a magical purse which never runs empty and the magical cap, will eventually be the source for both his sons' miserable demises. Nevertheless, the one aspect of interest for us here is not the overall development of the certainly highly fascinating chapbook (Classen 1995), but rather the open-minded description of the foreign world and its people. The heathen rulers treat Fortunatus justly and with friendship, whereas the Christian rulers, with the exception of the Cypriot king, appear as unreliable, tyrannical, and unjust. The narrator praises the exotic world of the Orient by means of the exordia topos, indicating that many Europeans would go there if they had the same financial means as Fortunatus (Müller 1990, 491). In particular, he observes that those foreign peoples have many different customs and beliefs which make them no worse or better than the Europeans (491). One reason, however, why they do not travel to Europe is simply that "sy wurden für toren geschâtzt / das sy auß gûten landen in bôse zugen / vnd gût vmb bôß gâbenn" (491; they would be considered fools if they traveled from good countries to bad countries). In a way, the narrator almost idealizes the East, completely disregarding the religious difference, although he also refers to the messianic and mystical Prester John who allegedly brought Christianity to the heartlands of Asia (490).

Certainly, Fortunatus explains to Marcholando that he would keep the stolen cap because of the eternal hatred between Moslems and Christians (Müller 1990, 503), but his own actions on his travels, especially his personal contacts with the Sultan indicate the opposite. In other words, this chapbook reveals that religious conflicts no longer concern European readers; instead the fascination which the foreign world exerts on the audience dominates this early modern novel (Kästner 1990, 105-106). European protagonists, whether Herzog Ernst in the *Lied* version (King 1959) or Fortunatus, experience the Orient no longer as a threatening and dangerous world which needs to be converted. Christian zeal has been discarded, and has given room to forms of tolerant attitudes. Whereas in the Middle High German romances the heroes win the love of Saracen princesses and make them convert to Christianity, in the fifteenth- and sixteenth-century texts the European travelers visit the Orient, marry and live there for lengthy periods, explore the countries and report back to their audiences. The absence of imperialistic attitudes is remarkable, and, we might add, so is the considerable degree of tolerance toward the foreigners. They are no longer a danger, but simply different people who would be ill-advised to travel to Europe and to leave their own beautiful countries behind. As the narrator in Fortunatus emphasizes, both the weather and the cultural climate in Europe would be detrimental to his Asian contemporaries. Nevertheless, the attractive Orient remains just that, attractive, but it does not convince the European traveler to stay there either.

## REFERENCES

Bartsch, Karl, ed. 1871. *Reinfried von Braunschweig*. Bibliothek des litterarischen Vereins in Stuttgart, 109. Stuttgart: Litterarischer Verein.

Beckingham, C. F. 1983. *Between Islam and Christendom. Travellers, Facts and Legends in the Middle Ages and the Renaissance*. London: Variorum Reprints.

Behr, Hans-Joachim. 1989. *Literatur als Machtlegitimation. Studien zur Funktion der deutschsprachigen Dichtung am böhmischen Königshof im 13. Jahrhundert*. Forschungen zur Geschichte der älteren deutschen Literatur, 9. Munich: Fink.

Bertau, Karl. 1983. Das Recht des Andern. Über den dichterischen Ursprung der Vorstellung von einer Schonung der Irrgläubigen bei Wolfram. In Karl Bertau, *Wolfram von Eschenbach. Neun Versuche über Subjektivität und Ursprünglichkeit in der Geschichte*. 241-258. Munich: Beck.

Classen, Albrecht. 1995. *The German Volksbuch. A Critical History of a Late-Medieval Genre*. Studies in German Language and Literature, 15. Lewiston-Queenston-Lampeter: The Edwin Mellen Press.

———. 1996a. Multiculturalism in the German Middle Ages? The Rediscovery of a Modern Concept in the Past: The Case of *Herzog Ernst*. In *Multiculturalism and Representation. Selected Essays*, ed. John Rieder and Larry E. Smith, 198-219. Honolulu: College of Languages, Linguistics and Literature, University of Hawaii.

———. 1996b. Marco Polo's "Il Milione/Le Divisament dou Monde": Der Mythos vom Osten. In *Herrscher, Helden, Heilige*, ed. Ulrich Müller, Werner Wunderlich; collaborator and editor Lotte Gaebel, 423-436. Mittelalter-Mythen, 1. St. Gallen: UVK.

———. 1998. Confrontation with the Foreign World of the East: Saracen Princesses in Medieval German Narratives. *Orbis Litterarum* 53: 277-95.

Flasch, Kurt, and Udo Reinhold Jeck, eds. 1997. *Das Licht der Vernunft. Die Anfänge der Aufklärung im Mittelalter*. Munich: Beck.

*Fortunatus* = Müller 1990.

Gerhardt, Christoph. 1973. Verwandlung eines Zeitliedes. Aspekte der deutschen Herzog-Ernst-Überlieferung. In *Verführung zur Geschichte. Festschrift zum 500. Jahrestag der Eröffnung der Universität Trier*, ed. Georg Droege, Wolfgang Frühwald, and Ferdinand Pauly, 71-89. Trier: NCO-Verlag.

Goss, Vladimir P., and Verzar Bornstein, eds. 1986. *The Meetings of Two Worlds. Cultural Exchanges between East and West during the Period of the Crusades*. Studies in Medieval Culture, 21. Kalamazoo, Michigan: Medieval Institute Publications.

Heer, Friedrich. 1961. *The Medieval World Europe 1100-1350*. Trans. from the German by Janet Sondheimer. New York-Toronto: The New American Library.

Heinzle, Joachim. 1994. Die Heiden als Kinder Gottes. Notiz zum "Willehalm." *Zeitschrift für deutsches Altertum und deutsche Geschichte* 123, 3: 301-08.

Höcke, Holger. 1996. *Willehalm-Rezeption in der Arabel Ulrichs von dem Türlin*. Europäische Hochschulschriften, Reihe 1: Deutsche Sprache und Literatur, 1586. Frankfurt a.M.-Berlin-et al.: Lang.

Johann von Würzburg, *Willhelm von Österreich* = Regel [1906] 1970.

Kästner, Hannes. 1990. *Fortunatus. Peregrinator Mundi. Welterfahrung und Selbsterkenntnis im ersten deutschen Prosaroman der Neuzeit*. Rombach Wissenschaft. Reihe Litterae. Freiburg: Verlag Rombach.

Kinoshita, Sharon. 1995. The Politics of Courtly Love: *La Prise d'Orange* and the Conversion of the Saracen Queen. *Romance Review* 86, 2: 265-87.

King, K. C., ed. 1959. *Das Lied von Herzog Ernst*. Kritisch herausgegeben nach den Drucken des 15. und 16. Jahrhunderts. Texte des späten Mittelalters, 11. Berlin: Schmidt.

Kühnel, Harry. 1993. Das Fremde und das Eigene. Mittelalter. In *Europäische Mentalitätsgeschichte. Hauptthemen in Einzeldarstellungen*, ed. Peter Dinzelbacher, 422. Stuttgart: Kröner.

Larner, John. 1999. *Marco Polo and the Discovery of the World*. New Haven – London: Yale University Press.

*Das Lied von Herzog Ernst* = King 1959.

Mielke, Andreas. 1992. *Nigra sum et formosa. Afrikanerinnen in der deutschen Literatur des Mittelalters. Texte und Kontexte zum Bild des Afrikaners in der literarischen Imagologie*. Helfant Texte, T 11. Stuttgart: Helfant.

Müller, Jan-Dirk, ed. 1990. "Fortunatus." In *Romane des 15. and 16 Jahrhunderts*. Bibliothek der frühen Neuzeit, 1: 385-585. Frankfurt a.M.: Deutscher Klassiker Verlag.

Müller, Ulrich. 1996. Toleranz zwischen Christen und Muslimen im Mittelalter? Zur Archäologie der Beziehungen zwischen dem christlich-lateinischen Okzident und dem islamischen Orient. In *Kulturthema Toleranz. Zur Grundlegung einer interdisziplinären und interkulturellen Toleranzforschung*, ed. Alois Wierlacher, 307-353. Munich: iudicium, 1996.

Regel, Ernst, ed. [1906] 1970. *Johann von Würzburg. Willhelm von Österreich*. Deutsche Texte des Mittelalters, 3. Berlin: Weidmann; rpt. Dublin: Weidmann.

Reichert, Folker F. 1992. *Begegnung mit China. Die Entdeckung Ostasiens im Mittelalter*. Beiträge zur Geschichte und Quellenkunde des Mittelalters, 15. Sigmaringen: Thorbecke.

*Reinfried von Braunschweig* = Bartsch 1871.

Rodinson, Maxim. 1980. *La fascination de l'Islam*. Petite Collection Maspero, 243. Paris: F. Maspero. Trans. Roger Veinus as *Europe and the Mystique of Islam*. London: Tauris, 1988.

Said, Edward. [1978] 1995. *Orientalism*. Harmondsworth: Penguin.

Schröder, Werner. 1984. *"Arabel"-Studien III. Arabel und Willehalm auf west-östlichem Divan.* Abhandlungen der Geistes- und Sozialwissenschaftlichen Klasse, 1984/9. Wiesbaden: Akademie der Wissenschaften und der Literatur.

Schroder, Werner. 1989. "Deswar ich liez ouch minne dort." Arabel-Gyburgs Ehebruch. In *Wolfram von Eschenbach. Spuren und Werke. Kleinere Schriften 1956-1987.* 1: 472-485. Stuttgart: Hirzel.

Schwinges, Rainer Christoph. 1977. *Kreuzzugsideologie und Toleranz. Studien zu Wilhelm von Tyrus.* Monographien zur Geschichte des Mittelalters, 15. Stuttgart: Hiersemann.

Singer, Samuel, ed. 1968. *Ulrich von dem Türlin. Willehalm.* Bibliothek der Mittelhochdeutschen Literatur in Böhmen, 4. Hildesheim: Georg Olms.

Southern, Richard William. 1962. *Western Views of Islam in the Middle Ages.* Cambridge, Mass.: Harvard University Press.

Stanesco, Michel. 1992. Le chevalier médiévale en voyage: du pèlerinage romanesque à l'érrance dans l'autre monde. *Diesseits- und Jensseitsreisen im Mittelalter*, ed. Wolf-Dieter Lange, 189-203. Studium Universale, 14. Bonn: Bouvier.

Tolan, John Victor, ed. 1996. *Medieval Christian Perceptions of Islam. A Book of Essays.* Garland Medieval Casebooks. New York-London: Garland.

Ulrich von dem Türlin, *Willehalm* = Singer 1968.

Wentzlaff-Eggebert, Friedrich-Wilhelm. 1960. *Kreuzzugsdichtung des Mittelalters. Studien zu ihrer geschichtlichen und dichterischen Wirklichkeit.* Berlin: de Gruyter.

# 6

# Dreams and Visions: A Comparative Analysis of Spiritual Gifts in Medieval Christian and Muslim Conversion Narratives[*]

*Linda G. Jones*

> The examples for our life are found in contemplation of the dangers that befall others.
> Pirro Ligorio, *Della antichità di Roma*

MEDIEVAL CHRISTIAN AND MUSLIM WRITERS of autobiographical conversion narratives invariably sought to edify, encourage, counsel, and even entertain their readers through the examples of their own lives. Their autobiographies differ in many respects, however. For example, the nominal audience for Christian authors is frequently God or the Virgin Mary, whereas Muslims typically address their fellow Muslims. Structurally, chronological order is normative in Western Christian autobiography; in Muslim autobiography thematic organisation is more common, although chronological structuring is not entirely absent.

---

[*] I would especially like to thank Dr. Dwight Reynolds, Professor of Arabic Literature and Folklore at the University of California at Santa Barbara, for his encouragement and guidance on this project. I would also like to acknowledge and thank Carol Lansing, Professor of Medieval Christian History, also at Santa Barbara, for her insightful comments and valuable feedback. Naturally any shortcomings or omissions are my own.

Despite these and other differences, dreams, visions and occurrences of supernatural phenomena play a pivotal role in some conversion narratives in both traditions. Medieval people, whether Christian, Muslim or Jewish, considered many of these experiences to be divinely inspired and thus authoritative, or demonically influenced sources of temptation and therefore heralds of spiritual perdition.

The inclusion of these experiences in both Christian and Muslim medieval conversion narratives is remarkable, considering that the two literary traditions developed independently of one another. Many Western scholars have commented upon the role and proliferation of dreams and visions in medieval western literature, including conversion narratives (e.g., Parman 1991, Kruger 1992, Lynch 1988, Hieatt 1967, Gregory 1985, and Le Goff 1980). Until very recently, however, little attention has been given to their contemporary Muslim and Arabophone counterparts.[1] Only a handful of western scholars have investigated the Arabo-Muslim autobiographical tradition and fewer still have undertaken a serious comparison with the Western tradition (*University Library of Autobiography* 1918, Misch 1949-69, Scaglione 1984). This study cannot address the full range of issues stemming from such a comparison – the question of origins, genre(s), the construction of an individual "self," to name just a few.[2] Here I compare the content and interpretation of the dreams and apparitions in the Muslim and Christian autobiographies, and examine their function and deployment, especially as they relate to the author's conversion and to the construction of the narrative. This comparison is particularly intriguing because of the independent development of the two sub-genres.

---

[1] A welcome addition may be found in a recent volume of *Religion*, which was dedicated entirely to the investigation of dreams and visions in Islam. See especially the articles by Hermansen 1997a, 1997b; and Katz 1997.

[2] The recent work *Interpreting the Self: Autobiography in the Arabic Literary Tradition*, edited by Dwight F. Reynolds and coauthored by Kristen E. Burstad, Michael Cooperson, Jamal L. Elias, Nuha N. N. Khoury, Joseph E. Lowry, Nasser Rabat, Dwight F. Reynolds, Devin J. Stewart, and Shawkat M. Toorawa, explores many of these issues (Reynolds ed. 2001).

I examine the conversion narratives of two Christian authors, St. Augustine and the French Benedictine monk Guibert of Nogent, and three Muslim authors, the celebrated theologian and religious reformer Abu Hamid al-Ghazali, a Jewish convert to Islam, Samau'al al-Maghribi, and the Moroccan Sufi Ahmad ibn 'Ajiba. I intend to probe both the similarities and differences that emerge from a close reading of the dreams and spiritual apparitions in the various texts. Some similarities may be readily explained in terms of related scriptural traditions in which dreams and miracles intervene as authoritative discourses. I argue, however, that the differences reveal a more profound contrast between conversion narratives in the Christian tradition of confessing one's sins, and those in the Muslim traditions of enumerating God's blessings and homologizing one's life-narrative with that of the Prophet Muhammad.[3]

I. THE CONVERSION NARRATIVE IN CONTEXT:
AUTOBIOGRAPHY "NORTH" AND "SOUTH"

Geoffrey G. Harpham's exploration of conversion and autobiography argues that "conversion appears as an exemplary plot-climax, a reversal of a certain way of being and a recognition, an awakening to essential being, to one's truest self." In contrast, the autobiography in which the conversion is embedded "confirms the understanding of the self as an

---

[3]The tradition of enumerating God's blessings is based upon the Surat al-Duha (The Glorious Morning Light) 93.11: "But the Bounty of thy Lord – Rehearse and proclaim!" (*wa-ammā bi-ni'mati rabbika, fa-ḥaddith*). The longest known pre-modern Arabic autobiography is by the Egyptian Sufi 'Abd al-Wahhāb al-Sha'rani (d. 1565); entitled *Laṭā'if al-minan wa-l-akhlāq fī wujūb al-taḥadduth bi-ni'mat Allāh 'alā al-itlāq*, it is over 700 pages long and structured as one long list of God's blessings. Reynolds et al. explain that "[the] motivations for presenting one's life as an act of thanking God and so that others might emulate one stand in marked contrast to the confessional mode of many medieval and pre-modern European autobiographies which emphasized the public recognition of one's faults, sins, and shortcomings as a warning to others" (Reynolds ed. 2001, 3).

imitation or repetition of other selves" (Harpham 1988). Although Harpham's study focuses on the *Confessions* of St. Augustine, his comments apply to all the conversion narratives under consideration. The exemplary impulse is present in both the Christian and Muslim traditions, with dreams and visions portrayed as playing an essential role in the author's own conversion and in the anticipated conversion of his intended audience.

What I wish to emphasize here, nevertheless, is that the two autobiographical traditions of works containing conversion narratives developed largely independently from one another. It is possible, as some scholars have surmised, that the Arabo-Muslim autobiographic tradition found a precursor in the pre-Islamic autobibliographical writings of Galen, Pseudo-Aristotle, and the Persian scholar and physician Burzôê (e.g., Rosenthal 1939; al-Ghamdi 1989, 42-51). Yet more plausible arguments have been made for the primacy of indigenous Arabic literary roots (von Grunebaum 1946, 261ff.).[4] Reynolds et al. have demonstrated that Arabic autobiography derives primarily from two distinct but indigenous cultural traditions. Narratives of the life of the Prophet Muhammad and the amassing of the biographical data of his companions and later scholars who transmitted the prophetic traditions, in combination with a scholarly tradition that privileges classification, categorization and description, gave birth to the Arabic autobiographical genre (Reynolds ed. 2001, 36-48). By contrast, the Western autobiography finds its closest paradigms in literary fiction, the ancient and chivalric epics, medieval hagiography, and the nineteenth-century novel (Scaglione 1984, 467; Pascal 1960, 52, quoted in Reynolds ed. 2001, 246).

Some examples of cross-fertilization between European and Arabic autobiographies exist. The tenth-century philosopher al-Razi [Rhazes], the eleventh-century philosopher Ibn Sina [Avicenna], and the twelfth-

---

[4]Reynolds et al. recognize that pre-Islamic texts by Galen, Aristotle, and Burzôê constitute "one thread of the early historical development of the Arabic autobiography," although he argues that "a far stronger impulse" may be found in the indigenous Arabic biographical traditions, the *sira* and the *tarjama* (Reynolds ed. 2001, 47-48).

century Jewish convert to Islam, Samau'al al-Maghribi, whose autobiography I shall examine below, acknowledged familiarity with the autobiographies of Galen and Pseudo-Aristotle (Reynolds ed. 2001, 45). An even more fascinating instance of cross-cultural influence occurs in the autobiography of King James I of Aragon (1208-1276), the *Llibre dels Feys* (*Book of Deeds*). Some scholars have asserted that this rare example of a medieval European royal autobiography "may have been influenced by Arabic heroic *sira* literature," – the earliest genre of Arabic biography (Reynolds ed. 2001, 31; Burns 1984, 285-288; Armistead 1990; Vernet 1978, 333).

Arabic influences have also been noted in the interpretation of dreams in European medieval literature. According to Steven F. Kruger, some of the most influential medieval European commentators on dreams, including Vincent of Beauvais and Albertus Magnus, cited al-Ghazali, and philosophers Ibn Sina, al-Farabi and Ishaq [Isaac] ibn 'Imran alongside Aristotle and Augustine in their commentaries (Kruger 1992, 100, 101, 104, 106). The spiritual autobiographies of converts to an entirely different religious tradition provide further intriguing examples of cross-cultural influences. We shall see in the following discussion how skillfully Samau'al al-Maghribi deploys a vision of a personal encounter with the Prophet Muhammad in order to persuade his audience of the sincerity of his conversion. Similarly, a thirteenth-century Spanish Christian convert to Islam, Anselmo Turmeda, explicitly modelled the experience of his own conversion after that of a Jewish convert to Islam, 'Abdallah b. Salam, as described in Ibn Ishaq's biography, *The Life of Muhammad* (Ibn Hisham 240). (Turmeda's fascinating autobiography falls outside the scope of this study, due to the absence of visionary or miracle narratives.) While it is indeed intriguing to observe converts such as al-Maghribi and Turmeda self-consciously borrowing the religious, cultural, and literary motifs of their chosen religious tradition, the fact remains that medieval Christian and Muslim autobiographical conversion narratives developed separately *as genres*.

The very act of constructing one's life into a conversion narrative presupposes a conscious understanding by the author of his or her own life as an example to others. This mimetic impulse is apparent in both Christian and Muslim autobiography, whether or not the author voices his/her motivations. In both cases, the exemplary, edifying and instructive functions of the conversion narrative in general, and of dreams in particular, remind us that the act of conversion is not merely personal, it is also a social phenomenon. Part of the allure of conversion in Augustine's *Confessions* stems from his reading of Athanasius' hagiographical account of another Christian convert in the *Life of Anthony*. In turn, Augustine's dramatic conversion spurs his companion Alypius to convert. Although Guibert of Nogent does not mention the *Confessions* in his memoirs, it is apparent from their confessional mode and his insistence upon his own sinfulness and iniquity in contrast with his mother's piety, that his autobiography, and indeed his conversion, owes much to his spiritual predecessor. Similarly, al-Ghazali, Samau'al al-Maghribi, and Ibn 'Ajiba each in his own way conforms to the Islamic traditions of adopting the Prophet Muhammad as a spiritual role-model and of recounting the blessings which God has bestowed upon the author's life. In so doing, the author consciously offers his own spiritual life-story as a model to his followers and inserts himself into a genealogy of religious and literary ancestors.[5] Moreover, the Islamic literary device of addressing one's fellow Muslims immediately suggests the social relevance of autobiography.

Harpham states that "conversion appears as an exemplary plot-climax" in the autobiography (Harpham 1988, 43). I would add that dreams and visions sometimes play a climactic role in the conversion itself. Kruger has observed that "[the] association between dreams and conversion is an ancient one" which may be traced back at least to the circumstances surrounding the Emperor Constantine's conversion to

---

[5]Indeed, as Reynolds et al. show in their discussion of al-Suyuti's autobiography, a Muslim intellectual undertook the act of writing an autobiography as a strategy for inserting oneself into a centuries-old intellectual and cultural tradition. Al-Suyuti's preamble includes a list of eminent intellectuals who penned their autobiographies and whom he "emulates in this" (Reynolds ed. 2001, 1-2).

Christianity. An even earlier paradigm is found in Saul/Paul's vision of Jesus on the road to Damascus (Kruger 1992, 221 n. 5; Parman 1991, 33).[6] This association applies also to the inclusion of dreams in Muslim conversion narratives. A hadith, recorded on the authority of the Prophet's wife 'A'isha, establishes the relationship between dreams, divination, and prophecy. She reported that: "[t]he beginning of the prophecy of the Messenger of God, when God wished to make him His agent and the instrument of His mercy towards creatures, (was manifested) by veracious dreams (*ru'yā ṣādiqa*); every dream which he saw in his sleep was as clear as the dawn. This made him love solitude; nothing was more pleasant to him than to be alone" (Ibn Hisham 151; Ibn Sa'd i/1: 129). The same source records another saying of Muhammad relating to dreams: "There exist no signs announcing prophecy other than the good dream [*al-ru'yā al-ḥasana*]; the Muslim sees it or it is seen for him" (Ibn Sa'd ii/2: 18; cf. Ibn Khaldun 3: 81/115). Not surprisingly, traditions recording Muhammad's dreams exist in the vast corpus of literature about the Prophet's life that appeared in the years and centuries following his death (Fahd 1999a, 1999b and [1966] 1987). Such hadiths, coupled with the traditions describing Muhammad's heavenly ascension, and the initial revelation and subsequent visionary encounters with the angel Gabriel, served as models for the spiritual progression of Sufi mystics.

In both the Christian and Muslim cases, the dream or vision appears as a locus of power in the process of conversion. The author's placement of the dream within the conversion narrative demonstrates that he is aware of its pivotal function. Structurally it marks the transformation of the former self into a new spiritual individual. Other scholars have noted the potentially transformative power of dreams and visions. Kruger considers dreaming to be "an anomalous experience, a kind of consciousness present only during unconsciousness ... [and thus] both a

---

[6]In addition to the example of Constantine, Parman also mentions the Frankish conqueror Clovis who "converted to Christianity when his own pagan gods did nothing to help him in battle" (1991, 33).

locus of danger and a source of power." Kathryn Lynch, invoking the language of anthropologist Victor Turner, understands the dream as a "liminal" experience (Kruger 1992, 150).[7] The following examination of the occurrence of dreams, visions, and other spiritual charisms in the autobiographical conversion narratives of St. Augustine, Guibert of Nogent, al-Ghazali, Samau'al al-Maghribi, and Ahmad ibn 'Ajiba aims to understand the nature of these phenomena, how and why they function as locuses of power (or otherwise) in the authors' conversion experiences, and how and why the authors chose to deploy them in the texts.

## II. Dreams and Visions in the Medieval Conversion Narrative

### *Augustine of Hippo (354-430), "The Confessions"*

Beginning with the *Confessions* of St. Augustine, the dreams and visions recounted in the following autobiographies are not only of the authors, but also those of "significant others" – a parent, teacher, spiritual guide or spouse. The dreams of others fulfil as powerful and transformative a function in the life of the author as the author's own, albeit, as we shall see, with some significant differences between the Muslim and Christian narratives. The centrality of Augustine's relationship with his mother Monica, his depiction of her as a paragon of Christian piety in contrast with his own sinfulness, and her ardent desire for his conversion to a Christian life suffice to explain Augustine's inclusion of her dreams in his conversion narrative.

Monica's first dream is recounted at the climax of Book 3: 11 in which Augustine confesses his sins. He describes his soul as having plunged into a "deep darkness" from which God, employing his mother,

---

[7]Kruger derives his understanding of anomalies from anthropologist Mary Douglas' study *Purity and Danger* (1966), especially chapters 2 and 6. See also Lynch 1988, 46-52.

was working to extricate him. It is in this context that he relates her dream: she was standing on a sort of wooden ruler, weeping for her son's perdition, when a "very beautiful young man with a happy face" came upon her and comforted her saying, "where she was, I was too." She then saw Augustine standing close by her on the same ruler (Augustine 1963, 66).

Initially, Augustine misinterprets the dream and his misunderstanding contrasts with his mother's spiritual clarity:

> I tried to twist it to a different meaning, namely, that it was she who need not despair of being one day what I was. But she at once and without the slightest hesitation said, "No; for what was told me was not, 'Where he is, you are too.' It was 'Where you are, he is too'" (1963, 66).

The contrast between his misinterpretation and his mother's clarity is crucial for understanding Augustine's self-perception as a sinner and the confessional mode of his autobiography. Monica was granted this vision and immediately understood its meaning *precisely because she was holy and pious*, whereas he misunderstood it because he was still wallowing in the "deep darkness" of sin. Augustine employs his mother's dream to illustrate the relationship between God and humanity – God hears the prayers of the faithful. Dreams are one way in which he answers their prayers and comforts them in their distress. Augustine reinforces this belief by identifying this dream as an answer to his mother's prayers.

The passage of some nine years between the occurrence of Monica's dream and Augustine's conversion, during which time he explored other paths, continuing to wallow "in the mud of the pit and in the darkness of falsehood," would seem to argue against a direct link between the two events. Yet in the structure of his life narrative Augustine unequivocally relates his conversion to her dream. Assessing the event he writes: "I was now standing on that rule of faith, just as you [i.e. God] had shown me to her in a vision so many years before. And so you had changed her mourning into joy" (1963, 183).

Two of Augustine's own experiences bear mentioning. The first occurs in Book 8: 11, during the pre-conversion storm when he is wrestling with his nemesis Continence. She appears before him in "chaste dignity ... calm and serene ... enticing me to come to her without hesitation ... as though she were saying, 'Can you not do what these men and these women have done?'" (1963, 181). The second experience is a mystical encounter with Wisdom, which occurs in the presence of his mother long after he has converted to Christianity. As the two of them were conversing about God, Augustine writes that "we raised ourselves higher and step by step passed over all material things, even the heaven itself ... and we came to our own souls, and we went beyond our souls to reach that region of never-failing plenty.... And as we talked, yearning toward this Wisdom, we did ... just lightly come into touch with her" (1963, 201). The contrast between Augustine's pre-conversion misunderstandings and vision, and this post-conversion mystical encounter with Wisdom strikingly affirms the profound spiritual transformation that he had undergone.

## *Guibert of Nogent (1055-1125): A Monk's Confession*

Guibert of Nogent, a twelfth-century Benedictine monk from northern France, spent much of his life in the monastery of Saint-Germer-de-Fly and was elected abbot of the monastery at Nogent in 1104. Like Augustine's mother Monica, Guibert's mother acted as the dominant and omnipresent spiritual force in his life. Also like Augustine, Guibert possesses a deep sense of his own ontological sinfulness and frequently contrasts himself, "an evil being," with his mother, "this good woman, who became even holier as time went on" (Guibert of Nogent 1996, 38). In the absence of a father, Guibert's private tutor functioned somewhat as a father figure, although their relationship was marred by his sadistic approach to teaching.

Guibert's memoirs contain fascinating accounts of dreams – his own as well as those of his mother and tutor, episodes of "the workings of the Devil," and the "miracles of the saints" and of Mary. They reveal both his own sense of iniquity and sinfulness vis-à-vis his pious mother, and his anxieties as a novice. They also reflect medieval devotion to the saints and Mary, beliefs in a celestial hierarchy and purgatory, obsessions with the devil, and concerns about monastic piety being addressed simultaneously by the Gregorian reforms.

Unlike Augustine's conversion, which takes place in one climactic scene, Guibert's memoirs present a series of pivotal moments in which he is tempted to stray and which are resolved through a dream or apparition, whether his own or someone else's. Such visions not only resolve conflict, they also indicate the potential of the dream to function as a "rite of passage" from sin to redemption, doubt to faith. During his youth, Guibert defied his mother's wishes and prematurely became a monk while residing in the monastery at Saint-Germer-de-Fly. His initial fervor proved to be no match for his "penchant for sin" and "weak nature" which led him into an infatuation with the "vain and ludicrous activity of studying verse-making and composing poetry" (1996, 58). His "inner turmoil" heightened as he became increasingly torn between the rigors of his monastic vocation and the seduction of composing "lascivious" poetry which prompted "immodest stirrings of [his] flesh" (1996, 59). The crisis was resolved when Guibert's tutor dreamt that an old man with "beautiful white hair" appeared to him and addressed him sternly, saying: "I want you to render an account of these poems that were composed; the hand that wrote them is not that of the man who drew these letters." Both Guibert and his tutor interpreted the dream as a clear sign that he "would not persevere in these shameful activities."

On another occasion the temptations of the secular and sensuous world seduced Guibert to "satisfy [his] ... lusts and other needs" and thus he resolved to transfer to a presumably less restrictive monastery. Although his intentions were initially unbeknownst to his mother, she had a dream warning her of his fate and used it to persuade him to remain at Saint-Germer-de-Fly. She dreamt that she entered the church at Germer-de-Fly and found it completely deserted, the monks scattered, dwarfed in size, and "dressed in clothes entirely out of keeping with the rules of the faith." Mary then entered, followed by her "lady-in-waiting," and declared, pointing directly at Guibert, that she would neither permit the church to be forsaken nor Guibert to leave, and miraculously restored both church and monks to their former splendor. For Guibert, the meaning of the dream is so clear that he "was never again attracted by the thought of changing monasteries" (1996, 56-57). This dream serves three purposes. It illustrates the thaumaturgic power and majesty of Mary, consonant with contemporary notions of Marian spirituality; it demonstrates Guibert's attempts to portray his mother's singular piety and devotion to Mary; and it reconfirms the nature of such dreams as exemplary and authoritative. On this final point, Guibert explicitly acknowledges the ultimate authority and didactic purpose of dreams and infers that this is commonly understood: "... dreams are known to 'come with much business' [Eccles. 5.3], and *nobody doubts this* ..." (emphasis added) (1996, 54).

Guibert experienced grave spiritual anxieties while he was still a novice – anxieties that vividly manifested themselves one night as an encounter with the devil. Seized by panic, he heard a violent clamor of incoherent voices which knocked him unconscious. He then discerned an enormous shadow, the "very contour of the devil," standing before him. He explains this apparition by his conviction that "demons are more vehement in attacking recent converts" (1996, 52). For Guibert, the recent convert or novice is in a liminal position. Lacking the spiritual maturity and fortitude of a more experienced monk, the initiate finds him- or herself caught between the danger of temptation to return to his or her previous life and the power of spiritual enlightenment. The anthropomorphized devil represents this fear of temptation.

Finally, it is notable that Guibert's memoirs include many miracle stories and tales of the devil tormenting sinners. They are highly moralistic and edifying and emphasize the power of good over evil, the certain perdition of those who fail to confess their sins, and the limitless rewards of those who do repent. Guibert is absolutely unrelenting in his condemnation of ecclesiastical avarice and simony, which, judging from the numerous vignettes he recounts of these sins, must have been rife within his contemporary monastic community. One such vignette recounts the fate of a monk who secretly kept two *sous* he had received from a woman. He was immediately seized with dysentery and became so ill that

> the wretched fellow had neither the opportunity nor the will to confess his sin and be absolved. The abbot withdrew, and the monk made his way from the pail to the bed to rest, but he had hardly laid himself down when the Devil suffocated him. You could see his chin and his long neck being violently crushed against his chest as if under some violent pressure. And so he died unconfessed and unanointed, having done nothing about that cursed money (1996, 77-78).

In the miracle of St. James and Mary, a man who was "living in sin" decides to repent by undertaking the pilgrimage to Santiago de Compostela. While en route, the Devil, disguised as St. James, convinces him that pilgrimage is futile and that he can only expiate his sins by castrating himself. He does this and dies and, once in purgatory, he is transported to the throne of God where the real St. James and Mary, acting as celestial barristers, intercede on his behalf and miraculously restore him to life.

## *The Islamic Tradition of Dreams and Visions*

Dreams and visions occupied a special place in ancient Near Eastern religious literature. The Islamic inheritance of this legacy may be seen in the scriptural references to the Prophet Muhammad's own visionary experiences and to the dreams of the other prophetic heroes.[8] Dreams often prefigure critical events in the prophets' lives. We are given to understand, for instance, that prior to the Battle of Badr, God granted Muhammad a dream of the victory. "Remember in the dream God showed them [the Muslim war victims] as few: if he had shown them to thee as many, ye would surely have been discouraged ... " (VIII: 43). In describing the Prophet's triumphal entrance into Mecca, the Qur'an mentions that "Truly did God fulfil the vision of His Apostle: Ye shall enter the Sacred Mosque, if God wills, with minds secure, heads shaved,

---

[8]For an overview of dreams in the Qur'an, see Fahd 1999a.

hair cut short, and without fear" (XLVIII: 27). The Surah that relates Muhammad's Night Journey and ascension to heaven (*isrā'*) shows God addressing Muhammad saying, "Behold! We told thee that thy Lord doth encompass Mankind round about: We granted the Vision which We showed thee, but as a trial for men ..." (XVII: 60).⁹ Regarding the dreams and visions of other prophets, one could mention the story of Joseph and his vision of the eleven stars and the sun and the moon prostrating themselves to him. Joseph's father took this as a sign that "thus will thy Lord choose thee and teach thee the interpretation of these stories ..." (XII: 4, 6). The Qur'anic telling of Abraham's sacrifice of his son presents the episode as the fulfilment of a divinely-inspired dream. Before the event Abraham says to his son, "Oh my son! I see in vision (*fi-l-manām*) that I offer thee in sacrifice." Just before he is about to commit the ritual murder God intervenes saying, "Thou hast already fulfilled the vision (*ru'yā*)" (XXXVII: 102, 105). T. Fahd also points out the *Sira*, Ibn Ishaq's biography of the Prophet, relates "a large number of dreams which marked the major events of the Prophet's life, those of his contemporaries and of his successors" (Fahd 1999a).

Oneiromancy, the classification and interpretation of dreams, was one of the few pre-Islamic sciences that the early Muslims retained, due no doubt to the Qur'anic allusions to prophetic dreams and visions.¹⁰ The most important Muslim interpreters of dreams include Ibn Sirin (d. 110/728), Ja'far al-Sadiq (d. 148/765), Ibn Abi Dunya (d. 281/894), Ibn Shahin (d. 873/1468), 'Abd al-Ghani al-Nabulsi (d. 1143/1731), Abu Sa'id al-Wa'iz (d. 407/1016) and al-Dinawari (d. 410/1020). Muslims conceptualised divinely inspired dreams or visions as "illuminations from God" visited upon them by an Archangel of Dreams. They

---

⁹Some Qur'anic commentators have asserted that in this verse the term "vision" (*ru'yā*) refers to the Prophet's ascension and have claimed on this basis that the entire episode was a dream. Other commentators have dissented, speculating that here the term *ru'yā* refers to other spiritual visions that the Prophet had and take the view that the mi'raj is to be understood literally.

¹⁰The following summary of dreams in the Arabo-Muslim tradition is taken from Gouda 1991, 1-37; and Katz 1997, 7-9. See also Fahd 1987 and Haddadou 1991.

distinguished these *ru'an* from demonically inspired dreams, known as *adghāth al-aḥlām* (lit. "jumbled dreams"), and codified the meanings of their symbols in encyclopedic collections.[11] The Qur'an and hadith established tenets about dreams that informed a separate tradition of Sufi dream interpretation and spiritual autobiography (Katz 1997, 7). Among them is the conviction that the devil is incapable of impersonating God, the Prophet Muhammad, his companions or the other prophets and saints. In the absence of any further prophecies after Muhammad, the "seal" of the prophets, God continues to provide spiritual guidance to human beings through "pious dreams."[12] The traditions and Muhammad's biographer Ibn Ishaq relate that the Prophet received his first revelation when he heard the voice of the angel Gabriel while meditating in the cave of Hira, a location noted for its "unusual spiritual activity" (Katz 1997, 1). Some of the hadiths suggest that the Prophet's night journey to Jerusalem and his ascension to heaven occurred as a powerful vision, although the canonical view is that it was an actual physical journey attesting to his miraculous and charismatic powers (Ibn Hisham 181-183). Many Sufi traditions have appropriated their conception of mystical illumination as successive, ascending stages (*aḥwāl*) from the descriptions of Muhammad's heavenly ascension. The apparition of the Prophet Muhammad or one's spiritual master in a dream is interpreted as a sign of spiritual progression. In some spiritual autobiographies, a

---

[11] The full names, biographical details and titles of their works on dream interpretation may be found in Gouda 1991, 29-37. Regarding the Arabic term *aḥlām* (sing. *ḥulm*), Fahd explains: "Concerned to distinguish the true dream, rendered by *ru'yā*, from the false dream, resulting from the passions and preoccupations of the soul, or furthermore the dream inspired by God from that inspired by Satan, Muslim tradition adopted h-l-m for the expression of the latter, on the basis of the following tradition: 'The *ru'yā* comes from God and the *ḥulm* from Satan'" (Fahd 1999a).

[12] According to the hadith transmitted by Malik ibn Anas, "And the Prophet said: 'There will not remain after me [anything] of prophecy except glad tidings.' Then they said, 'And what are glad tidings, O Messenger of God?' He said, 'The righteous dream which the righteous man sees or appears to him. [It is] one forty-sixth part of prophecy'" (Katz 1997, 21 n. 2).

dream or vision records the defining moment of the author's mystical illumination.[13]

## al-Ghazali (1058-1111), "al-Munqidh min al-Ḍalâl (The Deliverer from Error)"

One of the most prominent examples of a Muslim spiritual autobiography comes from the pen of Abu Hamid al-Ghazali, the great Muslim theologian, jurist, mystic and religious reformer. Born in Iran, he rose in prominence as the head of the Nizamiyya Institute in Baghdad, the most prestigious Sunni university at the time. Al-Ghazali lived in what was then part of the 'Abbasid Empire during a period when the dynasty was in decline. It was weakened internally by the Turkic Seljuks, who wielded the power behind the 'Abbasid Caliphate, and besieged externally by Isma'ili Shi'ite Fatimids, who controlled the whole of the Maghreb and were headquartered in Cairo. The Nizamiyya was founded in part to counter the spread of Shi'ism.

In 1095, having reached the pinnacle of his career, al-Ghazali suffered a psychological crisis of angst and doubt, which paralyzed his speaking faculties and made it impossible for him to lecture. As a result, he abandoned his post and "lived as a poor sufi often in solitude, spending his time in meditation and other spiritual exercises."[14] It was

---

[13]This appropriation reaches its zenith in the *al-Futūḥāt al-Makkiyya* of Ibn al-'Arabi (d. 1240). His conversion to the mystical path as a result of a vision causes him to regard his entire previous life as a period of Jahiliyya (i.e. the age of ignorance prior to the revelation of Islam). In the *Futūḥāt* all the decisive stages of his life are marked by dreams and visions of Muhammad and the Prophet al-Khidr. See Trimingham 1971, 190; and Ateş 1999.

[14]Some scholars believe that the true motivations of al-Ghazali's spiritual crisis were in fact political. The corruption of the 'ulama' of Baghdad, whom he criticizes in *Iḥyā'*, and the political machinations of the 'Abbasids and their rivals may have led him to believe that the only way to lead a spiritually uprightly life and avoid going to hell was to renounce his profession altogether (Watt 1999).

during this period of spiritual exploration that he composed his magnum opus, *Iḥyā' 'ulūm al-dīn* (*The Revival of the Religious Sciences*). The influence of *Iḥya'* on Sunni Islam compares with the writings of Sts. Augustine and Aquinas on Latin Christianity. Al-Ghazali's sudden departure undoubtedly dealt a devastating blow to his Sunni patrons. He returned to public life eleven years later and composed his autobiography shortly thereafter. The work is part autobiography, part polemical tract against Greek philosophy, scholastic theology and Isma'ili Shi'ism. In it he gives pride of place to Sufism – without ever rejecting the doctrines of the Sunni exoteric sciences – as the path of spiritual enlightenment. Al-Ghazali's influence on western European dream interpretation has been noted above. His descriptions of the various spiritual gifts, including dreams and visions, that one attains when following the Sufi path were influential to later generations of Sufi mystics. It is therefore ironic and surprising that al-Ghazali does not include a single detailed account of his own mystical experiences. He does, however, express the traditional Sufi belief that dreams, visions, and other spiritual charisms constitute signs of progression along the mystical path:

> From the time that [Sufi initiates] set out on this path, revelations commence for them. They come to see in the waking state angels and souls of prophets; they hear their voices and wise counsels. By means of this contemplation of heavenly forms and images they rise ... to heights which human language cannot reach, which one cannot even indicate without falling into great and inevitable errors (al-Ghazali 1981, 55).

These experiences are beyond the grasp of the rational mind and cannot be expressed in human language. Reason alone is insufficient to reach God; divine inspiration is also necessary (echoing the faith versus reason disputes of medieval Christianity). This explains his reticence in describing his own dreams and mystical charisms saying merely: "What I experience I shall not try to say. Call me happy, but ask me no more" (al-Ghazali 1981, 55).[15] Dreams are God-given "glimpses" of the divine will. They offer inspiration and guidance, and reveal the future. Al-Ghazali recalls, for instance, that the dreams of certain 'ulama' (Muslim scholars) validated his decision to return to public life after eleven years of mystic semi-seclusion: "Some sincere men had dreams in this regard on a number of occasions, foretelling the good and felicitous effects of my departure. Such was the will of God" (al-Ghazali 1981, 59, 114).

Finally, just as al-Ghazali accepted the reality of visions of angels and encounters with the souls of the prophets, so too did he believe in a devil who tempts human beings toward concupiscence through apparitions and dreams. He provides an example from his own life. Once, after he had decided to renounce his post at the Nizamiyya and to embark upon his spiritual journey, he was besieged by the devil:

> ... but the Tempter, returning to the attack, said, "You are suffering from a transitory feeling; don't give way to it, for it will soon pass. If you obey it, if you give up this fine position, this honorable post ... you will regret it later on ..." (al-Ghazali 1981, 50).

Note that this diabolic apparition intervened at a pivotal moment in al-Ghazali's life when he was "torn asunder by the opposite forces of earthly passions and religious aspirations" (al-Ghazali 1981, 50). The matter was resolved by a strange kind of miracle in which God caused an impediment to "chain" his tongue and prevent him from lecturing, thereby releasing him from his teaching duties.

*Samau'al al-Maghribi (1126-1175), "Ifḥām al-Yahūd (Silencing the Jews)"*

Samau'al al-Maghribi was a distinguished scholar, mathematician and physician. He was born in Iraq into a Jewish family of prominent

---

[15]Trimingham notes that elsewhere al-Ghazali does provide an account of an encounter with God in a dream at an advanced stage of his spiritual pilgrimage (1971, 191). This account is recorded in Muhammad al-Murtada's commentary on al-Ghazali's *summa* of theology, *Iḥyā' 'ulūm al-dīn* (al-Murtada 1: 9).

religious scholars. His father was a rabbi from Fez, "the most learned man of his time in Torah studies, and the most gifted and prolific stylist and exquisite extemporizer in Hebrew poetry and prose" (al-Maghribi 1964, 75). His mother was also learned, being one of three daughters of an eminent Levite family from Baghdad, all of whom were "well-versed in Torah studies and Hebrew writing." He was practising medicine in Azerbaijan when he converted to Islam in 1163. That very same day, he began to compose a polemical tract, *Ifḥām al-Yahūd* (*Silencing the Jews*). He appended his autobiography to the text some four years later (al-Maghribi 1964, 87). Despite his emphasis on reason as the final arbiter in his decision to convert to Islam, he presents two rather enigmatic dreams in his narrative as the catalyst for and climax of his conversion. They also very neatly resolve a conflict between Samau'al's desire to convert to Islam and his reluctance to hurt his father who "was very attached to him" (al-Maghribi 1964, 81).

In the first dream, Samau'al encounters his namesake the Prophet Samuel sitting beneath a mighty tree. The prophet greets him and passes him the Torah from which he read the following passage: "I will raise them up a prophet from among their brethren like unto thee; in him they shall believe" (Deut. 18: 15; al-Maghribi 1964, 81). Initially he "misinterprets" the verse according to the Jewish exegesis that it was a revelation to Moses foretelling the coming of the Prophet Samuel. However, the Prophet rebukes him, saying that the verse alludes to: "a prophecy that will be revealed ... on the mountains of Paran," which he "correctly" interprets as a reference to Muhammad's prophetic mission "because he is the one sent from the mountains of Paran, i.e. ... Mecca" (al-Maghribi 1964, 82).

This dream is a thinly veiled extension of his anti-Jewish polemic, which attempts to abrogate Judaism "from within" by illustrating the "errors" of traditional Jewish scriptural exegesis.[16] Samau'al would have us believe that he initially misinterpreted the dream *because* he was still

---

[16] For a parallel example of anti-Jewish polemics from a medieval Jewish convert to Christianity, see Steven Kruger's discussion of Hermann of Cologne (1992, 154-165).

Jewish at the time. Implicit here is a traditional Islamic polemic that the Jews distorted or deliberately concealed the messages allegedly referring to Muhammad in Jewish scripture. The dream functions as the catalyst which provokes Samau'al to consider conversion to Islam. The Prophet Samuel assumes the role of a true Muslim and Samau'al, as his namesake, is bound to follow in his footsteps.

The second dream describes his encounter with the Prophet Muhammad and serves to substantiate the sincerity of his conversion and to situate himself within the well-established Muslim tradition which greatly values such experiences as indicators of loyalty to Islam and the Prophet Muhammad and of spiritual enlightenment. In this dream he is led into a house by a Sufi to meet the Prophet:

> I walked behind [the Sufi], following in through a long corridor which was dark, but only slightly so. When I reached the end of the corridor and realized that I was about to meet the Prophet, I was overawed ... it seemed to me that most of [the Sufis there], though young, seemed to be preparing for travel ... Then I saw the Messenger of God standing between the two chambers.... When I entered and saw him, he turned to me, saw me, and came toward me smiling and benevolent. In awe of him I ... addressed him with an individual salutation saying: "Peace upon thee, O Messenger of God, and God's mercy and blessings," thus excluding the company, as my vision and my heart turned exclusively to him. He then said: "And upon thee peace, and God's mercy and blessings" (al-Maghribi 1964, 83).

Samau'al was overcome with emotion when the Prophet took him by the hand and he recited the Muslim testament of faith to him, pointedly changing the indirect statement that "Muhammad is the Messenger of God" into a direct proclamation that "thou art (*annaka*) the Messenger of God." The Prophet responds by inviting Samau'al to participate in the campaign to conquer Ghumdan in China (al-Maghribi 1964, 84).[17] Clearly, Ghumdan represents Samau'al's own campaign to convert the

---

[17] The editor notes that Ghumdan is probably Khumdân, "the capital of China, 'on the shore of the Green Sea.'"

Jews. He awakens from the dream and performs his ablutions and the dawn Islamic prayer "eager now to make public my conversion to the faith of Islam" (al-Maghribi 1964, 85).

When Samau'al entered the house of the Prophet, he noted that the long corridor was "dark, but only slightly so." Yet after he professed the Islamic credo directly to Muhammad and was leaving the house, he "[did] not find in the corridor the darkness that was there when [he] entered." I suggest that the slight darkness symbolizes Samau'al's liminal position vis-à-vis Islam. Although he had not yet publicly converted, he believed in the prophethood of Muhammad; thus he was not in total darkness. The absence of darkness following his profession of the faith intimates that he has grasped the light of Muhammad's prophethood. Moreover, his immediate public conversion to Islam identifies this dream as a rite of passage that initiates him fully into a new Islamic identity.

One other dream from Samau'al's autobiography merits comment. Samau'al's mother, Hannah, was named after the mother of the Prophet Samuel. Just as the Prophet's mother had been barren for many years and became pregnant after praying to God, so too was Samau'al's mother unable to conceive until she had the following dream:

> Now my mother had been with my father for some time, childless, until she was filled with fear of her barrenness, and saw a dream in which she was reciting the prayer of Hannah, mother of Samuel, to the Lord. She then vowed that if she had a son she would name him Samuel, as he name was the name of Samuel's mother. It came to pass that after that she conceived and I was born; she called me Samuel, which in Arabic is Samau'al (al-Maghribi 1964, 76).

In this brief anecdote, which is placed toward the beginning of his autobiography, Samau'al homologizes the circumstances surrounding his own birth with that of his namesake the Prophet Samuel. He also establishes his mother's piety and faith in God, which is a motif common in both Muslim and Christian autobiographies. Samau'al seems to be exploiting the coincidence between his and his mother's names and the names of revered biblical figures to convince his Jewish audience of the sincerity of his conversion, and the inevitability of their own. In other words, his re-imagining of the Prophet Samuel as a "true" Muslim is meant to signpost the eventual conversion of the Jewish community to Islam. That Samau'al should resort to autobiographic accounts of his dreams in his endeavor to "silence" the Jews by eliciting their conversion to Islam, illustrates the enormously persuasive and authoritative power of dreams in both the medieval Jewish and Muslim thought worlds.

*Ibn 'Ajiba (1747-1809): The Autobiography of a Moroccan Sufi*

Although Ahmad ibn 'Ajiba's autobiography falls outside the medieval period, I have included it as an example of the *longue durée* of the Arabic autobiographic tradition in general, and of a distinctly Andalusian/North African autobiographic tradition known as the *fahrasa* (Reynolds ed. 2001, 38-42). The author was born in Morocco in 1747 into a family descended from the Prophet Muhammad. He mastered the Islamic sciences and became a respected professor of Islamic theology and jurisprudence. In 1793, he entered the Darqawi Sufi order. His conversion to the Sufi path culminated when he renounced his teaching post and adopted the life of a mendicant. He was a mystic graced with the power to perform miracles and encounter spiritual beings at will, and many regarded him as a saint (*wali*) during his lifetime.

In contrast to the conversion narratives of Augustine and Guibert of Nogent, Ibn 'Ajiba's dreams present a unified commentary on the author's spirituality, as do the dreams of other Muslim converts. One's own dreams, visions and charisms, particularly of an encounter with the Prophet Muhammad or a powerful Sufi sage, play an important role in displaying the level of mystical power and enlightenment that one has attained. Such experiences are authoritative with respect to their content and meaning, and legitimate the authority of the person who experiences them. The dreams, visions and charismatic experiences that venerable Sufi personalities have about the protagonist are equally authoritative and edifying. Ibn 'Ajiba includes both types of dreams in his autobiography to illustrate his sharifian lineage (descent from the Prophet Muhammad's family) and his extraordinary mystical powers.

One of Ibn 'Ajiba's dreams describes a conversation with the Prophet. Its occurrence resolves a crisis involving the controversy over his family's alleged sharifian descent:

> One day, during a long dream, I saw the Prophet in his holy mosque. He said to me: "You are the *faqih* [a Muslim jurist] Ibn 'Agiba." "Yes, I am your servant Ahmad Ibn 'Agiba." The Prophet said to me: "You are my child, in truth! Do not doubt it!" (Ibn 'Ajiba 1969, 36).

A dream in which the Prophet Muhammad appears is absolutely authoritative. As proof, Ibn 'Ajiba quotes the hadith: "whoever sees me during his sleep has truly seen me, because Satan cannot assume my appearance" (Ibn 'Ajiba 1969, 37).

A second dream occurs at a pivotal point during Ibn 'Ajiba's progression toward conversion to the Sufi path. He has discovered Islamic esoteric literature on the Qur'an, and this inspires him to renounce the exoteric sciences in pursuit of mystical practices: "After this reading, I abandoned the exoteric sciences and dedicated myself to devotional practice, to the invocation of God and to praying for the Apostle of God" (Ibn 'Ajiba 1969, 42). He was filled with an ardent desire to enter into spiritual retreat away from the world, which he had come to detest (possibly in imitation of the Prophet's frequent seclusion in the cave at Hira). Ibn 'Ajiba had recently become a disciple of Shaykh al-Buzidi who initiated him into the Darqawi order and was set to abandon the world entirely when an apparition of a deceased Sufi master, Sidi Talha, intervened to prevent this premature decision:

> Once when I had situated myself next to the tomb of Sidi Talha, he appeared to me in a dream. He drew close to me until my face touched the whiskers of his beard. I thought: "I must consult him regarding what I intend to do." I had resolved at that time to sell my books in order to go into retreat in the mountain of Mawlay 'Abd al-Salam Ibn Mashis ... in order to consecrate myself to the devotion[al practice]. But God had not decided it to be so. I then said to Sidi Talha: "O Sidi! I wish to abandon

my studies and retreat in order to adore God without any preoccupations." "Study!" he responded. "The [exoteric] sciences?" I asked him. "Yes! Study the [exoteric] sciences in depth!" (Ibn 'Ajiba 1969, 46)

Structurally this dream resembles the one with the Prophet Muhammad. Ibn 'Ajiba confronts a specific problem, in this case whether to abandon his studies altogether and devote himself to God. Sidi Talha responds, like the Prophet, with a terse and unambiguous message. To abandon his studies at this point would be contrary to the will of God – "God had not decided it to be so" – and communicates His commands through Sidi Talha. The dream is clearly exhortative and Ibn 'Ajiba obeys at once: "Thus I resumed my studies." Divine orders and inspiration always prevail over human intentions, however sincere and pious they may be.

Ibn 'Ajiba also recounts manifestations of his thaumaturgic powers. One miracle features the distribution of food in a mosque, which, to the Christian reader, is certainly reminiscent of the Gospel accounts of the miracle of the five loaves and two fishes:

> While I was exercising the functions of the imam at the mosque of the Casba – I was at the time unmarried – it so happened that I finished the teaching of a book. In order to celebrate the event, I gave to the muezzin two or three small portions of wheat from which he made a dish. From the setting of the sun to the night prayer he did not cease to serve the guests; one group would get up, another would replace them; and mysteriously, there remained still some food for the muezzin to take home (Ibn 'Ajiba 1969, 135).

What is fascinating about this incident is that the mere presence of Ibn 'Ajiba produces the miracle. He has done nothing more than to give the muezzin a small bit of wheat, but his spiritual presence, his *baraka*, ensures that all will be provided for. Stories from Ibn Ishaq's *Life of Muhammad* describe similar miraculous phenomena (*karāmāt*) associated with the Prophet from his birth (Ibn Hisham 69-80). The inclusion of this miracle in Ibn 'Ajiba's narrative provides another example of the well-established tradition of taking the Prophet as a role model (*qudwa*) of Muslim piety and spirituality. After listing all the charisms that he can recall, Ibn 'Ajiba includes himself among those who have attained an elevated spiritual state, endowing them with the ability to heed the divine directives. "Those who understand the Will of God, who obtain the perfect union (*al-tawhīd al-khass*), attain that state if they have the perseverance (*ta'annī*) and know how to listen to the divine teachings. 'God possesses infinite grace!' [Qur'an, II: 105]" (Ibn 'Ajiba 1969, 138).

Ibn 'Ajiba also describes several dreams, visions and miraculous events experienced by others which attest to his spiritual gifts. One of these shows that he regarded himself as the "Pole" (*quṭb*), the head of the hierarchy of saints believed to be the *axis mundi* in Sufi cosmography (Trimingham 1971, 163).

> ... a virtuous man of the Baqqal family said: "I had in my heart a profound desire to meet the Pole [the spiritual master, i.e., Ibn 'Ajiba]. I went to sleep and was transported in a dream to the mosque of Sidi 'Ali al-Ja'idi. The yard was filled with plates [of] honey. Sidi Ahmad Ibn 'Agiba arrived and began to distribute the plates to his assistants. He gave one to me also" (Ibn 'Ajiba 1969, 129-130).

This visionary transportation to a mosque probably intends to evoke Muhammad's nocturnal journey to Jerusalem. Also, according to traditional Muslim dream interpretations, honey symbolizes the "merits of piety, the beauty of religion, the reading of the Holy Qur'an, and philanthropy" (Gouda 1991, 214).

## III. CONCLUSION

Both Muslim and Christian traditions share an understanding of dreams, visions, and other supernatural gifts as divinely or demonically inspired, and as one way in which "the sacred" intervenes in the course of human affairs. This ability to negotiate and transform human destiny illustrates how such phenomena function as loci of power. We have seen in all the texts that the divinely inspired experiences resolve conflicts, provide spiritual guidance, buttress one's faith, reveal the future, and serve as rewards or sign-posts of the visionary's piety and spiritual growth. Such experiences are authoritative by virtue of their perceived emanation from God. They also reify the authority, spiritual power and sincerity of the visionary, whether the author or a spiritually significant other.

Yet I detect a significant difference in how the Christian and Muslim authors deploy the dreams of others in their spiritual autobiographies. The Muslim accounts of dreams, apparitions and other celestial experiences draw attention to the author's own piety and spiritual power. The experiences of Ibn 'Ajiba and his followers attest to his spiritual graces or *baraka*. The dreams of the religious scholars ('ulama') confirm al-Ghazali's divinely guided decision to resume his career. Hannah's dream validates Samau'al's own understanding of the connection between himself and his namesake. This is also true of Samau'al's encounter with the Prophet Samuel, for the author's comprehension is not mediated through another human being, rather it emanates from divine inspiration. By contrast, in the Christian narratives, the dreams of Augustine's and Guibert's mothers, and their ability to interpret them correctly, attest to their own piety and underscore their sons' sinfulness and spiritual immaturity. This is not to suggest that the Christian authors exhibit no spiritual gifts. One could mention Augustine's mystical encounter with Wisdom or Guibert's lurid descriptions of the workings of the devil against sinful monks, with which he implicitly contrasts his own spiritual maturity and probity as Abbott of Nogent. Yet we do not find in the Muslim narratives a contrast between the author's own iniquities and another's piety.

This distinction may be explained by a difference in orientation between the two spiritual autobiographic traditions. The Christian narratives are written within a confessional mode whereby the author *confesses* his sins so that the reader may learn from his errors. By contrast, the Muslim narratives adhere to the Qur'anic injunction to enumerate the blessings that God has bestowed upon the author in reward for leading a life modelled after the Prophet Muhammad (Reynolds ed. 2001, 3). Pious dreams, visions and miracles and other spiritual gifts figure among the blessings to be counted. Both traditions are exemplary, although from different orientations.

It is also apparent that the power of the dream or vision inheres in its liminality, at least in cases such as St. Augustine and Samau'al al-Maghribi, where such experiences played a climactic part in the "rite of passage" that constituted the author's conversion and initiation into a new self-identity. Samau'al's public confession of Islam immediately upon awakening from his dream characterizes this as a liminal experience. Augustine's fleeting mystical adventure of being transported, along with his mother, out of the bounds "even of heaven itself" toward eternal Wisdom may also be regarded as a liminal experience that initiated them both into a realm of new understanding. The nightmare in which Guibert's mother beheld a deserted monastery and dwarfed monks could also be described as a liminal episode, insofar as it occurs at a crucial moment when Guibert was tempted to abandon the monastery. At the same time, it would be an exaggeration to apply Kruger and Lynch's notion of the liminality of dreams and visions to every such experience in a spiritual autobiography. We have seen that the autobiographies of Augustine, Guibert of Nogent and Samau'al al-Maghribi contain several other spectral apparitions and dreams. Many Arabic autobiographies are especially prolific in this regard. Al-Sha'rani related over 100 dreams in his autobiography and Ibn al-'Arabi's *al-Futūhāt al-makkiyya* is comprised of a series of dreams, revelations and other spiritual gifts.[18]

Both the Christian and Muslim conversion narratives demonstrate the capacity of the dream or vision to function as a source of peril. This potential for danger hovers as a dire consequence of the author's failure to recognize and heed the authority of the divinely inspired dream or to understand its message, especially when it occurs in the context of a personal crisis. This is most clearly articulated in the dreams of Guibert's mother and tutor. It is also implicit in Augustine's fear of damnation should he persist in concupiscence, in Samau'al's entrapment

---

[18]Dwight Reynolds alerted me to this in a personal communication.

in the liminal status of a crypto-Muslim had he failed to convert publicly, and in al-Ghazali's and Ibn 'Ajiba's inability to reach the zenith of mystical enlightenment had they not followed the traditional Sufi path, where such dreams and other charisms are the *sine qua non* of advancement in the journey toward union with God.

Diabolic dreams or encounters also constitute loci of danger. For al-Ghazali, the devil appears as an amorphous tempter who whispers into his ear to dissuade him from pursuing the ascetic, mystical path. His encounter entraps him in a state of turmoil between his earthly and spiritual passions, which is only alleviated by a miraculous intervention. Guibert likewise portrays the devil as a tempter who seduces the novice, the exceptionally devout or the spiritually weak toward concupiscence. Yet in Guibert's memoirs, the devil assumes a corporeal form and possesses extraordinary powers: he (or she) is capable of physically attacking, even murdering unrepentant sinners and of embodying or impersonating a holy figure such as St. James. This stands in marked contrast with the Muslim hadith tradition, reiterated in Ibn 'Ajiba's autobiography, that the devil cannot disguise himself as God, the Prophet Muhammad or a saint. This discrepancy between the Christian and Muslim imaginings of the devil may derive in part from a greater emphasis on sin and guilt in medieval Latin Christianity in general and particularly in monastic culture, which demanded celibacy, poverty and absolute obedience of its members.

If in the Christian narratives visions of the devil appear to be embodied and more graphic, in the Muslim narratives, personal dreams and apparitions of holy figures are far more vivid. Samau'al and Ibn 'Ajiba actually *converse* with the prophets and saints, experience physical contact with them, and provide detailed descriptions of their encounters. For all his devotion to Mary, nothing comparable is found in Guibert's autobiography, or, for that matter, in Augustine's confessions. This absence in the Christian conversion narratives is striking, considering the well-known paradigms of Paul's and the Emperor Constantine's conversion to Christianity. One must await the emergence of the later medieval mystics to encounter similarly tangible and vivid encounters with the sacred in Christian spiritual autobiographies and hagiographies.

Another fascinating difference lies in the gender issues raised in the Christian narratives. For both Augustine and Guibert, the female represents the model of spiritual piety and power, whether it be the mothers, Mary, Continence, or Wisdom. In the Muslim narratives, genealogy, rather than gender, seems to fulfil this function. By this I mean that a dream of an encounter with the Prophet Muhammad serves to insert the author into the spiritual genealogy of Muhammad, who is by far the greatest model of spiritual piety in Islam. We have seen that Ibn 'Ajiba's dream of Muhammad corroborated his claims to sharifian descent in the eyes of his community. Similarly, Samau'al's dream of the Prophet Muhammad integrates him into the spiritual family of the prophet and his contemporary Sufi companions. The apparition of other Sufi masters, illustrated by the example of Ibn 'Ajiba's encounter with Sidi Talha, fulfils a similar function of integrating the visionary into the spiritual genealogy of a particular Sufi order. As for the inclusion of the dreams of female relatives in the conversion narrative, it is notable that these compliment, rather than contrast with, the author's piety and spirituality.[19]

Each of the texts examined above suggests that the grace of God ultimately makes the author's conversion possible. The act of writing down one's own conversion experience for others to read characterizes conversion as a social act informed and buttressed by the examples of one's fellow Christians or Muslims. Whether stated explicitly or not, each of the author's conversions imitates the example of others, often those who appeared in their dreams or who had dreams about them. In turn, they composed their conversion narratives to influence their

---

[19]The Muslim conversion narratives do include dreams by women and portray them as models of piety, e.g. Samau'al's mother Hannah, and Ibn 'Ajiba's mother Rahma, and another of his ancestors, Sayyida Fatima, who was considered a saint. Ibn 'Ajiba also portrays his mother as a paragon of piety and devotion: "Ma mere était une femme pieuse, dévote, remplie de la crainte de Dieu le Tres-Haut" (Ibn 'Ajiba 1969, 268).

audience. Dreams, visions and other spiritual charisms often played a pivotal role in the conversion of the author. By recounting them in their autobiographies to dramatic effect, the author harnesses their discursive power and authority to persuade the reader to emulate his example. As Guibert of Nogent remarked, "dreams come with much business" and seemingly no one – Christian, Muslim, or Jew – doubted this.

## REFERENCES

*Primary Sources*

Augustine. 1963. *The Confessions of St. Augustine*. Trans. Rex Warner. New York and Toronto: The New American Library of World Literature, Inc.

al-Ghazali = Abu Hamid Muhammad al-Ghazali. 1981. *The Confessions of Al Ghazzali (al-Munqidh min al-Ḍalāl)*. Trans. S. H. Muhammad Ashraf. Lahore, Pakistan: Ashraf Press.

Guibert of Nogent. 1996. *A Monk's Confession: The Memoirs of Guibert of Nogent*. Trans. and intro. Paul J. Archambault. Pennsylvania: The Pennsylvania State University Press.

Ibn 'Ajiba = Ahmad ibn 'Ajiba. 1969. *Le Autobiographie (Fahrasa) d'un Soufi Marocain: Ahmed ibn Agîba (1747-1809)*. Trans. and intro. J.-L. Michon. Leiden: E. J. Brill.

Ibn Hisham. [1955] 1978. *The Life of Muhammad: A Translation of Ibn Ishaq's Sirat Rasul Allah*. Trans. Alfred Guillaume. Lahore: Oxford University Press.

Ibn Khaldun. 1958. *The Muqaddimah*. Trans. F. Rosenthal. 3 vols. New York: Pantheon.

Ibn Sa'd. 1904-40. *Kitâb al-Tabaqât al-Kabîr*. Ed. Eduard Sachau et al. 9 vols. Leiden: E. J. Brill.

al-Maghribi = Samau'al al-Maghribi. 1964. *Ifḥām al-Yahūd (Silencing the Jews)*. In Arabic; Eng. trans. and intro. Moshe Perlmann. New York: American Academy for Jewish Research.

Muhammad al-Murtada (d. 1205/1790). 1311 A.H. *Ithāf al-sāda* (a commentary on al-Ghazali's *Ihyā' 'ulūm al-dīn*). Cairo.
*The Holy Qur'an.* 1983. Text, Translation and Commentary by A. Yusuf Ali. St. Brentword, MD: Amana Corp.
al Sha'rani, 'Abd al-Wahhab. 1938/1357 A.H. *Latā'if al-minan wa-l-akhlāq fī wujūb al-tahadduth bi ni'mat Allah 'ala al-Haqq*. Cairo: 'Alam al-Fikr.
*University Library of Autobiography.* 1918 (rpt. 1927). Vol. 2: *The Middle Ages and Their Autobiographers.* Intro. Charles Bushnell. N. P.: F. Tyler Daniels Company. Reprint National Alumni.

*Secondary Sources*

Armistead, Samuel. 1990. An Anecdote of King Jaume I and its Arabic Cogener. In *Cultures in Contact in Medieval Spain: Historical and Literary Essays Presented to L. P. Harvey*, ed. David Hook and Barry Taylor. London: King's College.
Ateş, A. 1999. Ibn al-'Arabi, Muhyi 'l-Din. *Encyclopaedia of Islam 2.* CD-ROM Edition. Vol. 3: 707b.
Burns, Robert I. 1984. *Muslims, Christians, and Jews in the Crusader Kingdom of Valencia.* Cambridge: Cambridge University Press.
Douglas, Mary. 1966. *Purity and Danger: An Analysis of Concepts of Pollution and Taboo.* London: Routledge and Kegan Paul.
Fahd, T. [1966] 1987. *La divination arabe. Etudes religieuses, sociologiques et folkloriques sur le milieu natif de l'Islam.* Paris.
———. 1999a. Ru'yā. *Encyclopaedia of Islam 2.* CD-ROM Edition. Vol. 8: 645a.
———. 1999b. Nubuwwa. *Encyclopaedia of Islam 2.* CD-ROM Edition. Vol. 8: 93b.
al-Ghamdi, Saleh Mued. 1989. Autobiography in Classical Arabic Literature: An Ignored Literary Genre. Ph.D. dissertation, Indiana University.
Gouda, Yehyia. 1991. *Dreams and Their Meanings in the Old Arab Tradition.* New York: Vantage Press.

Gregory, Tullio, ed. 1985. *I sogni nel medioevo*. Seminario Internazionale, Rome 2-4 ottobre 1983. Rome: Edizione dell'Ateneo.

Haddadou, Mohand Akli. 1991. *La rêve et son interpretation dans l'Islam*. Alger: E.N.A.L.

Harpham, Geoffrey Galt. 1988. Conversion and the Language of Autobiography. In *Studies in Autobiography*, ed. James Olney, 42-50. New York & Oxford: Oxford University Press.

Hermansen, Marcia K. 1997a. Introduction to the Study of Dreams and Visions in Islam. *Religion* 27: 1-5.

———. 1997b. Visions as "Good to Think": A Cognitive Approach to Visionary Experience in Islamic Sufi Thought. *Religion* 27: 25-43.

Hieatt, Constance B. 1967. *The Realism of Dream Visions: The Poetic Exploitation of the Dream-Experience in Chaucer and his Contemporaries*. Paris: Mouton and Co.

Katz, Jonathan G. 1997. An Egyptian Sufi Interprets His Dreams: 'Abd al-Wahhâb al-Sha'rânî 1493-1565. *Religion* 27: 7-24.

Kruger, Steven F. 1992. *Dreaming in the Middle Ages*. Cambridge Studies in Medieval Literature 14. Cambridge: Cambridge University Press.

Le Goff, Jacques. 1980. Dreams in the Culture and Collective Psychology of the Medieval West. In *Time, Work, and Culture in the Middle Ages*, trans. Arthur Goldhammer, 201-204. Chicago and London: University of Chicago Press.

Lynch, Kathryn L. 1988. *The High Medieval Dream Vision: Poetry, Philosophy, and Literary Form*. Stanford: Stanford University Press.

Misch, Georg. 1949-1969. *Geschichte der Autobiographie*. 4 vols. Bern and Frankfurt.

Parman, Susan. 1991. *Dream and Culture: An Anthropological Study of the Western Intellectual Tradition*. New York: Praeger Publishers.

Pascal, Roy. 1960. *Design and Truth in Autobiography*. Cambridge, MA: Harvard University Press.

Rosenthal, Franz. 1939. Die Arabische Autobiographie. *Studia Arabica* 1: 1-40.

Reynolds, Dwight F., ed. 2001. Coauthored by Kristen E. Burstad, Michael Cooperson, Jamal L. Elias, Nuha N.N. Khoury, Joseph E. Lowry, Nasser Rabat, Dwight F. Reynolds, Devin J. Stewart, and Shawkat M. Toorawa. *Interpreting the Self: Autobiography in the Arabic Literary Tradition*. Berkeley and Los Angeles: University of California Press.

Scaglione, Aldo. 1984. The Mediterranean's Three Spiritual Shores: Images of the Self between Christianity and Islam in the Later Middle Ages. In *The Craft of Fiction: Essays in Medieval Poetics*, ed. Leigh A. Arrathoon, 453-473. Rochester, MI: Solaris Press.

Watt, W. Montgomery. 1999. Al-Ghazali. *Encyclopaedia of Islam 2*. CD-ROM Edition. Vol. 2: 1038b.

Trimingham, J. Spencer. 1971 (rpt. 1998). *The Sufi Orders in Islam*. Oxford: The Clarendon Press.

Vernet, Juan. 1978. *La cultura hispanoárabe en Oriente y Occidente* Barcelona: Ariel.

von Grünebaum, G.E. 1946. *Medieval Islam: A Study in Cultural Orientation*. Chicago: University of Chicago Press.

# 7

# Venetian Commerce in the Later Middle Ages: Feast or Famine?

## *Alan M. Stahl*

IN NOVEMBER OF 1417, the three Procurators of Saint Mark's, among whom was the future doge Francesco Foscari, called for a great reform of the silver mint of Venice (ASV SM, 52: 54v-56; Bonfiglio Dosio 1984, 90-98; Papadopoli 1893, 1: 356-62).[1] They declared that the mint was in disarray and reduced almost to nothing, with the result that the market for silver in Venice had been badly disrupted. They noted that the value of the gold ducat had risen against the silver coinage to the extent that the only way the mint could attract silver was by minting the coinage below its prescribed standards. The steps which they proposed, and which were adopted by an overwhelming margin of the Senate, called for a major reorganization in the way in which silver was sold within Venice, was processed by the mint into ingots and coins, and was paid back to the importing merchants; the weight of the silver coinage was also reduced by about seven percent.

Two years later, in December of 1419, one of the doge's councilors reported to the Senate that this reform of the silver mint had been a complete failure (ASV SM, 53: 18). Whereas 40,000 marks of silver (about 10 metric tons) had been imported into Venice each year before the reform, only one-quarter of that amount had been coming in since then. In typical Venetian manner, the problem was referred to a

---

[1] Archival research for this study was made possible by a series of grants from the Gladys K. Delmas Foundation.

committee, which responded by relaxing restrictions on the sale of bullion and reducing the duty on imported silver (Bonfiglio Dosio 1984, 101-3). A year later, the councilors reported that the silver mint was in such a bad state that it could not be worse and would be reduced to nothing unless further action were taken (ASV SM, 53: 104v). A new committee was appointed, which proceeded to debase the silver coinage in fineness as well as weight and cut the staff both of the mint and of its silver refinery (Bonfiglio Dosio 1984, 103-6). The main result of these reforms seems to have been the circulation of great quantities of counterfeit and clipped coins within Venice (ASV SM, 53: 141). The Senate, after much debate, decided against a general recoinage of the circulating medium, but undertook to remint bad coins collected by the state (ASV SM, 53: 152-2v; Bonfiglio Dosio 1984, 106-7). A year later, this measure was deemed to have brought down the value of the ducat to a reasonable level vis à vis the silver coinage, and the reminting was suspended (ASV SM, 54: 92). Finally, in 1429, the crisis was deemed to have passed, and the strict regulation of imported silver in effect in the fourteenth century was re-instated (Bonfiglio Dosio 1984, 111-12).

This period from 1417 to 1429 was not the first time that the Senate had been alarmed by the lack of silver coming to Venice (Stahl 2000, 69-96). In 1382, just after the costly War of Chioggia waged against Genoa, it was noted that silver was in short supply in Venice, as were copper, tin, soap, and cloth (ASV SM, 37: 75). This situation seems to have resolved itself, as the committee appointed to deal with it never presented its report. In 1390, to attract silver to the Venetian market, the Senate forbade citizens to export silver directly from Ragusa (Dubrovnik) to the Levant without bringing it to Venice for refining and minting (ASV SM, 41: 48v). In 1407, the preference accorded the gold ducat over silver coinage in the Levant was blamed for the low price paid for silver bullion in Venice and a decline in its importation (Bonfiglio Dosio 1984, 80-83; Papadopoli 1893, 1: 349-51). There are no surviving mint records from medieval Venice with which to control or quantify these reports of low levels of silver coinage in the period between 1375 and 1425.

It was not only the silver coinage of Venice which was under pressure in the late fourteenth and early fifteenth century; its gold ducat was also experiencing difficulties. For the most part, the troubles of the ducat seem to have stemmed not so much from the lack of supply of gold to Venice as from problems with keeping the coin's fineness intact in the face of a flood of base imitation ducats, some of quite convincing appearance, in the Eastern Mediterranean.[2] There are, nevertheless, indications of a shortage of gold bullion in some years. In 1387 the Senate exempted two of the Soranzo brothers from a ban on bankers engaging in overseas trade on the basis of their plea that the dearth of gold in Venice had hurt their business (ASV SM, 40: 56v). The gold mint was the object of continuous reforms from 1411 to 1421, one of which specified that it was occasioned by the lack of gold which occurred every year in the mint (ASV SM, 50: 95). On the other hand, in 1402, the mint's blacksmith requested and was granted a raise in view of the large quantity of gold which was being processed at the mint; as the man had been working at the mint for 28 years without a raise and none of the other employees got one, the justification cannot be given too much weight (ASV GR 19: 26). Other evidence, both documentary and numismatic, suggests that the production of Venetian ducats in the late fourteenth and early fifteenth century was at a moderate level, neither as restricted as that of silver coins nor as heavy as in the boom years of the 1340s ( Stahl 1995, 292-8; Stahl 2000, 369-406).

The measures which the Venetian Senate adopted to deal with the crisis in minting were administrative in the case of the ducat and monetary for the silver denominations. The gold mint underwent a series of regulations aimed at insuring that the masters could not produce coins of substandard alloy and reducing the time which suppliers of bullion had to await payment. To attract silver, the import fees on bullion were decreased, export regulations relaxed, and on occasion the production costs of turning bullion into coinage were underwritten by the state

---

[2]Cf. Bachrach 1983, 168-9; Grierson 1988, 95-104, where it is argued that the ducats found by Bachrach to be substandard were actually imitations.

rather than being charged to the customer. The fact that these measures appear to have had little effect on the flow of precious metal into Venice suggests that the problem was not a local one.

The steps which Venice took to attract silver and gold were undertaken within the context of a highly competitive minting regime in the Western Mediterranean, and especially in Italy. Suppliers of bullion, chiefly from across the Alps, could choose to bring their metal to whichever mint offered them the best coins under the most advantageous conditions. These northern merchants usually carried off imported goods in exchange for their bullion, so minting activity was closely tied into the market for the objects of Mediterranean trade. The production of coins was also crucial for merchants trading in the Levant, where Venetian coins, especially ducats, had become the preferred medium of exchange.[3] The strategy of the Venetian Senate was to offer terms which would attract holders of bullion to Venice away from other mints.

However, in the half-century from 1375 to 1425, there was comparatively little bullion going to competing mints which could have been lured to Venice. In Genoa, Venice's chief commercial rival, the production of gold coinage in this period was at a rate well under half of that documented for the earlier fourteenth century and usually about one-quarter of it (Fig. 1) (Felloni 1978, 152-3). For Florence, the chief commercial center of Italy, data for the minting of the gold florin are lacking from 1391 to 1423, but the quantities from the decades just before and after these dates indicate a rate of minting well below that of the middle of the fourteenth century (Fig. 2) (Bernocchi 1976, 67-70). The production of both of these mints appears to have been considerably below that of Venice; neither Florence nor Genoa is known to have minted at a rate of more than 200 kilograms of gold per year, while the rate in Venice seems to have ranged between about 500 and 1400

---

[3]For example, the account of Emanuel Piloti in 1420 that Venetian grossi were current in Egypt and Syria and that Venetian ducats were the only gold coins accepted there (Piloti, 1958, 108; 149-50).

kilograms a year (Stahl 1995, 292-93).[4] Figures for the minting of silver in the same period also fail to show the mints of Florence and Genoa capitalizing on the loss of production in Venice; at no time between 1375 and 1425 is the silver coinage produced in either mint anywhere near as high as the 12,000 marks (2,856 kg) documented as minted in Venice in the years around 1400 (Figs. 3 & 4) (Stahl 1995, 294-95; Felloni 1978, 152-53; Bernocchi 1976, 252-55).

In fact, the problems at the Venetian mint coincide with what has been called the Great Bullion Famine of the later Middle Ages, in which most major European mints are reported to have seen declines in production (Day 1987). According to this analysis, great quantities of precious metal, both gold and silver, flowed from Europe to the Levant and beyond in two waves, the first reaching its height in 1395 to 1415, and the second in 1440 to 1460. The flow is seen as the result of a deficitory balance of trade between West and East, with bullion carried east to pay for pepper and other valuable Asian commodities. Venice is viewed as having been at the apex of this movement, with much of the bullion flowing out of Europe recoined at its mint into the coins preferred by Levantine merchants, the silver grosso and gold ducat. Certain figures on the high output of the Venetian mint and the flow of its coinage to the East have been used to reinforce the theory of a drain of bullion out of Europe (Day 1987, 28-29; Lane 1984, 36-40).

Yet, as we have seen, the picture of the Venetian mint which arises from the scattered surviving archival sources points to a period of crisis in the very same years as it is supposed to have been flooded with bullion, with the silver mint near desolation and the gold mint in disarray and struggling to maintain a level of output consistent with that of the fourteenth century. The prevailing view of the early-fifteenth century as a period of prosperity for the mint of Venice derives in large measure from data contained in the supposed deathbed oration of doge Tomaso

---

[4]The values of the pounds of Florence and Venice relative to the mark of Venice are derived from Pegolotti 1936, 146-7. The figure of 238.5 grams for the mark of medieval Venice is taken from Lane and Mueller 1985, 526.

Mocenigo said to have been delivered in 1423, but known from no contemporary documents or accounts. As I have argued elsewhere, the information in this source is inconsistent with archival and numismatic documentation not only for the level of production of the Venetian mint but for the very denominations said by it to have been coined in Mocenigo's reign (Stahl 1995). This analysis has lead me to the view that the supposed oration of Mocenigo is actually the invention of a later period, intended to depict the early 1420s as a golden age. The basic argument of the text is that Venice's close involvement in the politics and economy of mainland Italy would harm her maritime trade and hence her wealth. This view appears to reflect that of an anti-Foscari faction of the mid-fifteenth century.

If the crisis of the Venetian mint in the early fifteenth century is difficult to reconcile with the late medieval bullion famine, we must examine whether it can be tied to the other great *conjonture* of the age hypothesized by twentieth-century economic historians – the demographic and economic depression of the early Renaissance. This theory has even more proponents and detractors than that of the Bullion Famine, and has been elaborated in several ways over the past half century.[5] In its basic outlines, it sees the period following the Black Death of 1348 as a time of economic decline throughout Europe, with the demographic catastrophe of the plague followed by declines in productivity and real purchasing power, and genuine recovery achieved only in the early modern period.

The place of Venice in this scenario is again seen as exceptional, with her Golden Age in the early fifteenth century coinciding with the depths of the depression elsewhere. This anomaly has been explained as the result of a concentration of wealth in the hands of a small elite, whose tastes for luxuries sustained and even enlarged Venetian commerce with the East. Again, the evidence most frequently cited for the wealth of Venice in this period is the depiction in the Mocenigo deathbed oration

---

[5]It had its starkest presentation in Lopez 1952 ; and was refined in Miskimin 1975, 132-58. For a review of the state of the question, see Brown 1989.

(Miskimin 1975, 154-5; Luzzatto 1961, 164-67; Cessi 1981, 363-64.; Ashtor 1971, 65-67). Another oration supposedly delivered by this same doge cites the profit to Venice from its export of Levantine luxuries to Tuscany and Lombardy, accompanied by a modest importation of textiles from these areas (Luzzatto 1961, 166-67).

As I have taken a skeptical approach to the data from the supposed Mocenigo orations, it seemed necessary to me to re-examine the question of the strength of Venice's trade in this period, to determine whether the evidence for the prosperity of Venice as a whole in the early fifteenth century is as evanescent as that for the productivity of its mint. The crisis of the Venetian mint could then be understood not so much as the result of a European bullion famine, but as a sign that the trade of Venice was in a period of decline and that merchants were not bringing bullion there because there was decreased demand for the commodities which this metal had earlier bought. In this paper, I would like to examine sources other than the Mocenigo orations to investigate whether a decline in the volume and profitability of Venetian trade can, indeed, be discerned in the decades around 1400.

The best documented aspect of Venetian trade is the system of convoys of rowed galleys chartered by the state and sent to specific ports to transport the wares of Venetian merchants. In most years, the Venetian Senate set in advance the number of galleys for each destination, in accordance with its expectations of the volume of trade as well as various political and diplomatic considerations. It then offered each ship at auction, with the winning bidder having the right to the freight charges for the voyage, prorated for all of the ships in the convoy. Starting with the earliest unbroken series of surviving Senate records in 1330, the figures for the number of ships and auction results form a continuous series of data unusual for medieval economic history. Though these records have been published in a partial manner and discussed through the past century, they have only recently been made available in complete and fully documented form with the publication of Doris Stöckly's Sorbonne doctoral thesis (1995) (Fig. 5).

The data illustrate the variability of the number of merchant ships sent by the state; the convoys were totally suspended in the years of war with Genoa in the 1350s and 1370s both because of the danger of transport and the requisitioning of the galleys for military purpose. The galleys to Cyprus were suspended in the decades in which Genoa controlled its trade between 1372 and 1445, and the number of galleys sent to Romania, that is Byzantium and the Black Sea, responded to commercial successes of the Genoese in the region and military victories by the Ottomans.

All in all, however, significant trends are discernible in the figures. The total number of galleys chartered by Venice per year, when averaged over 5-year periods, stayed below 10 ships a year in most of the period before 1395. It rose slightly above 10 ships a year in the period just before and just after the Genoese War of 1351 to 1355, and declined markedly in the period of that conflict and of the War of Chioggia of 1377 to 1381. After 1395, the numbers of galleys per year are significantly higher, reaching an average of about 15 per year in most of the five-year blocks between 1410 and 1450. Not only did the number of galleys rise through the period in question, so did their capacity. It has been estimated that the largest merchant galleys of the fourteenth century had a capacity of 140 tons, but that this rose to as high as 250 tons per galley by the middle of the fifteenth century (Lane 1934, 15).

The aggregate number and capacity of galleys per year, however, conceal changes in the destinations of the galleys. There were declines in the number of galleys to Cyprus and the Black Sea brought about mainly by political situations; to some extent these were offset by the rising number of galleys to Alexandria and Beirut, which carried basically the same commodities that were reaching the Mediterranean from Asia by different routes. More significantly, the galleys which headed to the West from Venice, to the Barbary Coast, to Southern France and especially to England and Flanders, represented a totally new direction and nature of trade. These excursions were minimal before 1375, but by the first half of the fifteenth century they represented about one-third of all galleys chartered. To some degree, these galleys were carrying west from Venice some of the same objects which other galleys had carried to Venice from the Levant, so the rise in the total number of galleys after 1400 can be attributed in part to a duplication of shipping rather than to an increase in the amount of goods carried. On the other hand, the added shipping offered greater opportunities for profit by Venetian merchants by replacing German middlemen as the ones who brought their imports to northern markets, so thereby added to the prosperity of the Venetian economy.

The auction prices realized for the galleys can also serve as an index of the value of the commerce which they carried. By comparing the number of ships authorized (Fig. 5) to the total auction prices (Fig. 6) for most of the period before 1370, it can be seen that the average auction price per ship aggregated over a five-year basis remained under 800 ducats per ship most of the time, while in the period 1370 to 1420 it fluctuated greatly, and after 1420 settled at around 1200 ducats per ship. The total realized by the state from these auctions again fluctuated widely, reaching lows in the dangerous periods just after the two Genoese wars, and highs in the periods 1355 to 1359 and 1395 to 1399, finally settling in at a high level from 1420 through 1449 (Fig. 6). It should be recalled that these auction figures reflect not the expected profit from the sale of the merchandise carried by the galleys, but the anticipated profit to the shipper from freight charges, which were set by the state depending on the commodity carried. Moreover, in some years the Senate offered a subsidy to encourage prospective bidders in the auctions, though up until 1441 this was usually a loan rather than an outright gift (Stöckly 1995, 220-21).

Merchant letters in the Datini archives can be compared with the official figures to give some idea of the trade carried on by these convoys of merchant galleys (Heers 1955). In 1395, three ships were authorized for the convoy to Alexandria, with an auction price averaging 2,420 ducats per ship (Fig. 7). They returned with pepper worth over 100,000 ducats, ginger worth 31,300 ducats, cinnamon worth 13,600 ducats and other commodities worth under 10,000 ducats total; the average value of goods carried to Venice was 51,000 ducats per ship.

Five galleys went that year to Beirut, auctioned at 1,184 ducats each. They brought back a similar array of commodities (though here ginger out valued pepper), worth an average of 60,000 ducats per ship. Only two galleys went to the Black Sea, auctioned at 1,170 ducats each, which brought back mainly silk at a value of 93,000 ducats worth per galley.[6] For these three convoys of 1395, then, the auction figures on the galleys were respectively 4.7%, 2.0%, and 1.2% of the value of the cargo reported to have been carried back to Venice.

The cargo carried on the outbound voyages of 1395 is known for only one of these convoys; the three galleys which went to Alexandria carried over 200,000 pounds of copper, plus an unspecified amount of mercury, velvet, and glassware. At current prices, the copper was worth 14,000 ducats in Venice, less than 10% of the value of the merchandise brought back (Ashtor 1971, 117). It must be inferred that a good proportion of the balance of the value of the material acquired in the East was paid for with coins or precious metal ingots brought from Venice. Information on a few other convoys confirms that a good part of the merchandise brought from the east in Venetian galleys was paid for with a flow of gold from Europe. In the years 1422 to 1433, convoys east are reported to have carried amounts ranging from 200,000 to 600,000 ducats per year in coin (Lane 1984, 38).

The galleys which went from Venice to Western Europe also carried merchandise and coins, but apparently at a lesser rate. In 1399, when 10 galleys went to the East, only 5 went West to Flanders and these carried out with them only about 28% of the value of the goods brought into Venice from the Levant; much of the rest was probably dispersed overland to Germany and the rest of Italy (Heers 1955, 191). In 1402 the five Flanders galleys are reported to have carried goods worth over 280,000 ducats from Venice, with another 100,000 ducats worth of coins and jewelry (Luzzatto 1955, 150).

---

[6]Three galleys to Romania were authorized and auctioned in 1395, but only two in subsequent years, so it seems likely that in 1395 only two of them actually made the voyage: Stöckly 1995, 118-19.

Galleys, which had relatively small capacity and required large crews of oarsmen, accounted for only a small percent of Venice's merchant fleet. The activity of the other ships, however, was not usually controlled by the Venetian state, so has left far less documentation. The best continuous sequence of reports on other types of shipping are contained in the chronicle, still unpublished, of Antonio Morosini, but this is contemporary only for the fifteenth century and reports only on commercial activities which its compiler considered newsworthy.

The most important of these secondary ships were cogs, round-bottomed sailing ships with a larger capacity than the merchant galleys (Lane 1934, 15, 39-47). They chiefly carried bulkier and less valuable materials, but appear to have sailed in greater number. In 1399, when five galleys were auctioned for the Beirut trade, two cogs were added to the official convoy (Stöckly 1995, 151). Merchant sources, however, record a total of 24 Venetian ships in the Beirut harbor in that year, most of which must have been unregulated trading cogs (Melis 1970, 371-73). These cogs are reported to have brought back cotton and sugar worth at least 210,000 ducats, compared to the 440,000 ducats worth of spices brought back by the convoys to Alexandria and Beirut (Ashtor 1983, 188). In the years 1384 to 1421, Venice authorized 93 cogs to sail to the Levant, most in the range of about 500 tons (Hocquet 1979, 2: 108). In this same period, Venice is reported to have had at total of over 150 ships in the same weight class in the Western Mediterranean, and 36 in the North Sea (Melis,1984, 11-19).

There are few comparable data from before 1375 to determine whether this sector of Venetian trade had experienced a decline from the early fourteenth century. The chronicle of Nicolò Trevisan, who died in 1369, reports that in the period of 1330 to 1342, 48 sailing ships a year went to Syria for cotton, but even if this figure is accurate these ships may have been significantly smaller than those of the end of the century (Hocquet 1979, 2: 158, 104-08). The number of cog voyages authorized by the Venetian state, a small percentage of the total, rose steadily through the last decades of the fourteenth century, with the exception of the years around the War of Chioggia from 1378 to 1381 (Fig. 8)

(Ashtor 1983, 515). Within the years covered by the Morosini chronicle, the first three decades of the fifteenth century, the number of important cogs reported returning to Venice is at its height in the period 1415-1420, with a peak noted in 1417, the very year in which the Procurators declared the silver mint "reduced almost to nothing" (Ashtor 1983, 255, 267; Lane 1966, 148).

Like the galleys, the cogs often carried coins east from Venice to use for purchases abroad. The seven cogs which left for the Levant in 1417 took 60,000 ducats in coin as well as cloth, amber, and other commodities (Hocquet 1979, 158-59). Cogs to Egypt and Syria in 1423 are reported to have carried outbound about 70,000 ducats in cash, compared with merchandise worth about 20,000 ducats, while those of 1433 are said to have carried as much as a million ducats in specie compared to under 400,000 ducats worth of goods (Ashtor 1984, 328). But these sums appear to have been exceptional, and it is probably for that reason that they were conveyed by the chronicler.

For the most part, cogs appear to have carried a significant amount of goods on their voyages to the Levant as well as on the return trip. Some of this comprised base metal and wood, strategic items which had sometimes been subject to papal ban but nevertheless remained important trade commodities for Venice (Hocquet 1979, 2: 151; Heers, 1955, 167). In the early fifteenth century, however, textiles were increasingly being shipped to the east, such as the Florentine and English cloth which Andrea Barbarigo shipped to the Levant in 1433, along with sheepskins, canvas, and silver grosso coins (Lane 1944, 61). The expansion of this commerce has been explained as the result of a decline in textile production in the Near East resulting from demographic decline, heavy taxation, and technological stagnation, creating markets there for cheap European cloth (Ashtor 1984, 200-08).Though there are no continuous series of data as for the galleys, the evidence for Venice's commerce in large cogs shows no decline in the early fifteenth century and suggests a significant increase in the kind of bulk commerce for which such ships were best suited.

There is, in sum, no indication of a decline in the maritime trade of Venice in the decades around 1400; all indications are that it was thriving at a rate significantly above that of the first half of the fourteenth century. The activity of these galleys and cogs did not constitute, however, Venice's only trade. There was a significant land-based commerce between Venice and the towns of Northern Italy, which the increased role of their textiles in Venetian trade would only have strengthened. Another major component of the overland commerce was the activity of German and other transalpine merchants who came to Venice principally to buy the goods brought from the Levant. There is little in the way of direct data as to the volume of this trade, but there is at least the possibility that it was diminished in the 1410s and 1420s by the embargo which the emperor Sigismund placed on commerce between his subjects and Venice (von Stromer 1986, 61-84). To the extent to which this embargo had any effect, it would have disrupted the supply to Venice of gold and especially silver, which appear to have been the chief commodities which Germans brought to exchange for imported goods. This would have added to whatever general decline there was in European stocks of precious metal and contributed to the crisis which was evident in the Venetian mint.

The crisis that came to a head in 1417 can now be seen as resulting from a strong demand in Venice for capital to use in the Levantine trade in the face of a reduced supply of bullion coming into the city. The steps which the Senate took to attract bullion by making the mint more competitive and trustworthy seem to have done little to increase the availability of gold and silver. The primary compensation for the constrained supply of coins and bullion for use in overseas commerce appears to have derived from the success of Venetian merchants in increasing the level of exports from West to East, especially of European textiles. In 1420, Emmanual Piloti, a Venetian resident in Egypt, noted that it was only the export of European industrial products to the Levant that made it possible for Venetian merchants to make purchases there (Piloti 1958, 110). The increased involvement of Venice in the domestic Italian economy and trade in products of European manufacture was part of an extension of her activity on the mainland which, contrary to the words put in the mouth of doge Mocenigo, appears to have supported her position in international trade, rather than undermining it.

VENETIAN COMMERCE IN THE LATER MIDDLE AGES 153

FIGURE 1: Minting of gold in Genoa, 1330-1450

kilograms per year averaged over five-year spans

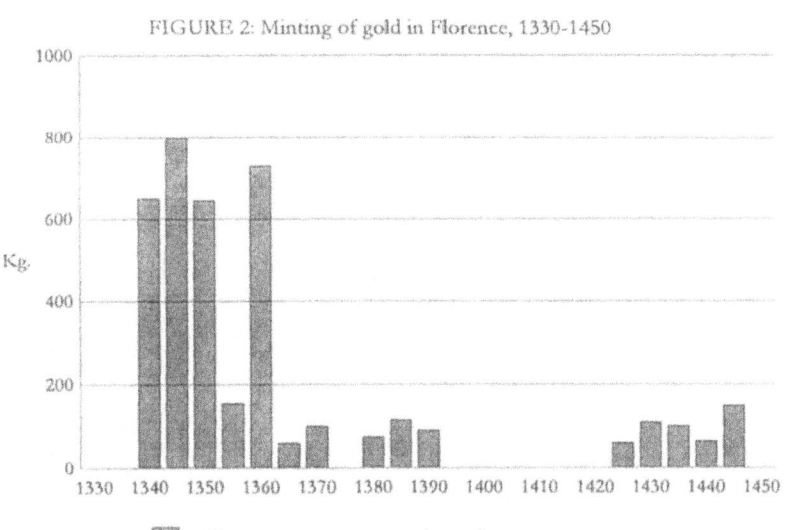

FIGURE 2: Minting of gold in Florence, 1330-1450

kilograms per year averaged over five-year spans

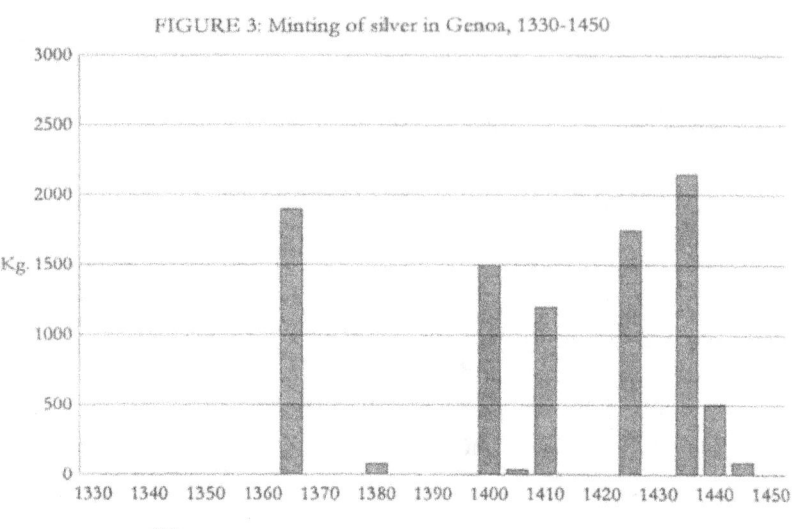

FIGURE 3: Minting of silver in Genoa, 1330-1450

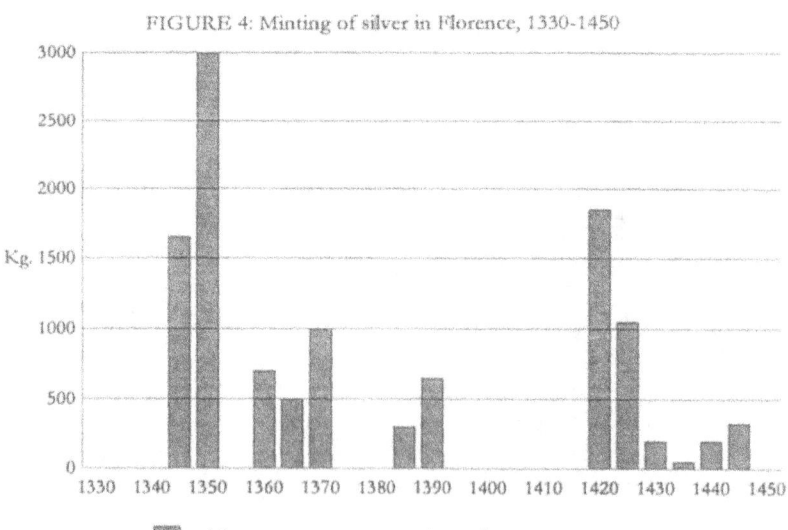

FIGURE 4: Minting of silver in Florence, 1330-1450

# VENETIAN COMMERCE IN THE LATER MIDDLE AGES 155

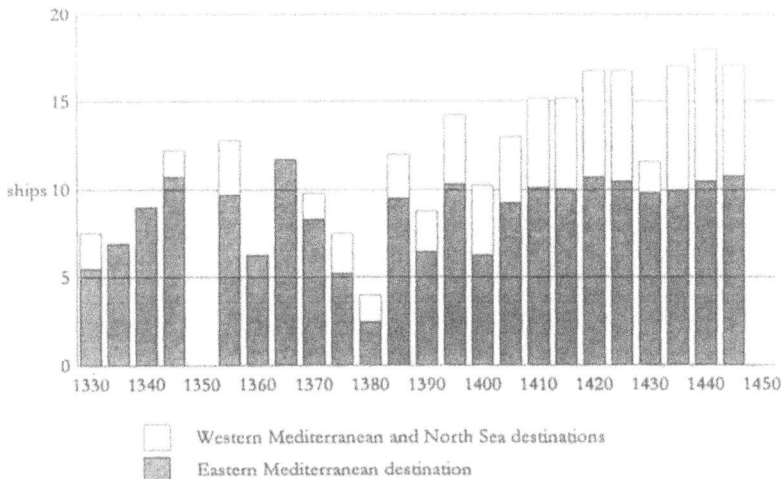

FIGURE 5: Venetian conveys authorized, 1330-1450
(number of ships per year averaged over five-year spans)

☐ Western Mediterranean and North Sea destinations
▨ Eastern Mediterranean destination

FIGURE 6: Venetian galley auction results, 1330-1450

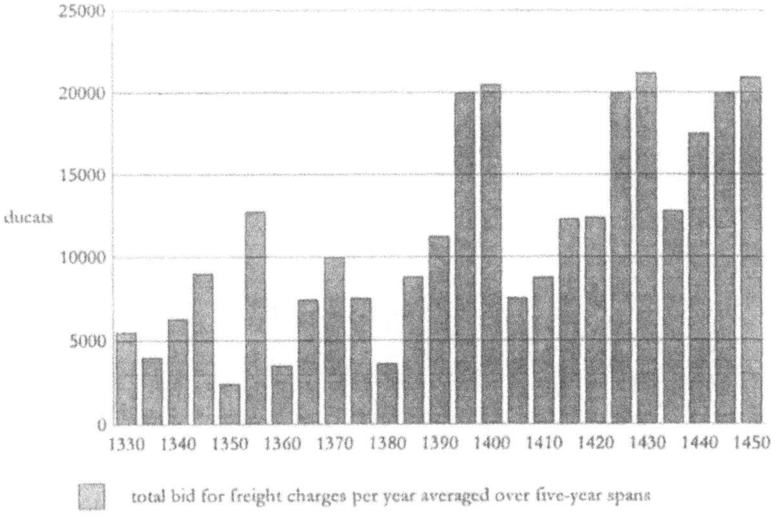

▨ total bid for freight charges per year averaged over five-year spans

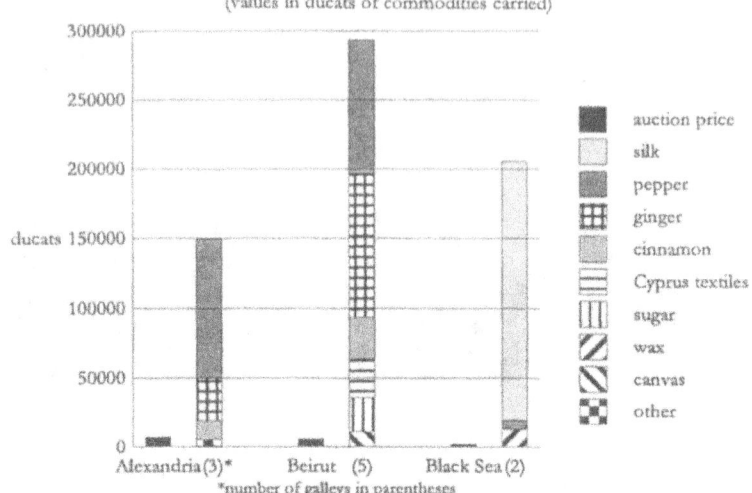

FIGURE 7: Venetian galley convoys of 1395
(values in ducats of commodities carried)

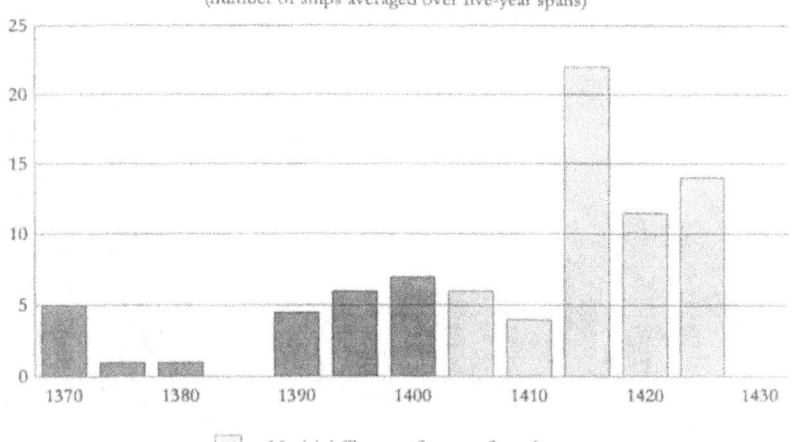

FIGURE 8: Cog voyages recorded, 1370-1430
(number of ships averaged over five-year spans)

## References

Ashtor, Eliahu. 1971. *Les métaux précieux et la balance des payements du proche-orient à la basse époque*. Paris: S.E.V.P.E.N.
———. 1983. *Levant Trade in the Later Middle Ages*. Princeton: Princeton University Press.
ASV SM = Venice. Archivio di Stato di Venezia. Senato Misti.
ASV GR = Venice. Archivio di Stato di Venezia. Grazie.
Bachrach, Jere L. 1983. Monetary Movements in Medieval Egypt, 1171-1517. In *Precious Metals in the Later Medieval and Early Modern Worlds*, ed. J. F. Richards, 159-181. Durham: UNC Press.
Bernocchi, Mario. 1976. *Le monete della Repubblica Fiorentina*. Vol. 3. Florence: Olschki.
Bonfiglio Dosio, Giorgetta, ed. 1984. *Il "Capitolar dalle Broche" della Zecca di Venezia (1358-1556)*. Padua: Antenore.
Brown, Judith C. 1989. Prosperity or Hard Times in Renaissance Italy? *Renaissance Quarterly* 42: 761-80.
Cessi, Roberto. 1981 [orig. ed. 1968]. *Storia della Repubblica di Venezia*. 2nd ed. Rpt. Florence: Martello.
Day, John. 1987. The Great Bullion Famine of the Fifteenth Century. In *The Medieval Market Economy*. Oxford: Blackwell.
Felloni, Giuseppe. 1978. Ricavi e costi della zecca di Genova dal 1341 al 1450. In *Studi in Memoria di Federigo Melis*, vol. 3: 141-153. Naples: Giannini.
Grierson, Philip. 1988. The Fineness of the Venetian Ducat and its Imitations. In *Metallurgy in Numismatics*, vol. 2, ed. W. A. Oddy, 95-104. London: Royal Numismatic Society.
Heers, Jacques. 1955. Il commercio nel Mediterraneo alla fine del sec. XIV e nei primi anni del XV. *Archivio Storico Italiano* 113: 157-209.
Hocquet, Jean-Claude. 1979. *Le Sel et la fortune de Venise*. Vol. 2: *Voiliers et commerce en Méditerranée*. Lille: PUL.
Lane, Frederic C. 1934. *Venetian Ships and Ship Builders of the Renaissance*. Baltimore: Hopkins.

———. 1944. *Andrea Barbarigo; Merchant of Venice, 1418-1449.* Baltimore: Hopkins.

———. 1966. The Merchant Marine of the Venetian Republic. Trans. and rpt. in his *Venice and History*, 143-162. Baltimore: Hopkins.

———. 1984. Exportations vénitiennes d'or et d'argent de 1200 à 1450. In *Études d'histoire monétaires*, ed. John Day, 29-48. Lille: PUL.

Lane, Frederic C., and Reinhold C. Mueller. 1985. *Money and Banking in Medieval and Renaissance Venice.* Vol. 1: *Coins and Moneys of Account.* Baltimore: Hopkins.

Lopez, Robert S. 1952. The Trade of Medieval Europe: The South. In *The Cambridge Economic History of Europe*, vol. 2, ed. M. Postan and E. E. Rich, 257-354. Cambridge: CUP.

Luzzatto, Gino. 1961. *Storia economica di Venezia dall'XI al XVI secolo.* Venice: Fantoni.

Melis, Federigo. 1970. Note sur le mouvement du port de Beyrouth d'après la documentation florentine aux environs de 1400. In *Sociétés et compagnies de commerce en Orient et dans l'Ocean Indien*, ed. Michel Mollat, 371-373. Actes du huitième Colloque International d'Histoire Maritime. Paris: SEVPEN.

———. 1984. Werner Sombart e i problemi della navigazione nel medioevo. Rpt. in his *I trasporti e le comunicazioni nel medioevo*, ed. L. Frangioni, 3-68. Prato: Istituto Datini.

Miskimin, Harry A. 1975. *The Economy of Early Renaissance Europe, 1300-1460.* Cambridge: CUP.

Papadopoli, Nicolo. 1893-1919. *Le monete di Venezia.* 3 vols. Venice: Ongania.

Pegolotti, Francesco Balducci. 1936. *La Pratica della Mercatura.* Ed. Allan Evans. Cambridge MA: Medieval Academy of America.

Piloti, Emmanuel. 1958. *Traité d'Emmanuel Piloti sur les passage en Terre Sainte (1420).* Ed. Pierre-Herman Dopp. Louvain: Nauwelaerts.

Stahl, Alan M. 1995. The Deathbed Oration of Doge Mocenigo. In *Intercultural Contacts in the Medieval Mediterranean: Studies in Honour of David Jacoby*, ed. B. Arbel, Mediterranean Historical Review 10: 284-301.

———. 2000. *Zecca: the Mint of Venice in the Middle Ages*. Baltimore: Hopkins.

Stöckly, Doris. 1995. *Le système de l'incanto des galées du marché à Venise (fin XIIIe-milieu XVe siècle)*. Leiden: Brill.

von Stromer, Wolfgang. 1986. Die Kontinentalsperre Kaiser Sigismunds gegen Venedig, 1412-1413, 1418-1433, und die Verlagerung der transkontinentalen Transportwege. In *Trasporti e sviluppo economico*, ed. A. V. Marx, 61-84. Settimane di Studio del Istituto Datini, Prato, 5. Florence: Le Monnier.

# 8

## *Quidam de Sinagoga*: The Jew of the *Jeu d'Adam**

### *Jennifer R. Goodman*

NEAR THE END OF THE ANGLO-NORMAN PLAY of Adam the prophet Isaiah is challenged by a character described only as *quidam de sinagoga* ("someone from the synagogue"), who bursts into the play out of nowhere. His interruption is as unexpected in the text as it would be in performance: the appearance of this character is not anticipated anywhere in the play's detailed Latin stage directions. This elusive being, *quidam de sinagoga*, has been too often neglected by students of this notable play. He is to be treated here not as a minor technical problem, but as a key figure integral to the meaning of the work as a whole.

The *Ordo representacionis Adae* ("The Service for Representing Adam," in David Bevington's translation), perhaps more familiar as the *Jeu d'Adam*, has long been acclaimed as a masterpiece of twelfth-century drama, commended successively by Gaston Paris, Henry Adams

---

*The intial version of this paper was presented at the 26th International Congress on Medieval Studies at Western Michigan University, in a session sponsored by the Medieval Academy of Judaeo-Christian Studies. I am grateful to the organizer, Professor Michael A. Signer of Notre Dame, for his encouragement. My first teacher in the field of medieval Jewish history, the late Professor Isadore Twersky of Harvard, was most helpful in answering my bibliographical inquiry. I owe special thanks to him and to Professor John Leyerle of Toronto, who first pointed me in the direction of the *Jeu d'Adam*, for their inspiration, to Dr. Richard Gyug of Fordham for encouraging me in the preparation of this revised version, and to Dr. Jeffrey Wollock for his help, kindness, and expert advice.

([1905] 1913, 205-206, citing Paris), and Erich Auerbach ([1953] 1971, 143-161).[1] Still this attractive play continues to perplex its readers. The *Jeu d'Adam* remains difficult to place, geographically or liturgically. Its problematic ending in the unique manuscript (Bibliothèque municipale de Tours 927), lost or transformed into a treatise on the Last Judgment (*Les Quinze Signes du Jugement*), raises issues of staging and social function.[2] Written in England or Northern France between 1146 and 1174, in liturgical Latin and debatably Anglo-Norman French, the *Jeu d'Adam* is made up of three parts: the Fall of Adam and Eve, the murder of Abel, and a procession of prophets. This final section of the play elaborates on the pseudo-Augustinian *Contra Judaeos, Paganos et Arianos, Sermo de Symbolo*. The play's prophetic speeches address a Jewish audience, which most critics assume to be figurative.[3]

This paper will suggest that the *Jeu d'Adam* is, on one level, an argument for the conversion of the Jews addressed to a contemporary Jewish audience. This theme links the scenes of the play, strengthening it as a dramatic structure. It also makes excellent sense in view of the interest in dialogues and disputations between faiths characteristic of the mid-twelfth century. Such a proselytizing effort accords with the conditions of life in many francophone Jewish communities at this time. Interpreted in this way, the *Jeu d'Adam* can be seen as an attempt to use the drama to communicate between cultures – even as it refuses to accept the cultural difference of the other.

---

[1]Auerbach remarks on "the scenes which render everyday contemporary life (the finest are the one between the Devil and Eve and the one here under discussion – two masterly pieces of incomparable purity, truly peers of the most perfect sculptures in Chartres, Reims, Paris, or Amiens) ..." ([1953] 1971, 156).

[2]Editions consulted in the preparation of this article include those of Aebischer 1963; Bevington 1975, 80-121; Noomen 1971; Odenkirchen 1976; and Studer 1918; except where otherwise noted, I use the translation and edition of Bevington. For a facsimile reproduction of the manuscript, see Sletsjöe 1968. For detailed discussions of the problems of location, the play's conclusion, and its staging, see Noomen 1968; Bevington 1975, 79-80; and Muir 1973.

[3]On the connections between Adam and the sermon *Contra Judaeos*, see Vaughan 1983; and Young [1933] 1962.

Key features support the inference that the *Jeu d'Adam* reflects an overt proselytizing effort. Much of it is written in French, the common vernacular of the twelfth-century Christian and Jewish communities both in England and Northern France. The play's biblical content would be familiar in its entirety to the Jewish community: Lynette Muir remarks on the "emphasis on the Jewish element" in the prophetic section, which she associates with the abbey of St. Victor, whose biblical interpreters were known for their consultations with Jewish scholars (Muir 1973, 118). The *Jeu d'Adam*'s performance on the church steps would render it potentially accessible to members of the Jewish community. Throughout the *Jeu d'Adam* the playwright anticipates such a Jewish audience and attempts to orchestrate its response to the play.

The bulk of critical writing on the *Jeu d'Adam* regards the initial Adam and Cain scenes as the heart of the play, and the Procession of Prophets as an unimaginative appendage. In fact, in this reading, Adam and Cain function as an historical prologue, an enticement into the Procession of Prophets.

The stories of Adam and Eve and Cain both contained well-established Jewish themes. The devil's temptation of Eve by way of her sense of mental superiority, her intellectual pride, may well reflect criticism of the Jews as overly proud of their own mental attainments: "mais neporquant tu es plus sage; / en grant sens as mis tun couraige" ("But notwithstanding you are wiser; your mind has discovered great wisdom"; ll. 233-234).[4] The play's psychology of sin develops from

---

[4] Accusations that the Jews sin through intellectual pride or an overreliance on human rationality can be found in Smalley [1952] 1970, 235: "'The Jews of our time are Parvipontani,' i.e. hair-splitting logicians, after a characteristic of the school on the Petit Pont." The presentation of Judaism in polemical literature, for instance Joseph Kimhi's *Book of the Covenant* (*Sefer ha-Berit*), as a religion notable for its rationality might also be pertinent here (trans. Talmage 1972). The twelfth-century Christian response ranged from accusing Jews of abject literal-mindedness (a view that dates back to Jerome; Smalley [1952] 1970, 170-173) to denying them any human rationality whatsoever, as in Peter the Venerable's polemical work of 1144-47, *Adversus Iudeorum Inveteratam Duritiem* (Friedman 1985).

Eve's intellectual pride by way of Cain's greed and avarice, to murderous envy. In her charmed acceptance of the devil's flattering image of herself as intellectually superior to Adam, Eve can be seen as the mother of the Jews.

The play's vivid depiction of the first couple's exile from Eden would have had a special resonance for twelfth-century Jews of the diaspora. The exile of the Jews from their ancient homeland had been seen as God's punishment, like the expulsion of Adam and Eve from Eden, by both Christian and Jewish writers.[5] Much of the *Jeu d'Adam* playwright's language of social declension as Adam and Eve descend the feudal hierarchy from God's trusted vassals to degraded serfs has analogues in the medieval church's Augustinian perception of the Jew's social status as similar to but baser than Christian serfdom (Langmuir 1990a, 293-295; and 1990b, 189, 190-191).[6]

The story of Cain was even more strongly associated with Judaism by twelfth-century writers. Cain's greed and murderous envy make him, here as in other twelfth-century works, a prefiguration of the contemporary Jews who were so often equated with him. The curse placed upon Cain was understood by many ancient and medieval Christians as identical to God's curse upon the Jewish people. Peter the Venerable's letter to Louis VII of 1146 asserts of the Jews, "God wishes them, not to be killed, but to be preserved in a life worse than death, like Cain the fratricide, for greater torment and ignominy" (Langmuir 1990b, 201; Constable 1967, 1: 327-330). This interpretation was not new to the

---

[5]By the twelfth century a substantial body of literature described the diaspora as God's punishment; for an overview and analysis of ancient and medieval Jewish attitudes to exile, see Patai 1971, 23-31. Patai observes a shift from the Biblical view that God had scattered the Children of Israel to punish their sins, to a sense that the Jews' banishment was intended to allow them to serve as "light to the nations," and was prolonged by the wickedness of the nations among whom they lived. For Christian interpretations of the exile of the Jews as divinely appointed punishment for collective Jewish guilt, see Augustine, *The City of God* 18: 46 (Dodds 1948, 2: 277-279).

[6]Langmuir distinguishes usefully between this theological doctrine and the question of "Jewish serfdom" in thirteenth-century legal terminology.

twelfth century; it was as old as Ambrose and Augustine. Ruth Mellinkoff's classic study, *The Mark of Cain*, explores this equation in detail (1981, 92-98). For audiences primed to recognize Cain as the Jew, the two sacrifices of the Cain and Abel scene would stand as theatrical emblems of Christianity and Judaism, the true and false worship of the same God.

The Jew, envisioned as a Cain, must repent his corporate responsibility for the murder of Jesus. The curse Figura places upon Cain in lines 736-40 echoes the Christian reinterpretation of the fifty-ninth psalm "Slay them not, lest my people forget; Scatter them by Thy power, let them wander to and fro" (Psalm 59: 11-15). The Jews, by their dispersion and abject suffering, are to serve as proofs of the truth of Christianity – a concept as self-evident to St. Bernard of Clairvaux in 1146 and Innocent III in 1205 as it had been to Augustine eight hundred years earlier (Langmuir 1990b, 133; Ladner 1971, 362).

Once the prophets arrive onstage, the focus on the Jews is relentless. The addition of Abraham, Aaron, David, Solomon, and Baalam to the prophets of the *Adversus Judaeos* text makes visible to the audience a much broader spectrum of Biblical history than usual in the tradition of the Procession of Prophets. The Hebrew Bible's historical narrative, as well as its complex prophetic material, is called upon to bear witness to Christian truth. The evocation of familiar figures of authority adds weight to the play's insistence that now the Jews have no kings or bishops of their own. "The sceptre is departed from Judah" (a reversal of Genesis 49: 10) is another familiar Christian (and Islamic) line of attack (Margolis and Marx [1927] 1973, 309). This argument echoes in Peter Damian's assertion of c. 1070 that the loss of temple, king, and priests demonstrates the failure of Judaism (Langmuir 1990b, 130). The most resplendent Jewish authorities of the Bible are depicted here enforcing the Church's message. Moses tells his Jewish audience that they should believe the one who is to come – Jesus – more than they do Moses himself. Repeated key words – appeals to reason – contrast with *quidam de sinagoga*'s later appeal to writing (*écriture*). The repeated consignment of the play's characters to the diabolical torments of hell adds force to the movement in the opposite direction – to heaven, into the church (Justice 1978). Read in this way, the entire *Jeu d'Adam* becomes a missionary drama; more than this, it serves as a Christian initiation, the prelude to baptism.

The prophet Isaiah's Jewish challenger is too often viewed as an afterthought, a footnote to the vivid biblical drama of the play's earlier scenes. The episode of Isaiah's debate with the Jew, *quidam de sinagoga*, has been read as the playwright's last desperate attempt to inject dramatic conflict into the undramatic, repetitive sermon structure of the play's concluding Procession of Prophets (MacDonald 1983, 113-114). But it is with this key scene that the proselytizing element of the play becomes most explicit.

In the *Jeu d'Adam*'s long series of prophets – Abraham, Moses, Aaron, David, Solomon, Balaam, Daniel, Habakkuk, Jeremiah, Isaiah, and Nebuchadnezzar – Isaiah stands out as a climactic figure. He is so important that the playwright gives him two prophetic speeches portending the birth of Christ: "Egredietur virga de radice Jesse" (Isaiah 11: 1-2; "There shall come forth a rod from the root of Jesse") and "Ecce virgo concipiet" (Isaiah 7: 14; "Behold, a virgin shall conceive"). In the twelfth century, as today, Isaiah remains the key prophet for Christological interpreters of the Hebrew bible. On theological grounds, this is the moment for a challenge. Right on cue, *quidam de sinagoga* turns up to object.

The designation *quidam de sinagoga* that identifies Isaiah's challenger itself poses a problem of interpretation. The word *sinagoga* may recall the long-standing medieval theme of the "dispute of Church and Synagogue."[7] However, *quidam* is the Latin masculine pronoun. The character who confronts Isaiah is not Synagogue herself, by well-established convention a feminine personification, as in the Bavarian *Ludus de Antichristo* of c. 1160 (ed. Young [1933] 1962, 371-384; trans. Wright 1967). Neither is he a named character like the Benediktbeuern

---

[7]For classic discussions of the theme, see Pflaum 1935; and Schlauch 1940.

Christmas Play's Archisynagogus.[8] Nor is *quidam de sinagoga* identified as a biblical personage. If he represents any abstract entity, he ought to stand for rabbinical Judaism, the Jew of the synagogue. Denying this speaker a name, either allegorical or personal, confines him to a middle ground between abstraction and individuality. As we shall see, the playwright does not give *quidam de sinagoga* a local habitation either.

The character of the Jew's challenge does offer some clues to his identity, while it plunges the student straight into the problem of staging the scene. "Tunc exurget," the single stage direction following line 882 states: "then let him stand up, rise up," or so a literal-minded reader might presume from the prefix *ex-*. The verb is "exurget" rather than "veniet," as for other characters. In the context of this play, "veniet" seems to mean, most often "let [somebody] come [into the playing area from outside]," as in "Tunc veniet diabolus" (following l. 590). "Exurget" suggests an outraged listener bounding to his feet or perhaps pushing himself forward, surging up. He does not merely come forward, or walk on, he rises from something or somewhere, with energy.

The auditor who rises to challenge a public preacher might have been familiar to a twelfth-century playwright from either Jewish or Christian experience. Marc Saperstein offers several pertinent examples. In one case, from the *Responsa* of Maimonides, the challenger was a local scholar who suddenly "rose and shouted, 'How long will this delirium last? All you have said is nonsense; it should not be heard, it cannot be understood.'" Saperstein also notes an episode from the life of Stephen Langton (d. 1228), then archbishop of Canterbury: "Langton ... once

---

[8] For the Latin text of the Benediktbeuern *Ludus de Nativitate* and an English translation, see Bevington 1975, 180-201. In this text Archisynagogus and his Jews ("Archisynagogus cum suis Judaeis") follows the speech of Balaam, the last in the procession of prophets (Bevington 1975, 183.) Here, too, the Jews respond to hearing the prophecies ("auditis prophetiis") and their response is noisy ("valde obstrepet"), disrupting the dignity of the proceedings. An inconclusive exchange involving Augustine, the Boy Bishop, the prophets, and Archisynagogus ensues (Bevington 1975, 183-189). For Bevington, this is "the most imaginative version of the Procession of Prophets to be found anywhere in medieval drama" (1975, 179).

began a sermon with the biblical verse 'My heart hopes in the Lord,' at which point someone in the congregation got up and shouted, 'You are a liar; your heart does not hope in the Lord.'" The outraged listener was a perennial hazard of religious life, one that would cause further trouble in the thirteenth century. Robert C. Stacey reports a later incident: a Jewish onlooker reacted to a 1268 Ascension Day procession down St. Aldates – the center of the Jewry of Oxford – by knocking down, trampling, and spitting on the processional cross. The pronouncement of 1280 that English Jews attend weekly Dominican sermons, cited by Stacey, stipulates perhaps with some apprehension that the Jewish auditors must listen "without tumult, contention or blasphemy" (Saperstein 1989, 55-58, esp. 55 and 58 n. 36; and Stacey 1992, 265, 267-268, 268 n. 27). The effect depicted in the *Jeu d'Adam* episode, then, may well suggest contemporary spontaneity, rather than allegorical stylization.

All we are told about the Jew who confronts Isaiah is "tunc exurget quidam de sinagoga disputans cum isaia" ("then let someone from the synagogue rise up, disputing with Isaiah"). Does *quidam de sinagoga* rise from among a group already present? Willem Noomen assumes a group of actors dressed as "Jews," performing the role of the Jewish auditors traditionally addressed by the prophets and indeed by the original pseudo-Augustinian sermon (Noomen 1968).[9] If so, they are specified nowhere else in the stage directions, though Jews are unmistakably addressed in the prophets' speeches, summoned by the choir: "Vos inquam, convenio, o Judei" ("You, I say, I do summon before a tribunal, O Jews"; Bevington 1975, 113). Noomen interprets this line as the cue for a group of stage Jews to come out (1971, note to l. 883).

---

[9]Muir discusses this problem, and agrees with Noomen that the most probable solution would be for a group of Jews to enter at the start of the prophets sequence so that the prophets can address them (1973, 33-34). She also considers the "not impossible, though ... very original" notion that "the author meant the audience to represent the Jews, so that the *quidam de sinagoga* would come out from the audience" (1973, 34). As Muir observes here, the *Jeu d'Adam* can be distinguished from liturgical drama proper in its awareness of an audience (*populum*) as distinct from the congregation.

There is no internal evidence to support this inference except the speeches throughout this section of the play, all addressing an unspecified group of Jews in the plural, as in Solomon's "Judeu, a vus dona Dex loi" ("O Jews, God gave you his law"; l. 791), or Daniel's "A vus, Judei, di ma raison" ("To you, O Jews, I deliver my sermon"; l. 827). Otherwise this theory can only rest on the practice of contemporary dramatists elsewhere, like the author of the Benediktbeuern Christmas Play. All that the internal evidence will bear out is that there is at least one actor portraying a Jew who appears in this play, the character *quidam de sinagoga*. Whether he appears from among a group of actors enacting the role of the prophets' Jewish audience, or whether he appears alone, is difficult to determine on the basis of the surviving text. If there is no group of actors, who, then represents the Jews addressed by the prophets?

Readers of *Jeu d'Adam* cannot be sure what happens to the Jew after his final speech. The play's stage directions specify that all the prophets are to be led into hell by devils following their speeches. "Dehinc ducetur a diabolo in infernum. Similiter omnes prophetae" ("Thereupon he will be led to hell by the devil. Similarly with all the prophets"; Bevington 1975, 114). It might seem logical to dispose of the Jew there, too. In fact we are not told anything about where he goes after his speech, or indeed, that he goes or is taken anywhere at all. For this reader, the undetermined fate of *quidam de sinagoga* lies at the root of the play.

Where the play of *Ludus de Antichristo* and the Carmina Burana Christmas play choreograph the movement of a specified group of actors representing the Jewish community, the text of *Jeu d'Adam* gives us instead, in apparent spontaneity, the sudden appearance of a single figure who proceeds to speak for this unseen group. This suddenness in the text might well support an equally sudden appearance in performance, in stark contrast to the author's careful advance preparation for the entrances of the play's other characters, who are all beautifully groomed, schooled, and located. The absence of symbolic costume, or of any deliberate, specified gestures, distinguishes this Jewish figure from everyone else in the play, as well as from other contemporary portrayals of Jewish entities in Christian drama.

In this reader's view, the only logical place for *quidam de sinagoga* to rise from is out of the audience, from among the people (*per populum*). No other place is assigned to him; none of the other playing places is suitable for him. He cannot come out of the church: the church has already been designated as the House of God, the mansion of *Figura*, and equated with heaven. As a living human being, he should not emerge from hell. That would make him a devil, which the play shows no sign of intending. Paradise or the waiting area where the prophets are dressing would provide an equally confusing entrance. The only places left are the open acting space in front of the church steps, the platea, which needs to be left clear for action, and the area set aside for the audience, "the people." The devil runs among the audience earlier in the play, during the temptation of Adam and Eve: "Post ea vero discursum faciet per populum" ("Thereafter he will make a foray among the people"; Bevington 1975, 90). In this diabolical interlude the playwright suddenly extends the playing area into the audience itself. By bursting out of the audience, *quidam de sinagoga* would capture the powerful dramatic effect of the unscripted intruder. In fact, *quidam de sinagoga* may best be identified as the Jewish audience of the play as imagined by the author. His interruption is a sign of the importance of this audience to the playwright. He is the only auditor who is brought into the play.

The real importance of *quidam de sinagoga* emerges in his dialogue with the prophet. *Quidam de sinagoga* seems to be conceived as a heckler in his jeering, sceptical response to Isaiah. The dignified prophet is, for this Jewish auditor, a cheap fortune-teller. *Quidam de sinagoga* orders the learned prophet around: "Ore repond, sire Isaias!" (a line I am tempted to translate, "Answer me here, Mr. Isaiah!"), "Ore le nus faites donches veer" ("Make us see it, then"), "Ore commence –" ("Now begin!"). The construction "or" ("Now"), with the imperative conveys a sense of immediacy, urgent demand, here as throughout the play. Characterizing Isaiah as a palm-reader, he demands "Or me gardes en ceste main!" ("Now look into this hand"). Thérèse and Mendel Metzger have published a Northern French palmist's diagram with Hebrew annotations dating from the late thirteenth century, establishing some Jewish interest in this form of fortune-telling – or is it medical diagnosis? The lines marked on the palm they reproduce do indeed reveal signs foretelling incurable disease – leprosy – as well as torture and martyrdom (Metzger and Metzger 1982, 217 [fig. 324: London, BL add. 11639, fol. 115r]). Isaiah's depiction of the Jew as diseased evokes associations of Judaism with contagion or pollution that would be accepted more and more literally as time went by, as in the fourteenth-century notion of the Jews as causers of the Black Death (Langmuir 1990b, 208).

The Jew pelts Isaiah with blunt questions: "Is it a tall story? Did you dream it or see it? Is this a joke? Is it written in a book?" He tells Isaiah that he must be senile: "Tu me sembles viel redoté." Isaiah responds to his attack by informing his disputant, as he looks at his hand, that he is incurably sick with "the disease of wickedness," and will never be healed. There may be an element of stereotypical characterization here, on a level far subtler than that of the Benediktbeuern Christmas Play. The Jew of the *Jeu d'Adam* is a materialist, interested in human physiology. The question being asked here is: whose mind is diseased, Isaiah's or the Jew's?[10]

At this point, the text offers contradictory signs of capitulation. After Isaiah's sharp reply, the Jew demands a repetition of the prophecy: "Or nus redi ta vision –" ("Go on, tell us your vision again"; l. 907), and

---

[10]For Archisynagogus' description, see Bevington 1975, 183: Archisynagogus charges out to the center of the action "movendo caput suum et totum corpus et percutiendo terram pede, baculo etiam imitando gestus Judaei in omnibus" ("agitating his head and his entire body and striking the ground with his foot, and imitating with his sceptre the mannerisms of a Jew in all ways"). The contrast between this physical level of ethnic caricature and the entirely verbal characterization of *quidam de sinagoga* may reflect a clear difference in the playwrights' approaches to these controversial characters. Paul Acker's recent studies of chiromancy in the Middle Ages, kindly pointed out to me by Linda Voigts, indicate that the reading of palms was a respectable branch of scientific study in the twelfth century (Acker 1994). *Quidam de sinagoga* should probably not be regarded as a crank in this respect.

states "Nus te tendrom puis por maistre / E ceste generacion / Escutera puis ta lecçon" ("We will regard you as a master, / and this generation / Will listen to your teaching from now on"; ll. 910-912).[11] This is the Jew's final speech. He disappears from the play with these words as mysteriously as he came, leaving Isaiah to present a second prophecy, traditional to the *Sermo contra Judaeos*, "Ecce virgo concipiet" ("Behold, a virgin shall conceive..." Isaiah 7:14). In the French exposition of this Latin text, some stress is placed on the urgency of the prophet's message "Prés est li tens" ("The time is near at hand") when "Jhesus, le nostre salvaor" ("Jesus, our redeemer"), will release Adam from great Sorrow and return him to paradise.[12] Isaiah tells his audience,

---

[11]The repetition of "puis" is not represented in Bevington's translation: "We will take you for our master / And this generation / Will hearken to your teaching" (1975, 120). Aside from its metrical utility, this doubling intensifies the passage's sense of "after that, then." In Wace's twelfth-century usage the word may also have the sense of the modern "depuis lors" ("ever since" or perhaps "ever after" something). For a complementary analysis of this passage that also stresses the Jew's positive response to Isaiah, see Muir 1973, 109-110, 110 n. 73, 166-167. In her note, Muir cites a number of instances of twelfth-century dialogues between Christians and Jews, in particular Peter the Chanter's report that a Master Gilbert, probably Gilbert de la Porrée, "sic convincit Judeos, et conversi sunt," though in that case the argument cited centers on the comparative merits of Jewish and Christian religious law; cf. Smalley [1952] 1970, 78 n. 2. Muir does not push her argument further than this.

[12]Isaiah's clear reference to the Harrowing of Hell locates that important event in the future. For the audience of the *Jeu d'Adam*, it may be the immediate future in a double sense. As several scholars have postulated, an enactment of the Harrowing of Hell might well have provided a neat conclusion to the play, though, as Bevington cautions (1975, 78), we have no evidence for any such dramatic material beyond Nebuchadnezzar. If the Easter liturgy is envisioned as a reenactment of the events of the Passion, the Harrowing of Hell also stands in the immediate future. If the play is indeed being enacted on Holy Saturday, the Harrowing of Hell could be imagined to be occurring somewhere during that very period between Good Friday and the celebration of the Resurrection at dawn on Easter Sunday. Like the Jew, then, this reference applies to both biblical past and the audience's present. Muir discusses the function of the concluding Nebuchadnezzar scene as "as an apocalyptic vision of the Harrowing of Hell" (1973, 110-112). Odenkirchen considers that "an ancillary theme" of the Procession of Prophets "is the concern of medieval Christianity with the conversion of the Jews" (1976, 25).

presumably including his Jewish challenger, "En ce devez tenir espeir" ("You ought to place your hope in this"; ll. 917-930). In the Jew's case, the implication of the line is "you ought to place your hope in this," in Jesus rather than in any other Messianic figure.

Can *quidam de sinagoga* be pinned down as an historical entity? In the context of this play, the character functions as a timeless being, potentially ancient and contemporary. He is a kind of "once and future Jew," a Jewish Everyman, perhaps. The Jews of Christian apocalyptic lore, who were supposed to accept Christianity as a necessary prelude to the Second Coming, might perhaps be relevant here.[13] This is the role Synagogue and her followers enact in the Latin *Ludus de Antichristo* of around 1160, passing through disputation to conversion, martyrdom, and Christian redemption. Because *quidam de sinagoga* is not anchored in any definite historical period, he remains free to perform multiple functions – as a twelfth-century Jew, possibly mingling with the play's audience, as the Biblical Jew, Isaiah's original listener seen from the Christian viewpoint of the play, and as the Jew of the apocalyptic era, pointing to the concluding section of the manuscript, the poem on the fifteen signs of the Last Days.[14]

In perhaps his most interesting line, *quidam de sinagoga* says "This generation will listen" ("E ceste generacion / Escutera puis ta lecçon"; ll. 911-912). Does "listen" imply acceptance of Christian belief, as Muir suggests (1973, 107, 166 n. 73)? "Escoutera" is the key word. This line responds to Isaiah, but also to the preceding series of prophetic appeals

---

[13] For the history of the idea that the conversion of any remaining Jews is a signal of the Apocalypse, see Adso's tenth-century *Libellus de Antichristo* glossing Apoc. 11: 24 (Wright 1967, 107-108), and Alcuin, *De fide sanctae et individuae Trinitatis* 3: 19 (PL 101: 51). The idea may go back to the late fourth-century Tiburtina, a Sibylline prophecy that specifies the conversion of the Jews as one in a series of events leading up to the coming of Antichrist (Wright 1967, 21).

[14] For the debate over the relationship between the *Quinze signes du jugement* and the *Jeu d'Adam*, see Aebischer 1963; and Cargill for arguments that the treatise on the Last Judgment ought to be seen as the conclusion of Adam (1930, 98-99); and Muir for arguments against this conclusion (1973, 167 n. 75).

to the Jews to hear, to listen, to believe. Is there another echo in these insistent demands, of *shema Yisroel*, "hear, O Israel," the Jewish declaration of faith, the most powerful and familiar of all Jewish prayers? Two alternative possibilities have been proposed by the interpreters of the play. One school of thought holds that no conversion is suggested; *quidam de sinagoga*'s reply is a mere device that allows Isaiah to go on talking. In a second approach to the line, a sarcastic tone is assumed – the Jew maintains his stance of mockery to the end (Odenkirchen 1976, 145). What happens if the reader defines "escouter" in the strongest sense of the word, as Muir does? Taking the idea of a Jewish audience seriously also means rereading the play as both an exhortation and a dramatic prelude to conversion. The baptism of a Jewish catechumen would tie together the play's apocalyptic potential and its atmosphere of penitential yearning for admission to the church on whose steps the performance took place.

Stephen Justice has argued that, for the Christian penitent excluded from the church on Ash Wednesday, the *Jeu d'Adam* dramatizes the sinner's exclusion and readmission to the community of worshippers, a movement climaxed by the liturgical ceremony of readmission on Holy Thursday (Justice 1987). The student of the *Jeu d'Adam* should also recall that in Christian theology the Jewish candidate for conversion was understood as a species of penitent. The Jew's position is not that of a heathen, reared in ignorance of Biblical history, but, for the Christian observer, of one with a perverted or incomplete form of belief. Caesarius of Heisterbach, writing in the first half of the thirteenth century, would classify his tales of Jewish converts under "contritio," contrition, not under "conversio," where he discusses "conversiones vitae," the decision to enter monastic life.[15]

---

[15]*Dialogus Miraculorum* (1222), Dist. 2 ("De Contritione"). This section includes a cluster of tales concerning Jews, who are infallibly refuted and frequently baptized: "De clerico, qui puellam Judaeam stupraverat (Strange 1851, 92-94); "Item de puella Judaea apud Lovaniam baptizata" (95-98; trans. Marcus 1973, 142-144); "De puella in Linse baptizata" (98-99). The preceding section, Distinctio prima: "De Conversione," concerns itself with "conversiones vitae," the conviction to abandon secular for religious life.

The Easter vigil Mass had traditionally been the moment designated in the church calendar for adult baptisms, a rite still practiced today. Pope John Paul II performed several such baptisms in 1991 (Associated Press). By the twelfth century adult baptism is often assumed to have lapsed into disuse, since most Christians were now baptised as infants. This was clearly not true of adult converts from Judaism or Islam. The most powerful conclusion for the play of Adam would be the entrance into the church, "through these doors," as Jeremiah urges, not only of those who were already members of the Christian community, but of a member or members of the Jewish community, of "somebody from the synagogue," for the enactment of the rite of baptism. Indeed, Vaughan details clear verbal associations between the language of the play and the pre-baptismal catechism during the Easter vigil lections (Vaughan 1983, 113 n. 63).[16] The play's thrust towards admission into the church, noted by Justice, gains in force when it is seen as operating on the permanently excluded Jewish community, not just on errant members of Christian congregation. The *Jeu d'Adam* playwright's ultimate goal is to reunite the divided human community within the church.

In this reading of his "disputation," *quidam de sinagoga* moves from derisive disbelief to exemplary acceptance – and acceptance not just for himself but for all his contemporaries: "this generation will listen." His response offers a model for others "from the synagogue." The drama seems admirably designed to instruct a Jewish audience, here imagined as in dire need of reeducation.

In their studies of the history of Christian proselytizing movements, Cohen (1982), Chazan (1989), and Stacey (1992) discern a shift towards more strenuous missionary efforts in the thirteenth century, coinciding

---

[16]Vaughan remarks several times on echoes of the pre-baptismal lections in the text of the *Jeu d'Adam*; he does not press the suggestion further: "*Adam* would not be an unsatisfactory means of catechizing those preparing for Easter Baptism ... . *Ordo L* directs that such catechesis take place specifically during the Vigil lections ... . Furthermore, the questions addressed to those requesting Baptism correspond quite strikingly with the range of topics treated in Adam – even to the point of excluding any mention of Jesus' Resurrection" (113 n. 64).

with the rise of the mendicant orders. Programs of compulsory sermon attendance date from the thirteenth century as well. Stacey points out that after 1280 all English Jews were required by the crown to attend a Dominican conversion sermon each week, and to listen "without tumult, contention, or blasphemy" (1992, 267-269). James I of Aragon established such a program of required sermons in 1242, and still another is documented in Lombardy in 1278 (Kedar 1984, 137; Abrahams [1896] 1969, 418). The *Jeu d'Adam* seems to reflect an intermediate stage leading towards more strenuous proselytizing efforts. It also fits well with the disputations between faiths that were being written in the mid-twelfth century: Judah ha-Levi's *Kuzari* of 1140 arguing for Judaism, and, on the Christian side, Peter the Venerable's *Adversus Judeorum inveteratam duritiem* of 1144-47, and Peter Abelard's (d. 1142) dialogue of a Christian, a Jew, and a gentile (Kedar 1984, 61; Schoeps 1963, 63-69).

As a practical matter, common sense and ecclesiastical legislation barring Jews from the streets during Holy Week would seem to eliminate the possibility of a Jewish presence in the vicinity of any church on Holy Saturday. According to Stacey, "Jews were forbidden to appear on the streets during the Christian Holy Week, because their very presence was likely to inspire violence" (1992, 265). But this may well be an anachronism. The earliest instance of such legislation to my knowledge is that of the Third Council of Orléans of 538, and the most celebrated, that of the Fourth Lateran Council of 1215, which also issued decrees concerning moneylending practices of Jews and demanded that Jews be identified by some distinctive form of dress: "Moreover, during the last three days before Easter and especially on Good Friday, they shall not go forth in public at all, for the reason that some of them on these very days, as we hear, do not blush to go forth better dressed and are not afraid to mock the Christians who maintain the memory of the most holy

Passion by wearing signs of mourning" (Marcus 1973, 139).[17] Innocent III's text bears witness that Jews not only appeared on the streets during Holy Week but might even taunt Christians, just as *quidam de sinagoga* taunts Isaiah. The text of the decree supports the inference that prior to 1215 in some places at least Jews were reported to "go forth" and mingle with the Christian populace during the last three days of Easter, the time when the *Jeu d'Adam* was designed to be performed. In the same way, the decrees of 1215 make it clear that up to this point Jews were not easily distinguished from the Christian population by any external characteristic; this is why the Council expresses the need for a distinguishing garment or badge to identify Jews on sight. Without the imposition of such a visual sign, the twelfth-century Jewish auditor would not necessarily stand out in a public gathering, as for instance, in the audience of a play.

Another possibility should be considered: the notion that the playwright of the *Jeu d'Adam* expected his play to be overheard by members of the local Jewish community. Robert Stacey (1992) follows Cecil Roth (1964) and Vivian D. Lipman (1967) in stressing that the Jews and Christians of medieval England lived among one another (also Richardson 1960); evidence from northern France marshalled by Robert Chazan (1973) and William Chester Jordan suggests the same thing.[18] Instances of churches situated in neighborhoods densely populated by Jews can easily be documented from the twelfth century. In twelfth-cen-

---

[17]On the Fourth Lateran, see Grayzel 1933, 85-143. The Lateran decree may be compared with the parallel decree of Alfonso X, el Sabio, in the *Siete Partidas* (1265), where the Jews are also enjoined to remain indoors between Good Friday and Saturday morning; the penalty is a loss of the right to reparations for any "injury or dishonor inflicted upon them by Christians" (Marcus 1973, 35).

[18]Jordan 1989, 4-9, 31-34, 43, on the Jewish population of the royal domain, especially the Parisian Jewish community before the expulsion of 1182 and after the readmission of 1198; 48-55, on the Jews of Normandy and western France in the late twelfth century. Especially pertinent to my study is Jordan's discussion of the social contacts between Jews and Christians, lamented by Philip Augustus's monastic biographer Rigord, and the absence of "essential segregation" of Jews in the northern Europe of this period (23-26).

tury Norwich the Jewish community lived in close proximity to the market and to the major church of St. Peter Mancroft. A London congregation of penitential friars complained of the persistent outcry from the yeshiva next door. Margolis and Marx describe a regulation of January 31, 1253 demanding that "Jewish worship in the synagogues should be carried on in a low voice, inaudible to Christians" ([1927] 1973, 389).[19] As Stacey also demonstrates, overhearing operated in two directions (1992, 264-265). The playwright might not have far to look in order to find Jewish auditors, voluntary or involuntary. Indeed, in such circumstances, it would be difficult for an outdoor performance to avoid making its presence known to a mixed population of Jewish and Christian listeners. How close the Jewish auditors would have been able to come to the scene would depend on local regulations. It is unlikely that they would be out of earshot.

*Quidam de sinagoga* makes the most sense when he is recognized as the incarnation of the play's Jewish audience. In fact, there are really two Jewish audiences involved here. The first, imaginary, is *quidam de sinagoga* himself. Paradoxically, he is the only audience member to be presented within the play as a character: of all the "people" the playwright envisions as gathered to view the drama, he is the only one to emerge as a distinct, fully visualized individual. He is a fictional Jew, not a real one, but he is the only one we have – indeed, he is the only audience member the author goes to the trouble of creating for himself. The second Jewish audience can only be inferred from the text – an anticipated audience of contemporary Jews, who are, from the play's point of view, potential candidates for baptism. The first audience, *quidam de sinagoga*, functions as an acknowledgement of their presence, a model that predicts their reaction and attempts to shape their response to the play. In a way, this fictional Jewish audience is the playwright's invitation to the real Jewish audience behind him to participate in the

---

[19]Jordan cites a substantial body of ecclesiastical literature on this theme in his discussion of the linguistic relations of northern French Jews and Christians (1988, 14-17); see also Baron 1952, 9: 35-36.

liturgical conclusion of the play. To realize its mission, the *Jeu d'Adam* must engage the second Jewish audience. Through *quidam de sinagoga*, the playwright attempts to anticipate and guide this second audience's interpretation of the play.

An impressive procession of scholars has interpreted the meaning of Adam for its twelfth-century Christian audience – Accarie, Adams, Auerbach, Bevington, Calin, Justice, Muir, Noomen, Vaughan, to mention only a few of these distinguished commentators. For this reader, it becomes increasingly clear in the text that the play also addresses a twelfth-century Jewish audience. To my knowledge the play has not yet been read with this audience's point of view in mind. It is instructive in itself to study a twelfth-century Christian dramatist at work imagining a non-Christian audience.

The *Jeu d'Adam*'s apparent restriction to the matter of the Hebrew scriptures, long recognized as a distinctive feature of this play, exploits the area of shared biblical literature that links Jew and Christian (Muir 1973, 53, 118). The play draws on material presumed to be familiar to both audiences, but the restriction lays stress on familiarity to the Jewish auditor as a principle of selection (Muir 1973, 118).

Attempts have been made to explain the *Jeu d'Adam*'s special focus on Jews, on the Hebrew Bible, and on an historical Jewish viewpoint as references the Christian audience, the "Verus Israel" of patristic interpretation, would be accustomed to ascribe to itself. As Berhard Blumenkranz puts it, according to Augustine, "Les chrétiens ne sont pas seulement le vrai Israel, ils sont finalement même les 'vrais Juifs'" ([1958] 1977, 234, 237-238).[20] This familiar equation might seem to stand in the way of any reader who wishes to discern an actual Jewish audience as a target of this or any other medieval Christian work. My reading does challenge this basic assumption in the case of the *Jeu d'Adam* by suggesting that the entire play speaks directly to a contemporary Jewish audience, ultimately personified as *quidam de sinagoga*. I

---

[20]For Joseph Kimhi's twelfth-century reaction to this subject, see Talmage 1972, 23, 67.

suggest that this anomalous twelfth-century play demands a multiple, "bicultural" audience. If this hypothesis is correct, the *Jeu d'Adam* becomes a unique example of its type, but the play has always been recognized as idiosyncratic in many respects. This approach helps to solve many of the play's mysteries.

With a hypothetical twelfth-century Jewish audience in mind we can discern the *Jeu d'Adam*'s project of rereading the Hebrew Bible from creation to trace a history of Jewish deviance from the "true faith." The play divides the personages of the Hebrew scriptures into "Sons of the flesh and sons of the spirit," in the Augustinian formulation. The medieval Christian envisioned himself as Abel, the virtuous worshipper. The medieval Jew was presented to the community as Cain (Mellinkoff 1981; Ruether 1979), but he is also *quidam de sinagoga*, the Jew who promises to listen (Langmuir 1990b, 201).[21]

Gavin Langmuir has pointed out that "the roots of the distortion of the history of the Jews at the hands of the majority go back to the Christian appropriation and reinterpretation of Hebrew scripture in the first century" (1990b, 25). The *Jeu d'Adam* can and should be read as a clear, purposeful example of this traditional Christian activity. One goal of the play is the systematic Christian redefinition of Jewish identity, in preparation for its replacement by a Christian one (Moore 1987, 152).

The play is distinctly positive in its assertion of a common humanity of Christian and Jew, both descendants of Adam and Eve. *Quidam de sinagoga*'s Judaism is identified as a disease, not a fundamental difference of nature. The point is worth noting perhaps in contrast to Peter the Venerable's ultimate exasperated denial of the common humanity of the Jew in his *Adversus Judeorum inveteratam duritiem* of 1144-47.

> It seems to me, Jew, that I ... judge in these matters ... as do all men. And if all men, then you also – if, nevertheless, you are human. For I dare not

---

[21]For the long-standing association of Jews and devils in Christian tradition, see Joshua Trachtenberg 1943.

declare that you are human lest perchance I lie, because I recognize that reason, that which distinguishes humans from ... beasts, is extinct in you or in any case buried ... . The ass hears but does not understand; the Jew hears but does not understand. Has not the same been said many centuries before [by your prophet]? ... And although it is fully proved by these sacred authorities that you are a domestic animal or beast ... (Langmuir 1990b, 207).

Contrariwise, the *Jeu d'Adam* begins with the common humanity of Jew and Christian. It proceeds to the point of divergence with Cain, the prototypical Jew, and Abel, the figure of proto-Christian virtue, and then continues on through Jewish history, imagined as a procession of prophets all berating the Jews for their failure to understand their own experience. In the *Jeu d'Adam* the establishment of Judaism parallels the fall of humanity through original sin. A virulent form of the common disease, it, too, is an incurable illness, for which baptism is the church's only remedy.

Such a rereading enhances our appreciation of the complexity of the role of the play and its author. It does not by any means invalidate readings of the *Jeu d'Adam* from the viewpoint of the Christian audience (Vaughan 1983, 113). It is still reasonable to presume that the author of the play is a Christian playwright with a message for his Christian contemporaries. But I am not sure that the message to the "certain one from the synagogue" is not expressed with more ingenuity, energy and urgency. The twelfth-century playwright might well regard his Jewish contemporaries as the play's most important critics.

Muir characterizes the play's Anglo-Norman French as the language of the Angevin aristocracy, while English remained the language of the folk (1973, 119-120). French was also the language of the Angevin Jewish community in England as it was the language of commerce between Jew and Christian in France. A playwright operating in England could communicate much more persuasively with the English Jew – often an English Jew with a French name – in French than in English. Trachtenberg remarked that "the use of French names was even more marked in England, where Norman French was the vernacular of the

Jews no less than of the aristocracy ... " (1943, 160). Similarly, as Beryl Smalley noted, communications between French and English Christian and Jewish scholars took place in French rather than in Hebrew or Latin ([1952] 1970, 155). Trachtenberg cites Jewish references to French as "our language" (1943, 160, 248 n. 3). This rereading of the *Jeu d'Adam* adds depth to our sense of the potential Jewish experience of vernacular literature, at this period especially French literature. It enables us to observe the sophistication of the pressures imposed by the majority Christian culture on this oppressed minority, portrayed here as a perverse relative in need of a drastic act of persuasion to conform. The French poetry of the *Jeu d'Adam*, rather than its liturgical Latin, would confront the Jewish auditor most subversively, putting familiar, sacred narrative into the common vernacular, while at the same time enforcing the Christian interpretation of that narrative. This playwright uses French as the common language of Christian and Jew.

Can this hypothesis lead us towards new evidence for the location of this elusive play? Possibly. Jewish communities were to be found throughout the Angevin empire – and they were invariably French-speaking Jewish communities (Richardson 1960, 6-14; Chazan 1973). Students of the play might look with renewed interest at the Angevin court and at Henry II's sponsorship of Jewish converts, who took his name after baptism (Muir 1973, 119-20; Richardson 1960). We might also look at the many English and French churches in the immediate vicinity of synagogues – like the London churches of St. Mary Colechurch and St. Olave Upwell in Old Jewry, or St. Peter Mancroft in Norwich (Richardson 1960, 8 n. 2; Lipman 1967).[22] The Jewish audience, as suggested earlier, may not be in the street, but if not,

---

[22]Not much later they might be confiscated synagogues like St. Mary's in Jewry, London (Stacey 1992, 265 n. 8). The problem of a Jewish presence in the immediate vicinity of the church was persistent. In a fourteenth-century legal deposition from Narbonne the canons of the cathedral would express discomfort that Jews, women, and other inappropriate parties went about their business in excessively close proximity to the high altar of the cathedral of St. Just. For this reason the enlargement of the building was essential (personal communication, Dr. Vivian Paul, Texas A&M University).

they are likely to be in their houses – an audience of overhearers and invisible watchers. The play's repeated calls on the Jews to listen may have been immediately applicable to these unseen ears.

Specialists in European vernacular literatures are not used to thinking about medieval audiences as belonging to more than one religious community. The mythic image of the Middle Ages as a monolithic Age of Faith – the Christian faith – continues to retain its charms. "The lost unity of the medieval world" can only be discerned from a safe distance; today, the pressing need for scholarship may be to recover the "lost diversity" of the medieval era. Modem Jewish readers of medieval texts attempt to suppress their personal system of belief, so as to read them from a sympathetic Christian viewpoint. This approach has clearly been overdone, and in this case negates the complexity of the text.

This reading of the *Jeu d'Adam* demands an enhanced awareness of the role played by vernacular languages as vehicles of communication between cultural communities and between faiths. French is the tongue at issue here, but the lesson applies elsewhere. This interpretation calls, in fact, for a redefinition of the cultural community. Here the audience of French poetic drama is clearly not envisioned as coterminous with the community of Christian believers. As Gavin Langmuir remarks, in much of existing medieval scholarship "the Jews have continued to be viewed as an alien element of little importance" (1990b, 39). My larger argument is for a Jewish audience of Old French literature, not an audience of eavesdroppers, always subordinate to the majority Christian audience but in this case at least as a recognized group, a principal target of this major work.

Of course, *quidam de sinagoga* is not a real twelfth-century Jew. He is a purely fictional confection, like the Jew of Abelard's disputation, created to be refuted with the minimal amount of debate. Still, his presence at the climactic moment of the play reflects a real desire for a Jewish audience and a Jewish response to the play. *Quidam de sinagoga* anticipates the resistance and hostility of that audience, as well as enacting the desired final modulation into docile receptivity. *Quidam de sinagoga*'s abrupt reaction to all that has gone before, the mounting pressure of the drama, is the *Jeu d'Adam*'s true moment of catharsis. The scene mirrors the playwright's vision of the drama's power to move its spectators. By assimilating the *Jeu d'Adam* to other vernacular plays of the same era, scholarship obscures the inventiveness of this playwright and the distinctive nature of his work.

To put my concept in the simplest possible form, I argue that the *Jeu d'Adam* needs to be reread as a play for Jews and about Judaism. This re-reading unifies and lends new focus to the play and its manuscript. By ignoring the Jew we misinterpret the play.

## REFERENCES

Abrahams, Israel. [1896] 1969. *Jewish Life in the Middle Ages*. New York.

Acker, Paul. 1994. "The Book of Palmistry." In *Popular and Practical Science of Medieval England*, ed. Lister M. Matheson, 141-183. East Lansing.

Adams, Henry. [1905] 1913. *Mont-Saint-Michel and Chartres*. Boston.

Aebischer, Paul, ed. 1963. *Le Mystère d'Adam (Ordo representacionis Adae)*. Textes Littéraires Français. Geneva.

Alcuin. *De fide sanctae et individuae Trinitatis*. PL 101.

Associated Press. 1991. Report of vigil Mass baptisms by Pope John Paul II. Bryan-College Station Eagle.

Auerbach, Erich. [1953] 1971. *Mimesis: The Representation of Reality in Western Literature*. Trans. Willard R. Trask. Princeton.

Augustine, *The City of God* = Dodds 1948.

Baron, Salo W. 1952. *A Social and Religious History of the Jews: High Middle Ages, 500-1200*. New York.

Bevington, David. 1975. *Medieval Drama*. Boston.

Blumenkranz, B. [1958] 1977. Augustin et les juifs, Augustin et le judaïsme. In *Juifs et Chrétiens: Patristique et Moyen Age*. London [orig.: *Recherches augustiniennes* 1].

Cargill, O. 1930. *Drama and Liturgy*. New York.

Caesarius of Heisterbach, *Dialogus Miraculorum* = Strange 1851.
Chazan, Robert. 1989. *Daggers of Faith: Thirteenth-century Christian Missionizing and Jewish Response*. Berkeley.
———. 1973. *Medieval Jewry in Northern France: A Political and Social History*. Baltimore.
Cohen, Jeremy. 1982. *The Friars and the Jews: The Evolution of Medieval Anti-Judaism*. Ithaca and London.
Constable, Giles, ed. 1967. *The Letters of Peter the Venerable*. 2 vols. Cambridge, Mass.
Dodds, Marcus, ed. and trans. 1948. *Augustine. The City of God*. New York.
Friedman, Yvonne, ed. 1985. *Peter the Venerable. Adversus Iudeorum Inveteratam Duritiem*. Corpus Christianorum, continuatio medievalis 58. Turnhoult.
Grayzel, S. 1933. *The Church and the Jews in the XIII Century*. Philadelphia.
Jordan, William Chester. 1989. *The French Monarchy and the Jews: From Philip Augustus to the Last Capetians*. Philadelphia.
Joseph Kimhi, *Book of the Covenant (Sefer ha-Berit)* = Talmage 1972.
Justice, Steven. 1978. The Authority of Ritual in the *Jeu d'Adam*. *Speculum* 62: 851-864.
Kedar, Benjamin Z. 1984. *Crusade and Mission: European Approaches Toward the Muslims*. Princeton.
*Ludus de Antichristo* = Young [1933] 1962, 371-387.
*Ludus de Nativitate* = Bevington 1975, 180-201.
Ladner, Gerhart B. 1971. Reflections on Medieval Anti-Judaism 1: Aspects of Patristic Anti-Judaism. *Viator* 2: 355-363.
Langmuir, Gavin I. 1990a. *History, Religion, and Antisemitism*. Berkeley.
———. 1990b. *Toward a Definition of Antisemitism*. Berkeley.
Lipman, Vivian D. 1967. *The Jews of Medieval Norwich*. London.
MacDonald, Peter F. 1983. Religious Drama: The Ordo representacionis Ade. In *The Revels History of English Drama*, ed. A. C. Cawley,

Marion Jones, Peter F. McDonald and David Mills, vol. 1: *Medieval Drama*, 113-114. London.

Marcus, Jacob R. 1973. *The Jew in the Medieval World: A Source Book, 315-1791*. New York.

Margolis, Max L., and Alexander Marx. [1927] 1973. *A History of the Jewish People*. New York.

Mellinkoff, Ruth. 1981. *The Mark of Cain*. Berkeley.

Metzger, Thérèse and Mandel. 1982. *Jewish Life in the Middle Ages*. Fribourg.

Moore, R.I. 1987. *The Formation of a Persecuting Society: Power and Deviance in Western Europe, 950-1250*. Oxford.

Muir, Lynette R. 1973. *Liturgy and Drama in the Anglo-Norman Adam*. Medium Evum Monographs, n.s. 3. Oxford.

Noomen, Willem. 1968. Le Jeu d'Adam: Étude déscriptive et analytique. *Romania* 89: 95-117.

———, ed. 1971. *Le Mystère d'Adam*. Classiques Français du Moyen Âge 99. Paris.

Odenkirchen, Carl J., ed. 1976. *The Play of Adam (Ordo Representacionis Ade)*. Medieval Classics: Texts and Studies 5. Brookline, Mass.

Patai, Raphael. 1971. *Tents of Jacob: The Diaspora – Yesterday and Today*. Englewood Cliffs, N.J.

Peter the Venerable, *Letters* = Constable 1967.

Peter the Venerable, *Adversus Iudeorum Inveteratam Duritiem* = Friedman 1985.

Pflaum, H. 1935. *Die Religiöse Disputation in der Europäischen Dichtung des Mittelalters. I. Erste studie: Der allegorische Streit zwischen Synagoge und Kirche*. Geneva and Florence.

Ruether, Rosemary Radford. 1979. The *Adversus Judaeos* Tradition in the Church Fathers: The Exegesis of Christian Anti-Judaism. In *Aspects of Jewish Culture in the Middle Ages*, ed. Paul E. Szarmach, 27-50. Albany, NY.

Richardson, H.G. 1960. *The English Jewry under Angevin Kings*. London.

Roth, Cecil. 1964. *A History of the Jews in England*. 3rd ed. Oxford.

Saperstein, Marc. 1989. *Jewish Preaching, 1200-1800: An Anthology.* New Haven.
Schlauch, Margaret. 1940. The Allegory of Church and Synagogue. *Speculum* 14: 448-464.
Schoeps, Hans Joachim. 1963. *The Jewish-Christian Argument: A History of Theologies in Conflict.* Trans. David E. Green. New York.
Smalley, Beryl. [1952] 1970. *The Study of the Bible in the Middle Ages.* Notre Dame.
Sletsjöe, Leif, ed. 1968. *Le Mystère d'Adam. Édition diplomatique accompagnée d'une reproduction photographique du manuscrit de Tours et des leçons des éditions critiques.* Paris.
Stacey, Robert C. 1992. The Conversion of Jews to Christianity in Thirteenth-century England. *Speculum* 67: 263-283.
Strange, Joseph, ed. 1851. *Caesarius of Heisterbach. Dialogus Miraculorum.* Cologne.
Studer, Paul, ed. 1918. *Le Mystère d'Adam. An Anglo-Norman Drama of the Twelfth Century.* Manchester.
Talmage, Frank, trans. 1972. *Joseph Kimhi. Book of the Covenant (Sefer ha-Berit).* Toronto.
Trachtenberg, Joshua. 1943. *The Devil and the Jews: The Medieval Conception of the Jew and its Relation to Modern Antisemitism.* New Haven.
Vaughan, M.F. 1983. The Prophets of the Anglo-Norman "Adam." *Traditio* 39: 81-114.
Wright, J., trans. 1967. *The Play of Antichrist.* Toronto: Pontifical Institute of Mediaeval Studies.
Young, Karl. [1933] 1962. *The Drama of the Medieval Church.* Oxford.

# 9

# Minstrel Meets Clerk in Early French Literature: Medieval Romance as the Meeting-Place Between Two Traditions of Verbal Eloquence and Performance Practice

*Evelyn Birge Vitz*

THE MAJORITY OF THE PAPERS in this collection address contacts between cultures which are geographically, linguistically, religiously, or ideologically separated from one another. By contrast, my paper[1] focuses on contact between two groups of people who, while markedly divergent in training, culture, and general ethos, frequently inhabited the same space – the court – and had similar interests and ambitions: I am speaking of minstrels and clerks. It is, indeed, my view that the birth of French romance in the twelfth century is the result of the coming together of the interests and the skills of these two groups in the court setting. Specifically, while it is generally believed that romance is the invention solely of clerks, I will argue that the contribution of minstrels to the birth and early development of romance needs to be recognized, and its importance appreciated.

---

[1] This paper develops with a different focus material and arguments that I presented in Chapters 1, 3 and 4 of *Orality and Performance in Early French Romance* (Vitz 1999).

We need to examine these two groups. First, I will lay out a few essential features of the court clerk – for this is the sort of clerkly figure who interests us.

The clerk was defined in large part by his education, his learning. He had studied the Liberal Arts – the Trivium and the Quadrivium – in school. He had read the Bible and was familiar with classical texts. He was aware of and indeed traded on, the authority and prestige of the book and book-learning.

From the mid-twelfth century on, clerks began to be present in significant numbers in courts (e.g., Clanchy 1993, 44ff.). As they poured out of the schools, they increasingly filled positions outside of ecclesiastical institutions. Their roles in court were by no means exclusively, or even primarily, religious: they were not merely chaplains, but were archivists, court functionaries, secretaries, official readers, and the like. We can think of them as the "resident intellectuals" of the court; and they are also writers, in Latin and in French. It is to such figures that the invention of romance is ascribed.

Now let's look at the situation of the minstrel and jongleur (Faral [1910] 1970). But first, I need to address these two terms briefly. Jongleurs are generally defined today as performers who traveled from place to place – they were thus itinerant entertainers; by contrast, minstrels were entertainers attached to a particular court and patron. We will be generally more concerned with minstrels than with jongleurs, but medieval usage of these terms was very loose – and, after all, the same person could go from being a jongleur to a being minstrel, and back again. I will not emphasize distinctions between the two terms and will use them almost interchangeably.

I will be primarily concerned with entertainers who specialized in story and song: the arts of language. There were, of course, other essentially non-verbal kinds of entertainers, such as acrobats and tumblers. (There were also fools, puppeteers, people who showed animals such as bears, etc. See, for example, Southworth 1989.) I will try to set these figures aside – but they will occasionally pop back up.

Minstrels had, as their primary social and esthetic function, to provide entertainment: to make people laugh and cry, to give pleasure. And they transmitted important cultural values by telling stories and singing songs.

Their repertory was variable. It was dictated in part by tradition, but also in large part by the desires of patrons and audiences: at various historical moments, we see new subject matters – new kinds of stories – entering the minstrel repertory: for example, the story of Tristan and Iseut, and the Arthurian material.

While some minstrels were apparently what we today might call "school dropouts" and had had some rudimentary education, most of them in the twelfth and early thirteenth centuries were illiterate by any definition of the term. What this means is not that they were stupid or ignorant, but that their art was an oral one, rooted in apprenticeship and memory (Lord 1960; Ong 1982). Their authority was not based on the text, but on the compelling quality of their voice, their human presence, and the appeal of their stories.

We turn now to the issues of similarity and interaction between these two groups.

Minstrels had always been present in courts – and jongleurs welcomed at feasts – time out of mind. Such story-tellers and musicians provided entertainments and pleasures of many natures for many temperaments and many occasions. But, as I noted earlier, now – that is, from the mid-twelfth century on – clerks were there in court too (Benson and Constable 1982). Clerks and minstrels were thus thrown together, along with men and women of the nobility, in the courts in France and England. Indeed, this is the picture throughout Western Europe.

The situation of minstrels and clerks was obviously different in important ways. Their training was different. So were the nature of their authority, their respectability and relation to the Church, and many other things. But their situation was also similar in a number of respects that are important for the birth of romance.

Both minstrels and clerks had to please their patrons: they were there at the pleasure of the lord and lady. It is important to remember that the word "minstrel" comes from the Latin *ministerialis* meaning "servant." And these clerks as well were there primarily to serve, not the *Church*, but rather their secular lords.

Moreover, both minstrels and clerks were story-tellers. Clerks certainly made themselves useful and entertaining by providing narratives; in particular, they made new narrative material available in the vernacular to their patrons and to the other members of the court. Most of this "new" material was, of course, classical in origin, such as stories from the Latin epics, and from Ovid. Clerks also translated Arthurian material from the Latin of such figures as Geoffrey of Monmouth. Finally, clerks were commissioned by magnates to tell stories from history – or, as we might say, to "rewrite" history – to make the dynastic past, and present, look good.

But of course minstrels were story-tellers too – what could be more obvious? They, as well, told stories, and sang songs, at least some of which they had apparently made up themselves. In other words, illiterate minstrels, like clerks, were frequently "trouvères": inventors, makers, of songs and tales.

In this framework, we can now return to the issue of the birth of romance. We can see that clerks and minstrels were together – they coexisted – in court settings, and they had some similar functions; in particular, figures from both groups made up and told stories.

Now there is general scholarly agreement that romance is a court phenomenon: that it arose and developed in a court context. I have no quarrel with this assumption. But what *is* odd, I think – and unwarranted by the evidence available to us – is that it is generally believed that in the "invention" of romance the clerks had all the "beaux rôles," and that minstrels played little if any part. It is believed that early romance was a learned, a clerkly, phenomenon, up and down the line. But let me be more specific. First, it is thought that the poetic form in which virtually all early romances were composed – the octosyllabic rhymed couplet – was a clerical invention. Secondly, it is supposed that clerks were the authors of all the great early romances: thus, that the poets who composed the "antique romances" were all clerks; that Chrétien de

Troyes was a clerk; and so forth. (Some of these poets were certainly clerks – but not all!). And, finally, it is claimed that romances were perceived, received, by their audiences as "books." I think that no one today now believes, as many scholars did in the past – as recently as, say, Eugène Vinaver (1971, 4) – that romances were intended for private, silent reading. (The work of Paul Saenger, especially 1982, makes such a performance mode for early romances even harder to believe than it was previously.) But many, perhaps most, scholars still think of romances as primarily read aloud – and as written with this sort of performance in mind.

Most of these issues I must set aside for the present. What I will focus on is the question of performance. What I would like to demonstrate – and I do think it is possible to demonstrate this – is that minstrels were vitally involved in the performance, and thus in the cultural transmission, of early romance. In fact, romances were not generally read aloud – and they were hardly ever read privately; rather they were most commonly recited from memory by minstrels; they were recited, even played, in quite a dramatic way, and sometimes sung. Romances were, from the very earliest period – from the second half of the twelfth century – part of the minstrel repertory.

We turn now to some of the evidence for this argument. I am going to present relevant passages with some abundance, even perhaps a certain redundancy. There is a good reason for this: while there are in fact very few references to the reading of romances – which is why scholars come back over and over to the same tiny handful of lines – references to the festive performance of romance are quite numerous. It is important to recognize how many references there are to the recitation of romances from memory by minstrels. I want to draw such passages to your attention.

We begin with a highly interesting and rather amusing quote from Peter the Chanter, an important late-twelfth-century clerical figure. This quote comes from a Bible commentary where Peter is talking about priests who sing the mass up to the Offertory, but then stop and begin again – sometimes over and over – if no one has given any money yet. Peter says of such priests:

> Hi similes sunt cantantibus fabulas et gesta. Qui videntes cantilenam de Landrico non placere auditoribus, statim incipiunt de Narcisso cantare: quod si nec placuerit, cantant de alio. (Migne, 205: 101)

> They are like those who sing fables and stories, who, seeing that the song about Landry [hero of a story which has not survived] is not pleasing their listeners, immediately start singing about Narcissus; because if it will not please, they sing about something else. (Translations are mine unless otherwise indicated.)

Thus, the story of Narcissus – generally thought of as "antique" and therefore learned and clerical subject-matter – was already part of the repertory of minstrels and popular singers. This interesting passage also documents the need that entertainers had to adapt their performance to the interests of their audience. Landry is "out"; Narcissus is now "in."

We can hear story-tellers and minstrels brag about the quality of their story or the extent of their repertory. First, a couple of passages from the *Roman de Renart*. In the 1170s, Pierre de Saint-Cloud began a story about Renart (Branch 2) by saying:

> Seigneurs, oï avez maint conte,
> Que maint conterre vous raconte
> Conment Paris ravi Elaine,
> Le mal qu'il en ot et la paine,
> De Tristan que la Chievre fit
> Qui assez bellement en dist
> Et fabliaus et chançons de geste.
> Romanz d'Yvain et de sa beste
> Maint autre conte par la terre.
> Mais onques n'oïstes la guerre,
> Qui tant fu dure de grant fin,
> Entre Renart et Ysengrin,
> Qui moult dura et moult fu dure … . (Dufournet 1970, ll. 1-13)

> Lords, you have heard many a tale,

> Which many story-tellers tell you
> About how Paris stole Helen away,
> The evil that he had from it and the pain,
> About Tristan, a story that [the poet] La Chievre told
> He told about it very beautifully,
> And fabliaux and chansons de geste.
> The romance of Yvain and his beast
> Many others tell throughout the land.
> But you have never heard about the war,
> That was so extremely hard
> Between Renart and Ysengrin,
> It lasted very long and was very hard ... .

This passage is all about what people have heard told by story-tellers, and about the repertory of minstrels. And this repertory includes *contes*, *fabliaux*, *chansons de gestes* and *romans*. So here we have clear references to different narrative genres, all of which have been heard by the audience that Pierre aims to please with a new story. Note that, among the works mentioned is the story about Yvain and his beast: this is apparently a reference to one of Chrétien's romances.

In another important passage from the *Roman de Renart* – Branch 1b, dating from the end of the twelfth century – the fox disguises himself as a Breton jongleur. Speaking with a fake Breton accent, and in garbled French, he describes his repertory:

> – Ya, ge fot molt bon jogler.
> Mes je fot ier rober, batuz
> Et mon vïel fot moi toluz.
> Se moi fot aver un vïel,
> Fot moi diser bon rotruel,
> Et un bel lai et un bel son
> Por toi qui fu sembles prodom...
> Ge fot saver bon lai Breton
> Et de Merlin et de Noton,
> Del roi Artu et de Trisran,
> Del chevrefoil, de saint Brandan. (Dufournet 1970, ll. 2370-77, 2389-92)

> ... I were very good jongleur.
> But I were yesterday robbered, beaten,
> And my viel was taken from me.
> If me have viel,
> Make me saying a good rotrouance,
> And a beautiful lai and a beautiful melody
> For you who seem worthy man...
> Me know good Breton lai
> And about Merlin and Noton,
> About King Arthur and about Tristan,
> About the honeysuckle, about Saint Brendan.

Thus Renart, as a jongleur, declares then that he can perform romance material along with such lyric works as *rotrouanges*, *lais* and a saint's story. Later on, he adds *chansons de geste* to the list:

> Fotre merci, dist-il, bel sire,
> Moi saura fer tot ton plesir.
> Moi saver bon chancon d'Ogier,
> Et d'Olivant et de Rollier
> Et de Charlon le char chanu".... (Dufournet 1970, ll. 2851-55)

> Pegging your pardon, he said, my lord,
> Me know how to do all your pleasure.
> Me know good song about Ogier,
> And about Olivant and about Rollier [*sic*: the names are garbled]
> And about Charles with the white skin [should of course be white hair].

It might be argued that if Renart so garbles the heroes of epic, he may be garbling genres as well. But in fact this sort of mixed-bag list is common even in entirely *un*-garbled repertories. And what we might call these "generic malapropisms" – these errors and reversals – are clearly intended for an audience that knows its genres and its stories well and will be able to appreciate the comic effect. But in short, minstrels represent their repertory as large, and as including romance.

The joking jongleurs of the famous text called the "Deux Bourdeurs Ribauds" give us a very similar picture. One of the jongleurs claims to know, first, many *chansons de geste*, and then a variety of romances as well:

> Tu ne sez dire nul bon mot
> Dont tu puisses en pris monter;
> Mais ge sai aussi bien conter
> Et en roumanz et en latin,
> Aussi au soir come au matin,
> Devant contes et devant dus,
> Et si resai bien faire plus
> Quant ge sui a cort ou a feste.
> Car ge sai de chançon de geste.
>   Chanteres el mont n'i a tel:
> Ge sai de Guillaume au Tinel,
> Si com il arriva as nés
> Et de Renouart au cort nés
> Sai ge bien chanter com ge vueil;
> Et si sai d'Aïe de Nantueil
> Si com ele fu en prison;
> Si sai de Garin d'Avignon,
> Qui mout estore bon romans; ...
>   [further enumeration of *chansons de geste*, ll. 74-80]
> Mais de chanter n'ai ge or cure.
> Ge sai des romanz d'aventure,
> De cels de la Reonde Table,
> Qui sont a oïr delitable.
> De Gauvain sai le malparlier,
> Et de Quex le bon chevalier;
> Si sai de Perceval de Blois:
> De Pertenoble le Galois
> Sai je plus de .LX. laisses.
> Et tu, chaitis, morir te laisses
> De mauvaitie et de paresce:
> En tot le monde n'a proesce
> De quoi tu te puisses vanter;

Mais ge sai aussi bien chanter
De Blancheflor comme de Floire;
Si sai encore moult bone estoire,
Chançon mout bone et anciene:
Ge sai de Tibaut de Viane. (Faral 1910, ll. 56-98)

You don't know how to say anything witty
By which you could rise in esteem;
But I know how to tell stories
Both in French and in Latin,
In the evening, as in the morning,
Before counts and dukes,
And I also know how to do more
When I am at court or at a feast,
For I know chansons de geste.
 And there is no such singer in the world:
I know about Guillaume with his Big Stick,
And how it landed on his nose,
And about Rainouart with the short nose
I know how to sing well, when I want:
And I know about Aie de Nantueil
How she was in prison;
And I know about Garin d'Avignon,
Which is a very good romance ...
But I don't care about singing now.
I know adventure romances,
The ones about the Round Table,
Which are delightful to hear.
I know about Gauvain who talked so badly,
And about the good knight Kei;
And I know about Perceval of Blois,
About Partonpeu the Welshman
I know more than 60 laisses.
And you, wretch, let yourself die
Of wickedness and laziness:
In the entire world there is nothing of value
About which you can brag;
But I know how to sing

> About Blancheflor, and about Floire;
> And I know many a good story,
> Many a good and ancient song:
> I know about Tibaut de Vienne.

Let us look toward the south, toward the Occitan world: the famous troubadour Raimon Vidal, in "Abril issi'e" evokes yet another jongleur who describes his repertoire. Here too the blend of romances in with other genres is completely explicit.

> Senher, yeu soy un hom aclis
> a joglaria de cantar
> e say romans dir e contar
> e novas motas e salutz
> e autres comtes espandutz
> vas totas partz, azautz e bos,
> e d'En Guiraut vers e chansos
> e d'En Arnaut de Maruelh mays,
> e d'autres vers e d'autres lays
> que ben deuri' en cort caber. (Huchet 1992, 40 ll. 38-47)
>
> My lord, I know as a knowledgeable man
> how to sing with jonglerie
> and how to tell and recount romances
> and new melodies and 'love salutes'
> and other well-known stories,
> to all esteemed and good places,
> and different kinds of songs by En Guiraut
> and by En Arnaut de Maruelh even more
> and other songs and lays,
> so that I should find a good place in court.

Here too, we see the "saying and telling" of romances mixed in with a general lyric and narrative repertory.

Thus far we have looked at the *Renart*, at unpretentious jongleresque works, and at Occitan texts from the thirteenth century. But what of courtly romances, and the courtly scene in the north of France and Anglo-Norman England in the twelfth century? What of Chrétien de Troyes himself?

Here is a quote from one of the manuscripts of *Erec et Enide* – B.N. fr. 1376 – recently edited in the Lettres Gothiques/Poche edition of Chrétien's entire *oeuvre*. This passage deals with wedding festivities:

> Quanz la corz fu tote assenblee,
> N'ot ménestrel an la contree
> Qui den seüst de nul deduit,
> Qui a la cort ne fussent tuit.
> En la sale mout grant joie ot,
> Chascuns servi de ce qu'il sot:
> Cil saut, cil tume, cil enchante,
> Li uns conte, li autres chante,
> Li uns sible, li autres note;
> Cil sert de harpe, cil de rote,
> Cil de gigue, cil de vïele,
> Cil fleüte, cil chalemele
> Cil gigue, li autres vïele,
> Puceles querolent et dancent;
> Trestuit de joie fere tencent.
> N'est riens qui joie i puisse faire
> Ne cuer d'ome a leesce trere,
> Qui ne soit as noces le jor.
> Sonent timbre, sonent tabor,
> Muses, estives et fretel
> Et buisines et chalemeles. (Fritz 1994, ll. 2031-2050)

> When the court was all assembled
> There were not any minstrels in the region
> Who knew how to do anything to give pleasure,
> Who weren't all at court.
> In the hall there was great joy,
> Each one served up what he knows how to do:
> One jumps, one tumbles, one does tricks,
> One tells stories, another sings,
> One whistles, another one sings the notes,
> This one plays the harp, that one the rote,

> This one the gigue, that one the viele,
> Girls sing and dance;
> They all try to make joy.
> There is nothing that can bring joy
> Nor draw happiness to the heart of man,
> Which was not that day at the wedding.
> The tambour sounds, the tamborine sounds,
> Bagpipes, flageolet and panpipes
> And trumpets and flutes ...

Here again we have a multitude of kinds of entertainers and entertainment. Amidst all these kinds of entertainers – the acrobats do again pop up – we have singers and story-tellers: *conteurs*. And "conter" is a verb that Chrétien uses repeatedly to speak of what *he* does.

A similar passage in the late-twelfth-century romance by Renaut de Beaujeu, *Le bel inconnu*, has in its opening lines an evocation of the festivities at King Arthur's court and refers to singers telling beautiful "adventures":

> La veïsiés grant joie faire,
> As jogleors vïeles traire,
> Harpes soner et estriver,
> As canteors cançons canter.
> Li canteor metent lor cures
> En dire beles aventures. ... (Williams 1983, ll. 21-26)

> There you would have seen great joy being made,
> With the jongleurs taking up their vieles,
> Playing and striving on harps,
> With singers singing songs.
> The singers put all their effort
> Into telling beautiful adventures ...

Here we seem to have several different narrative and musical genres, as well as different instruments, though specific genres are not referred to by name. It is commonly assumed that when reference is made to "singers telling beautiful adventures" (or the like), it is the *chanson de geste* that is being spoken of. But, in fact, the "dire" could be applied to the singing of epics, and romances are sometimes spoken of as sung. "Adventure" is a romance term.

Our next example has a slightly different thrust. This passage focuses on the responsibilities of lords, rather than on the claims of the minstrels: in his early-thirteenth-century *Roman des eles* the poet Raoul de Houdenc says that when a host is truly "courtois" you can tell by the way he treats minstrels:

> Le set l'en par les menestrex,
> Qui es places et es hostex
> Voient les honnors et les hontes,
> De qui l'en doit dire beax contes ...
> Quant li conteres a servi
> Et vient an point del demander,
> Larges ne puet contremander
> La larguece qu'il a el cors
> Que la point n'en saille hors ...
> Qu'a chevalier est cortoisie
> Qu'il oie volentiers chançons,
> Notes, et vïeles, et sons
> Et deduit de menesterex ... (Faral 1910, 293)

> You know it from the minstrels,
> Who in public places and in residences
> See the honor and the shame
> About which they must tell good stories.
> When the story-teller has finished his service
> And comes to the point of asking [to be rewarded]
> A generous [host] cannot deny
> The generosity that he has in himself [in his "body"]
> So that it doesn't spill forth ...
> For a knight has courtliness
> If he listens willingly to songs,
> And melodies, and vieles, and tunes
> And minstrels' entertainment ... .

This passage comes from a work on courtliness – "Cortoisie" – for the nobility, produced by a rather self-interested figure. Here too the blend of various kinds of narrative and musical material is apparent: we have here the work of *menestreleurs* and *contere*, with *chançons, notes, vïeles* and *sons.*

I cannot close without speaking at least briefly of the wonderful thirteenth-century Occitan romance *Flamenca.* Here, in the context of a wedding feast, the performance of many works – including various romans antiques and Chrétien de Troyes's romances – is clearly referred to. Chrétien's *Yvain* is first evoked in an explicitly musical context:

> Apres si levon li juglar:
> Cascus se volc faire auzir.
> Adonc auziras retentir
> Cordas de mantas tempradura.
> Qui saup novela violadura,
> Ni canzo ni descort ni lais,
> Al plus que poc avan si trais.
> L'uns viola[l] lais de Cabarefoil,
> E l'autre cel de Tintagoil;
> L'us cantet cel dels Fins Amanz,
> E l'autre cel que fes Ivans.
> L'us menet arpa, l'autre viula;
> L'us flaütella, l'autre siula;
> L'us mena giga, l'autre rota;
> L'us diz los motz e l'autrels nota;
> L'us estiva, l'autre flestella;
> L'us musa, l'autre caramella;
> L'us mandura e l'autr' acorda
> Lo sauteri ab manicorda;
> L'us fal lo juec dels bavastelz,
> L'autre jugava de coutelz;
> L'us vai per sol e l'autre tomba,
> L'autre balet ab sa retomba,
> L'us passet cercle, l'autre sail;
> Neguns a son mestier non fail.
> Qui volc ausir diverses comtes
> De reis, de marques et de comtes,
> Auzir ne poc tan can si volc.

Anc null'aurella non lai dolc,
Quar l'us comtet de Priamus
E l'autre diz de Piramus;
L'us comtet de la bell' Elena
Com Paris l'enquer, pois lan mena; ... (Hubert and Porter
    1962, ll. 593-625)

... The jongleurs now arose,
Each striving to make sure that he
Was heard. Out rang the melody
Of many tunes, and they made trial
Of songs new-written for the viol,
Essaying chant, descort and lay.
Each at his best did strum and play.
The Honeysuckle legend rang
From one, one of Tintagel sang,
One the True Lovers' tale related,
And one the tale of Yvain created.
One played the harp, and one the lute,
And one the fife and one the flute.
Some played the jigs and some the rotes,
Some sang the words, some twanged the notes.
With sackbut, fife and violin,
Bagpipe and whistle, song and din,
They blow and beat and pluck the cord
Of psalter and of monocord.
While one with mannequins contrives
Good sport, another juggles knives.
One tumbles, while another leaps
And somersaults, yet nimbly keeps
His feet. Some dive through hoops. Each man
Performs his stunt as best he can.
He who would hear diverse accounts
Of marquesses and kings and counts,
May hear as many as he will
And of such stories have his fill.
One told the tale of Priamus,
Another that of Piramus,

> One told of Helen, called the Fair
> and Paris, who made off with her ...

Note the tumblers and leapers. Note as well the performance of romances, including antique romances. This part of the *Flamenca* passage emphasizes the musical and entertaining quality of the performances. We pick this long list up again almost fifty lines later, where the stress shifts to the extent of the minstrel repertory:

> L'autre comtava de Galvain,
> E del leo que fon compain
> Del cavallier qu'estors Luneta.
> L'us diz de la piucella breta
> Con tenc Lancelot en preiso
> Cant de s'amor li dis de no.
> L'autre comtet de Persaval
> Co venc a la cort a caval.
> L'us comtet d'Erec e d'Enida
> L'autre d'Ugonet de Perida.
> L'us contava de Governail
> Com per Tristan ac grieu trebail.
> L'autre comtava de Feniza,
> Con transir la fes sa noirissa .... (Hubert and Porter 1962, ll. 666-679)

> Another told of Gawain; one
> Of the lion whose companion
> Was he whom Lunette liberated.
> One of that Breton maid related
> Who held in prison Lancelot
> When he her love accepted not.
> And one of Percival recounted,
> Who came into the king's court mounted
> One told of Erec and Enide,
> One of Ugonet of Peride.
> One told of Gouvernail, who bore
> For Tristan's sake misfortune sore.

> And one told of Fenice, whose nurse
> By drugs' aid made her seem a corpse ... .

In this second part of the passage emphasis falls on the range of the repertory rather than on the music. But in any event, this long passage can leave us in no doubt that many romances – including *all* of Chrétien's works – were indeed recited by minstrels and other performers in the thirteenth century.

I could keep going – there are a good many such texts – but I believe the point is made. It is clear that in the twelfth and thirteenth centuries minstrels and jongleurs were reciting romances right along with everything else in their capacious repertory: songs of all sorts, *chansons de geste*, and all manner of short narratives, sometimes enlivened with acrobatics. Furthermore, it is clear from some of these passages that minstrels weren't just *reciting* romances: they were often *singing* them.

***

What I hope to have shown is that early romance cannot properly be thought of as an art invented and practiced simply by clerks, or performed and transmitted primarily through books and reading. The genre – the art – of romance, which arose in the twelfth-century court milieu, was, to a significant degree, an art of *minstrelsy* as well as of *clerkliness*.

It is, in my view, highly likely that minstrels were sometimes the poets as well as the performers of these works – just as minstrels and jongleurs are known to have composed other sorts of stories and songs. It is hard to believe that minstrels sang and recited only works written for them by clerks.

It is also clear that in French and Anglo-Norman courts of the twelfth and thirteenth centuries, minstrels and clerks drew on each others' art – borrowed strings from each other's bow – as they competed for "authority," as well as for audience attention. For example, even jongleurs with few if any clerical pretensions, such as Béroul, may refer to the authority of a book – "I saw this written in a book." ("... Ne, si

comme l'estoire dit / Loü Berox le vit escrit," Payen 1974, ll. 1764-5: "
... Nor, as the story says it, / There where Béroul saw it written.")
Similarly – or rather, inversely – clerks may refer to oral sources as
conferring credibility to their compositions.[2] Moreover, clerks speak to
audiences of court listeners – to lords and ladies, *not* to their fellow
clerks – using forms of auditory appeal drawn from traditions of
minstrelsy.

Clerks and minstrels may actually have collaborated in the production
of romances, with the clerks providing the learning – that new intellectual "leaven" – and the minstrels providing what we could call the oral
patter, the entertainment skills, the ability to retain long songs and

---

[2]For example, Thomas refers to the authority – the oral authority – of a certain Breri:

> Entre ceus qui solent cunter
> E del cunte Tristran parler,
> Il en cuntent diversement:
> Oï en ai de plusur gent.
> Asez sai que chescun en dit
> E ço qu'il unt mis en escrit,
> Mé sulun ço que j'ai oï,
> Nel dient pas sulun Bréri
> Ky solt lé gestes e lé cuntes
> De tuz lé reis, de tuz lé cuntes
> Ki orent esté en Bretaigne. (Payen 1974, ll. 2113-23)

> Among those who are used to telling stories
> And to talking about the story of Tristan,
> They tell it differently;
> I have heard it from many people.
> I well know what each one says about it
> And what they have put into writing,
> But, according to what I have heard,
> They don't tell it according to Breri
> Who knows the *chansons de geste* and the stories
> Of all the kings, of all the counts
> Who have been in Brittany.

stories in memory.[3] But what is, I submit, quite certain is that the art of the minstrel and the scholarly lore of the clerk come together in early romance. We are seeing not the dominance of "clerkliness," but the coexistence – indeed the fusion – of clerkly and minstrel skills, pleasures, and notions of authority.

In short, minstrels were far more important in the invention and the early success of romance than is generally believed. They were *there* – and the time has come to recognize and appreciate their contribution to the birth of medieval romance.

## References

Benson, Robert L., and Giles Constable, eds. with Carol D. Lanham. 1982. *The Twelfth Century Renaissance: Renaissance and Renewal in the Twelfth Century*. Cambridge, Mass: Harvard University Press.

Dufournet, Jean, ed. 1970. *Le Roman de Renart (Branches I, II, III, IV, V, VIII, X, XV)*. Paris: Garnier-Flammarion.

Faral, Edmond, ed. 1910. *Mimes français du XIIIe siècle*. Paris: Champion. Pp. 93-111.

Faral, Edmond. [1910] 1970. *Les Jongleurs en France au moyen age*. New York: Burt Franklin.

Fritz, Jean-Marie, ed. 1994. *Chrétien de Troyes: Romans*. Gen. ed., Michel Zink. Paris: Poche/Lettres Gothiques.

Hubert, M. J., tr., and M. E. Porter, ed. 1962. *The Romance of Flamenca*. Princeton: Princeton University Press / University of Cincinnati.

Huchet, Jean-Charles, ed. and trans. 1992. "Abril issi'e." In *Novelles occitanes du Moyen Age*. Paris: Garnier-Flammarion.

---

[3] An analogous phenomenon occurs in the world of the visual and decorative arts: in this period, sculptors, painters, weavers, embroiderers, etc., acquired directly or indirectly from clerks "learned" subject matter – such as "the Liberal Arts," motifs from the Bible and from classical epics, and similar topics – that they then depicted in their works.

Lord, Albert B. 1960. *The Singer of Tales*. Cambridge, Mass.: Harvard University Press.
Migne, J. P., gen. ed. 1844-1882. *Patrologiae cursus completus series latina*. Paris: J. P. Migne. [Petrus Cantor] *Verbum abbreviatum* 27, 205: 101.
Ong, Walter J. 1982. *Orality and Literacy: The Technologizing of the Word*. London: Methuen.
Payen, J. C., ed. 1974. *Tristan et Yseut*. Paris: Garnier.
Saenger, Paul. 1982. Silent Reading: Its Impact on Late Medieval Script and Society. *Viator* 13: 367-414.
Southworth, John. 1989. *The English Medieval Minstrel*. Woodbridge (Suffolk, England): Boydell.
Vinaver, Eugène. 1971. *The Rise of Romance*. New York and Oxford: Oxford University Press.
Vitz, Evelyn Birge. 1999. *Orality and Performance in Early French Romance*. Cambridge: D.S. Brewer.
Williams, G. Perrie, ed. 1983. Renaud de Beaujeu, *Le bel inconnu*. Paris: Champion.

# 2
# Teaching Cultures in Contact

# 10

# Team Teaching the Literature of the European and Islamic Middle Ages: The European Perspective

*Kathryn L. Lynch*

THIS SHORT ESSAY concerns a course that I taught recently together with a colleague, Louise Marlow of the Wellesley College Religion Department, a course called "Images of the Other in the European and Islamic Middle Ages." As I generally find my home in the Wellesley English Department, the course was self-consciously interdisciplinary from the start; it was also geographically and culturally diverse. In this paper, I would first like briefly to discuss the origins of the course, as some of the issues the course raises have to do with its specific role in the Wellesley College curriculum and then to move on, by extension, to the lessons our course might have within our disciplines at large. Cultural diversity and, to a slightly lesser extent, interdisciplinarity are flashpoints in current debates about educational policy; in both its specific incarnation and in its general implications our course opens up some of the complexity of that debate, revealing a few of the problems as well as the rewards of cross-cultural pedagogy within an historical framework. In our two essays about the course, Professor Marlow and I attempt to speak very frankly not only about the rewards but also about the problems, in the hope of postponing premature closure in the discussion of multiculturalism and the Middle Ages, or of the relationship between medieval Europe and the medieval Islamic world, especially as these topics are of interest to today's American student.

About five years ago, I decided to use a regular changing topics slot in my department to teach a senior-level literature course that would bring together materials, some continental and some English, to explore the literary reputation that the "Eastern" world, very broadly conceived, enjoyed, or should I say "suffered," in the medieval "West." My motivations were loosely twofold: first, I had been fielding questions from my students in courses on Chaucer and Arthurian romance that had to do with the reputation of the Middle East and Africa in European poetry, and I had to confess that I knew little about this subject. My own intellectual curiosity was piqued, and I felt personally challenged by my students' questions; second, I knew that the students' interest partly reflected the growing international population in my classes and at Wellesley. I guessed that an East/West medieval course would attract its share, or more, of students. So I had institutional and pedagogical reasons for wanting to offer the course, in addition to personal and professional ones.

This first run-through of the course was indeed popular; I called it "The Exotic East in Medieval Literature," and limited the enrollment to twenty. I had to turn many students away, and ended up with a class that brought together far-ranging interests and national and academic backgrounds. We read large sections of the *Travels* of both Sir John Mandeville and Marco Polo, followed by troubadour and trouvère lyrics read alongside Ibn Hazm's *The Ring of the Dove*, parts of *The Arabian Nights*, Petrus Alfonsi's *Disciplina Clericalis*, *The Song of Roland*, *The Poem of the Cid*, four of the *Canterbury Tales*, sections of Boccaccio's *Decameron*, and finished up with Shakespeare's *Othello*. It was a grab-bag of a course; we read no "theory" to tie it together, and, though the students claimed to be satisfied at the end with the eclecticism of the syllabus, I was disturbed by it, disturbed by the confusing way in which the syllabus brought materials *from* the Arabic world, like *The Arabian Nights*, *The Ring of the Dove*, and the *Disciplina Clericalis*, into contact with materials *about* that world, without making space for a discussion of the fact that we were thus both looking *through* and also looking *at* the eyes of a different culture. I was also aware, of course, of the fact that the "East" was not a unity, and so I was uncomfortable with the way the "East," as a category, quickly became a mushy and undifferentiated mass about which we could make a series of facile generalizations. It troubled me too that I didn't know enough to answer many questions about the "real" Eastern regions of the Middle Ages, questions that I was also increasingly distressed to find that my students rarely asked.

But teaching this course on the "European perspective" was finally a more positive experience than a frustrating one. It did alter my professional and pedagogical outlook on my subject, which these days is mainly Chaucer, in ways that were going to fulfill both the personal and professional goals I had set when designing the course. I gained new perspectives on tales taught many times before in my traditional Chaucer classroom; I felt confident that I would be better able to respond to student questions about, say, the role of Islam in the Man of Law's Tale. And I was coming upon some research topics that I was eager to explore in a sabbatical scheduled for the following year. Part of that next year I spent writing an essay on the relationship between Chaucer's "Squire's Tale," long recognized as a locus of "orientalism" in Chaucer, and the tale that follows it in most manuscripts and printed editions of *The Canterbury Tales*, the "Franklin's Tale." I had become convinced that Chaucer probably was acquainted with some version of *The Arabian Nights*, to which I believe he is referring when Dorigen in the "Franklin's Tale," a European Shahrazad manqué, offers "mo than a thousand stories" (line 1412) in a diminished attempt to delay her own death. I published this interpretation in an essay the summer after I returned from leave (Lynch 1995), by which time I was again engaged in planning and revising the syllabus for the second run-through of my course. It was on the whole a satisfying instance of the mutual benefit that teaching and research can gain from each other, despite my discomfort with the way the course tended to simplify its diverse material.

The second time through the course I tried to correct some of what had troubled me before. To give the course more thematic and intellectual coherence, I eliminated all the material that was not of European Christian origin, except *The Arabian Nights*, which I simply could not bear to give up. I added the first one-hundred pages of Edward Said's book *Orientalism*, so that we would have an intellectual framework for the reading, and I retitled the course "Orientalism in Medieval Literature" (as opposed to "The Exotic East"); along with the new, less exotic title came a noticeable drop in student interest, for this time the course was slightly undersubscribed. Also, I still had some of my original dissatisfactions with it. While it offered a more coherent syllabus, we were still studying the European response to an alien tradition without first-hand knowledge *of* that tradition. At the same time, there was an announcement one week in Wellesley's Academic Council of a new fund, a "multicultural initiative," to support new courses, curricular development, and opportunities for team teaching.

At this point, I would like to step back from my narrative to discuss the specific institutional situation at Wellesley, because, while I don't think conditions at my own institution are universal, I wonder if they are not common enough to strike a chord of familiarity. To put the matter briefly, the curriculum at Wellesley has been in a fair amount of flux in recent years. Student interests are changing in ways that benefit some departments more than others. While we frequently invoke the value of a "liberal arts education" at Wellesley, many disagree about the fundamental meaning of that phrase, and one hears increasing concern from certain quarters that our students should be better prepared for the world they will find outside the ivory tower, prepared in a variety of ways – as producers and consumers, as citizens, and with the prominence of such graduates as Hillary Clinton ('69) and Madeleine Albright ('59), as leaders. Moreover, as I mentioned earlier, the College has been quite successful at making diversity at Wellesley a reality, and we are attracting an increasingly international student population. A recent report by an internal consultant at the College estimates that the number of students on our campus whose families live abroad, or hold citizenship in another country besides the U.S., may be as many as twenty-five per cent (Murphy 1997, 16). This same internal report, entitled, I think rather ominously, "An Agenda for Wellesley in a Changing World," recommends, among other things, that we shift the priorities of our curriculum rather dramatically in coming years, greatly increasing the number of courses that cover what this report calls "less-studied regions" of the world while consolidating courses that cover "well-studied regions" (Murphy 1997, 47-48) and counseling a policy of "the non-replacement of faculty with no regional or cultural specialty" (Murphy 1997, 49).

Now, this report is only an internal document representing the views of its single author, a political scientist, and it has not been in any way "adopted" as official policy at Wellesley College. I should add, too, that it includes many recommendations that do not affect the curriculum, and many curricular recommendations that are good common sense. But if faculty discussion of these matters is favorable to significant curricular change, student response is even more so, and a very vocal group of Wellesley students feels that even our sympathetic Administration is dragging its feet in globalizing the curriculum. It is probably not surprising, then, that as a medievalist with a European specialty, I find myself feeling defensive when reading or listening to campus discussion of these issues, that I wonder where my place is when the chief educational goal expressed is making our students good citizens of a contemporary "world city." More generally, how is an English Department, like the one of which I am a member, simultaneously to honor close reading of texts written in English and global diversity of subject matter? Without ignoring the existence of English literature written by writers in Canada, the U.S., Africa, India, Australia and other locations, one can still say that my particular corner of the college is somewhat "Eurocentric" of necessity, and all the more so in the early periods. Perhaps even more troubling, this internal report at Wellesley never mentions the role of history in creating the conditions of the modern world; nor does it consider the past as an object of interest in its own right. It is hard for those of us who teach in the humanities and especially for those of us who teach the art, thought, or literature of the European past, not to feel that our fields are in danger of being labeled "well-studied" and, hence, paradoxically, marked out for gradual extinction.

It was in this environment that I took the announcement of funds to support multicultural, team-teaching experiments as a welcome challenge to bring history into the discussion, to demonstrate that European civilization itself has a multicultural past, one that should be brought into dialogue with the present. Wherever one goes, one hears anecdotes of the curricular languishing of the Middle Ages, the demise of Anglo-Saxon studies, the poor enrollment in some medieval courses, the struggles in hiring committees over whether candidates who teach such central pieces of the canon as *Beowulf* or Chaucer can attract the number of students their departments need to flourish. And yet, in fact, while doubly marginalized, first by historical remoteness and second by lack of political cachet, the Middle Ages themselves existed before colonialism and fully developed nationalism had divided the modern world up into its contemporary regions and so composed a time when the boundaries of national literatures and languages were more fluid and when the religious message of universalism, propounded by both Christianity and Islam, made possible a philosophy of inclusiveness the modern world might find attractive. The "Eastern" world, loosely conceived, had not settled into the position of cultural and technological inferiority that Said describes (1978, e.g., 73-92), indeed rather the reverse, and Europe gladly if somewhat anxiously welcomed the influx of philosophical texts that were to make up its classical heritage. Until the late fourteenth century, the Mongol captivity of the Far East opened trade routes to Western travellers and missionaries, and the stories they brought back with them were far-fetched and extravagant but not unattractive to Western readers. Without trying to glamorize the European Middle Ages – this was, after all, also the age of the Crusades – I felt that the time and place might have something more interesting and appealing to say to our contemporary students than it is normally given credit for, and I wanted some of the available funds to go to open up the "less-studied" past to the "well-studied" present. I don't deny that I feel nervous about the complicated mix of personal and political motives that have characterized our course from the beginning, for I have also felt strongly that the course should stand or fall according to its fidelity to the primary material and not for its political usefulness.

Professor Marlow, for reasons she describes in her own essay, was enthusiastic too about joining forces, and so we came up with and were successful in winning approval for our "multicultural" course. Assisted by its interdepartmentalism, the course was again very successful at attracting students (we tried and failed to limit it to fifteen, and it had a significant wait list), and again it covered a wide range of materials – wider than ever – from parts from the *Qur'an* and *The Nasirean Ethics* to Shakespeare's *Othello*, from the travels of Ibn Battuta to those of Marco Polo, and from the chivalric verses of *The Song of Roland* to Ibn al-Marzuban's justification of "the superiority of dogs to many of those who wear clothes," in a text by that same name (see syllabus materials appended). But this time, there was an intellectual principle behind the chaos; we were looking at two parts of the world looking at and past each other. The theme of the cultural "other" tied the course together. Most importantly from my perspective, this team-teaching experience will continue to inform the way that I teach my other courses, even when my colleague is not standing beside me, and the way that I read canonical texts in the European tradition.

I would like to finish, though, by mentioning some other problems that emerged in part *from* the course's interdisciplinarity. Our course not only bridged two regions and two literary and cultural traditions; it also bridged two academic disciplines. Professor Marlow teaches from within a Religion Department and I from an English Department, but paradoxically it was not this division that was responsible for the most troubling sorts of disciplinary confusion in our course material, but problems that arose from the material we were studying itself. The category of the literary, for example, is defined differently in each tradition. Hostility to fiction-making and a resultant hewing to authority seem to have produced a body of medieval Islamic material that hedges against fabrication more aggressively and that is more overtly philosophical than the European Christian tradition. Partly for this reason, *adab* is a different sort of thing from the chivalric romance and so conveys different kinds of attitudes toward an event like the Crusades, attitudes less explicitly apologetic and more meditative. Similarly, in a literary hierarchy, *The Arabian Nights* and *The Book of the Wonders of India* occupy a less elevated niche than *The Decameron* and *The Canterbury Tales* do within their traditions. Not surprisingly, then, the structural asymmetries of our syllabus were a problem for our students; no sooner had they formulated a set of expectations appropriate to one body of material than they were asked to reformulate their expectations and interpret another body of material that operated by entirely different kinds of conventions.

We also attracted students with interests that were sometimes in conflict, and the different texts we were studying appealed to these students for differing reasons. The students from the English Department were at first frustrated by our lack of attention to aesthetic features, while other students were pushing to bring contemporary politics into the classroom. Because the Islamic material usually did not present itself as fiction, it raised questions of belief that do not normally come up in my literature classes, and as a result at least one Christian student, who had easily bracketed such questions the previous semester when studying *Beowulf* and the *Pearl*-poet, now felt intensely beleaguered by Muslim students in the class, or by students whose perspectives were resolutely secular; she felt personally threatened by the critical tone of their observations on the Christian tradition. She was not altogether wrong to feel this way either, for the culturally relativist pieties of some of the other students in the course often informed their value judgments, a fact that in turn came to bother *me* intensely when those judgments were not only cultural but aesthetic. One option we offered on the final paper was to imagine, dramatize – and finally to analyze – a meeting between two authors we had studied during the term – one from the Islamic world, the "East," and one from the Christian, the "West" (see assignments appended). A couple of students chose this topic, and selected as their authors Chaucer and the anonymous "author(s)" of the *Arabian Nights*. In contrast to the sophisticated traveler from the Middle East, named Ibn Fazim by one student, Chaucer emerges in her paper as a cultural and literary lout, "a great, fat man with a greying goatee" belching and laughing in a tavern, bouncing a buxom girl named "Molly" on his knee, completely flummoxed but also impressed by the innovation of framed narrative, which he sees as solving a problem of coherence in his *Canterbury Tales*. Not only did this student confuse and invert events in literary history that I thought we had covered thoroughly in class; in her analysis, the literary debt is all on the side of the Western author, whom she sees as unilaterally more primitive than his Middle Eastern counterpart. In our zeal to be open-minded and evenhanded, we seem to have given this student the impression that the West was in every way, culturally and artistically as well as scientifically and technologically, backward; indeed, to her this seemed to have been one of the messages of the course, and one that I fear was at least partly reinforced by the institutional politics of the course's history.

On the other side, the course's interdisciplinarity was a source of intellectual excitement, both for Professor Marlow, for me, and also for our students. I gained from it a far more vivid sense than I had had before, of the likelihood and importance of significant cultural contact between East and West. The maps that were constantly part of our study gave us all, I think, a tangible sense of the Middle Ages as one world criss-crossed by travellers who must have made some effort to understand each other, even across their linguistic barriers. The Islamic writers speak frequently of such encounters, as for instance when Usamah Ibn-Munqidh describes the "curious mentality" of a Frankish knight, a close friend, who offers to take Usamah's son back to Europe with him to learn manners and chivalry; "[t]hus," Usamah exclaims in exasperation, "there fell upon my ears words which never would have come out of the head of a sensible man" (Hitti 1929, 161). Despite Usamah's polite refusal of the offer, what emerges most powerfully from the scene is the bemused mutual respect the two men feel for one another. My own sense of the meetings that might have taken place between Chaucer and the merchants or scholars who brought him stories from the East is now I think more nuanced, more varied, and also more likely than before to include formal matters – for example, the peculiarly Islamic feel of the disavowals of authority in Chaucer's fiction.

Team-teaching the European Middle Ages has also, as I mentioned earlier, altered the way that I teach my other courses. To cite just a single example, in my Arthurian Legends course the following semester, I felt more aware than before of the importance of East/West distinctions in Geoffrey of Monmouth's story of Britain's foundation, which involves at the beginning the transplantation of the Trojan graft onto British soil and at the end the expulsion of the Romans, who are now driven into alliance with the Eastern kings of Spain, Parthia, Libya, Egypt and other exotic places both real and imaginary. By bringing two medieval cultures into contact in the classroom, I feel that we in some way visited these places, and were forced to confront those borders where the imaginary both fails to explain and also redeems the real. It was sometimes a troubling and problematic encounter, but the friction was also productive.

## REFERENCES

Chaucer, Geoffrey. 1987. *The Riverside Chaucer*. Ed. Larry D. Benson. Boston: Houghton Mifflin.

Hitti, Philip K., trans. 1929. *An Arab-Syrian Gentleman and Warrior in the Period of the Crusades: Memoirs of Usamah Ibn-Munqidh*. Princeton: Princeton University Press.

Lynch, Kathryn L. 1995. East Meets West in Chaucer's Squire's and Franklin's Tales. *Speculum* 70: 530-51.

Murphy, Craig N. 1997 (27 January). An Agenda for Wellesley in a Changing World: A Report of an Internal Consultant, Craig N. Murphy (M. Margaret Ball Professor of International Relations), to the Deans and President of the College.

Said, Edward W. 1978. *Orientalism*. New York: Vintage. Reprinted and expanded 1994.

# 11
# Team-Teaching the Literature of the European and Islamic Middle Ages: The Islamic Perspective

## *Louise Marlow*

AS THE BOUNDARIES of many academic fields and disciplines become less distinct, the feeling of defensiveness to which my colleague Professor Lynch has referred afflicts not only scholars of medieval European literature but also scholars who deal with the "less studied regions" of the world (Murphy 1997, 47-48), and in particular those whose work falls squarely into area studies. Indeed, by some assessments, the very future of area studies, at every level of scholarly activity, is in some doubt. The threat to area studies might seem surprising in an era when institutions such as Wellesley College, where Professor Lynch and I taught the experimental course under discussion here, have made an explicit commitment to global education and are accordingly engaged in a transformation of their curricula. It sometimes appears, however, that the global scope of the emerging curriculum may come at the cost of regional specificity.

In the case of Middle Eastern Studies, it is instructive, if chastening, to consider the unsettling issues that have been raised by the current and former Presidents of the Middle East Studies Association, the largest professional organisation in the field, over the past several years. These presidents have repeatedly warned their members that area studies generally, and Middle Eastern Studies in particular, must find new justifications for their existence in the face of the relentless downsizing and restructuring trends that are affecting educational institutions no less than other forms of business (see, for some recent examples, Kazemi 1996, 1; Fawaz 1997, 1, 6). As evidence of the ill-health of Middle Eastern Studies, observers have noted declining enrollments in undergraduate- and graduate-level courses, especially when these courses are offered in departments defined by geographical area rather than by discipline, and decreased funding for Middle Eastern topics by national and international organisations. Many scholars of the Middle East have felt that the field is too often either excluded from, or relegated to the peripheries of, discipline- and subject-based scholarly institutions; a glance at the programs of the annual meetings of the American Historical Association or the American Academy of Religion confirms this impression. In the areas of both teaching and research, the declining popularity of Middle Eastern Studies seems to be partially due to the field's perceived tendency, until recently, towards insularity, its general reluctance to address comparative topics or issues of concern to scholars in related fields (Said 1978, 271f). In order to attract students and to resist further cut-backs in their field, scholars who specialise in Middle Eastern Studies are urged to initiate effective interactions with other, more self-evidently "relevant" fields of study, and to claim actively a solid footing within the mainstream of academic and public discourse.

Edward Said's powerful book *Orientalism* drew attention to the complex history of Oriental Studies, the predecessor of Middle Eastern, South Asian, and East Asian Studies, and triggered a process of generally healthy reflection among scholars of the Islamic Middle East (see, for example, Hourani 1979, 27-30). Many of the first Orientalists were generalists who, in their eagerness to grasp as many facets of Middle Eastern history and culture as they could, sometimes constructed comprehensive interpretative frameworks for their findings and in so doing reduced and essentialised their subject matter (Said 1979, 255ff). The contemporary successors of these Orientalists have sought to avoid their predecessors' tendencies to reification by becoming specialists in more narrowly defined aspects of area studies, but they may have limited their readership to scholars whose expertise is similarly focused. The latest challenge to the field calls for regional specialists to relate their work to the concerns of a more general audience, while avoiding the essentialising tendencies of earlier scholars. To some extent, the crisis that area studies now faces can be considered an episode in the ongoing process of self-criticism initiated in particular by Said's analysis, as scholars continue to ponder the purposes of their work and their own relationships to the materials they study. In the first half of the twentieth century, educational institutions felt less pressed to cultivate a consumer-oriented outlook than many do today, and actual or quasi-colonial connections with the Middle East in themselves provided an incentive for numbers of students to aspire to learn the languages and explore the cultures of the region. Since the 1960s, these educational and political conditions have changed decidedly. Scholars of Middle Eastern Studies can no longer expect the importance of their work to be taken for granted by their students or their colleagues. They cannot, as some may have done in the past, study the Middle East in isolation from the major academic disciplines, as if the region defied the application of techniques or questions employed in other fields and required its own unique methods of scholarship. Instead, it is necessary that scholars of the Middle East demonstrate the relevance of their work to other fields of study, perhaps especially those in the social sciences, such as economics, sociology, and political science.

In significant measure, the insularity that contributes to the marginalisation of Middle Eastern subjects in academic settings may derive from the formidable barrier posed by the necessary language study. To those outside the field, the Middle East and the broader Islamic world can appear to be cut off from general scholarly interest by the boundaries created by its languages, while for Islamicists themselves, the sheer effort involved in attaining fluency in the appropriate languages may foster a sense of protectiveness, even proprietariness, about scholarship relating to the Middle East. The insecure status of area studies today suggests to some observers that the globalising curricular imperative may be at odds with the need for intense study of particular cultures in their own right. Although it is widely accepted that scholars with expertise in the Middle East would benefit from greater integration with other branches of scholarship, it would be unfortunate if we were to dismiss the importance of linguistic competence as a prerequisite for the study of Middle Eastern subjects, or to pretend that such proficiency is likely to be attained without sustained immersion in the literature and culture of the region.

Just as well established parts of the liberal arts' curriculum, such as English literature, find their status questioned on account of a perceived lack of global relevance, regional studies are increasingly seen as outmoded and lacking in disciplinary or "theoretical" rigor. It was for these reasons that Professor Lynch and I decided to join forces in an attempt to offer an undergraduate course that sought to provide both proper contextualisation for literary materials drawn from different cultures and also an authentic attempt at comparison and interdisciplinarity.

Specialists in area studies at liberal arts' colleges often find themselves obliged to go beyond the safe parameters of insularity and to attempt to address the interests of non-specialists. They may belong to a relatively small group of faculty members whose training and expertise prepare them to teach the aspects of the regions that fall into the "less studied" category. Particularly when a teaching area is not supported by the availability of relevant language instruction on the campus, such scholars are likely to be receptive to ways by which they might integrate their own areas of study into those of a broader community of scholars and students. For me, then, the opportunity to team-teach an undergraduate seminar on the literature of the European and Islamic Middle Ages was highly appealing. I saw the creation of the course as a chance for greater contact and integration between my area and a related field and department. The idea of increasing such contact with a focus on the Middle Ages was particularly appealing to me, since the sharp delineation of boundaries that until recently characterised so much of our modern approach to scholarship and teaching often seems at odds with the more fluid and sometimes creative interaction of European and Middle Eastern peoples in pre-modern times. It was also an opportunity, as Professor Lynch has already pointed out, to highlight the interconnectedness of the pre-modern Islamic and European worlds, to expose students to ways of thinking and associated aesthetic forms that predate the current divisions (geographical, political, cultural and disciplinary) that have been taken for granted.

One of the problems that we immediately faced in designing our course was, as Professor Lynch has already mentioned, the question of asymmetry. This asymmetry was apparent not only in our employment of literary genres, as Professor Lynch has noted, but also in the content and orientation of our materials. Whereas the European materials could be conveniently grouped together because they all involved some treatment of the Orient, the Islamic materials for the most part did not offer a mirror-image: in other words, Muslims during the Middle Ages were usually more engaged by cultures further east than by the cultures of the Mediterranean and western and northern Europe. When Muslim travelers wrote about the peoples of northern and western Europe, they often dismissed them as barbarians: the tenth-century writer Ibn Fadlan, for example, describes the Rus as filthy, unkempt, cruel, prone to drunkenness, and totally lacking in sexual modesty (McKeithen 1979, 127ff). For a closer parallel to European exoticisation, one has to look at Middle Eastern accounts of India, South-East Asia and China.

When we first discussed our plans for the course, Professor Lynch and I realized we faced a choice: either we could offer a team-taught course on the medieval history of European/Christian-Middle Eastern/Muslim relations, in which we could make use of literary sources and fiction where appropriate; or we could offer a course on literary treatments of otherness, even though the "others" in question would sometimes differ, in the two cultures. We opted for the latter path. There were some points at which the two groups of materials, European and Islamic, would provide mutual perceptions. For example, our section on the literature of the Crusades included Muslim views of Crusaders as well as Crusaders' views of Muslims. But surprisingly, these occasional instances of symmetry were not, in my opinion, necessarily more successful than the sessions in which we were unable to provide such symmetry of content. It seemed as if the lack of symmetry in content was less difficult for our students to negotiate than the lack of symmetry in the cultural and aesthetic assumptions underlying our different literary genres and styles.

In putting together the Islamic side of the course, I faced the practical problem of finding interesting and appropriate materials available in English translation. This constraint proved to be significant, and I was sometimes limited to brief anthologised excerpts of longer, untranslated works. If I were to redesign the course now, I should attempt to decrease the number of short readings and assign a smaller number of complete works in translation.

A major problem for presenting the Islamic materials, I found, was that students in many cases lacked a sound knowledge of the historical, cultural and religious background to the texts they were reading. I was concerned about this problem at every stage in the construction and teaching of the course: in organising the syllabus, in class meetings, and after the conclusion of the semester. I could have assigned yet more readings, and asked students to read general works on Islamic history and on Islam as a religious tradition; but my colleague and I agreed that we were already at the limits of reasonableness in the amount of reading we had assigned for each week. If, on the other hand, I had substituted historical and general readings for some of the texts included on the syllabus, without increasing the amount of reading overall, it would have detracted significantly from students' exposure to the primary literary materials under study in the course. So what I opted for in general was to provide relevant background information to the readings in each class session, and to attempt to tie this information to the assigned materials for that session. Professor Lynch in several cases adopted the same approach in presenting "her" materials. The creation of an electronic bulletin for the class further facilitated our presentation of contextual materials. Each week students posted their reactions to the readings on the bulletin, and they were able to conduct their own discussions of the material throughout the week. The bulletin was also extremely useful to us as instructors, in that we were able to provide background information to each of the readings for the week on the bulletin, so that students had at least a basic orientation and a sense of what to look for before they plunged in to some fairly challenging materials. Despite these measures, I was left with the feeling that many of our students lacked the context they needed to understand and appreciate the Islamic materials as fully as I would have liked. This was perhaps inevitable in a team-taught interdepartmental course for which we felt we could require neither previous work in Islamic Studies nor coursework in medieval European literature, let alone courses in both fields. In our first experimental offering of the course, it was the students who had had some prior exposure to Islamic materials who felt most able to react to them, comment on them, and criticise them.

Questions of genre were also, as my colleague has indicated, problematic in certain respects. There were a number of instances, however, in which our combinations of European and Islamic materials worked very well. One of the most successful sections of the course, in my opinion, was the section that dealt with travel literature. We included two sessions on travel literature, the first dealing with European travelers or pseudo-travelers (Marco Polo and Mandeville), the second with Middle Eastern travelers (Ibn Battuta, al-Biruni, Marvazi, al-Sharif al-Idrisi). Students seemed to feel comfortable with this combination of materials because, despite the unfamiliarity of the Muslim travelers' accounts, they had a genre in their minds against which they could compare the Muslim materials, which they found to concentrate less on personal narrative and more on practical information, such as flora and fauna, weights and measures, distances between places, and so on. Students' observations of these differences led very nicely to a discussion of the different worlds in which these travelers operated, the purposes of travel in each culture, the lack of water-tight political boundaries, and the different audiences assumed by writers in each culture. It also led our students to speculate in interesting ways about the applicability of Said's ideas about Orientalism to medieval materials, especially when some of our Middle Eastern travelers, such as al-Biruni, began to look decidedly imperialistic in outlook. Our session on portrayals of the marvelous in the two cultures was, in my view, equally successful. Thus in these instances I found the literature a helpful means of enhancing the students' understanding of the larger political and intellectual context in which it was produced, and a stimulus to creative and critical thinking about the functions of literature in the medieval world in both the European and the Islamic cultural settings.

In other cases, where the European materials were less well equipped to provide a standard for comparison and contrast, I was particularly aware of our students' need for more background before they could approach the Islamic texts. This was especially evident in the second half of the course, where the European and Islamic materials seemed to have less in common as we focused more on questions of genre than on themes such as travel or the marvelous. From the point of view of the evolution of European literary forms, it makes sense to study Chaucer together with Boccaccio, but it is harder to fit comparable trends in Islamic literary history into the same framework. In retrospect it might have been helpful to devote one or more sessions to some Islamic literary genres, such as the *maqama* or the romance, and to have returned to comparative questions after some more or less equal exposure to the two literatures on their own terms. But here too – Julie Scott Meisami's fine translation of Nizami's romance, the *Haft paykar*, notwithstanding – the lack of English translations presents a serious limitation.

Even in this second and generally more unwieldy section of the course, several units proved both valuable educationally and successful in the classroom. For example, our session on the *Thousand and One Nights* allowed us to discuss such questions as open and closed frame-tales and the characteristics of female narrative within an Islamic framework. In fact I am tempted to say that the *Thousand and One Nights* provided an orientation for the second half of the course in much the same way that Said's *Orientalism* established a direction for the first half.

For all its failings, our experimental course on medieval European and Islamic treatments of otherness was, in our opinion, a relatively successful example of curricular multiculturalism and interdisciplinarity at Wellesley College. It is perhaps worth noting that Wellesley, like some other liberal arts' colleges, has a "multicultural requirement": students are obliged to take at least one course in a "multicultural" field. The requirement is broadly defined, such that it may be fulfilled by taking a course not only in some aspect of a culture or cultures outside Europe and America but also in issues pertaining to racism and social justice. Since its inception, the multicultural requirement has been surrounded by controversy at both the conceptual and the practical levels. Our team-taught course, which attempted to bring together materials from the "well studied" and the "less studied" areas of the curriculum, fulfilled the requirement, but also, we hope, demonstrated that related materials drawn from different traditions can be inherently worthy of study.

## REFERENCES

Fawaz, Leila. 1997 (February). Regaining Control. *MESA Newsletter*. Tucson: University of Arizona. 19.1: 1, 6.

Hourani, Albert. 1979 (March 9). The Road to Morocco. *New York Review of Books*, 27-30.

Kazemi, Farhad. 1996 (May). Changes for Area Studies: Impact Could be Great. *MESA Newsletter*. Tucson: University of Arizona. 18.2: 1.

McKeithen, James E. 1979. *The Risalah of Ibn Fadlan: An Annotated Translation with Introduction*. Ph.D. dissertation. Indiana University.

Meisami, Julie Scott. 1995. *The Haft Paykar, A Medieval Persian Romance*. Oxford and New York: Oxford University Press.

Murphy, Craig N. 1997 (January 27). An Agenda for Wellesley in a Changing World: A Report of an Internal Consultant, Craig N. Murphy (M. Margaret Ball Professor of International Relations), to the Deans and President of the College.

Said, Edward. 1978. *Orientalism*. New York: Vintage. Reprinted and expanded 1994.

## Appendix

Sample Syllabus: ENGLISH 315/RELIGION 365
"Images of the Other in the European and Islamic Middle Ages"

### I. The Course

Kathryn Lynch  
Department of English

Louise Marlow  
Department of Religion

The ways in which communities envisage otherness are often closely related to their understandings of themselves. Historically, a community's sense of its own identity evolves in conjunction with its need to distinguish itself from its neighbors and from subversive-seeming elements within its own makeup. This new course examines, in a comparative framework, various conceptualizations of the other in the European and Islamic Middle Ages. In both contexts otherness was defined in religious, ethnic and cultural terms; at the same time, both cultures also invented marvelous and fantastic beings whose imagined reality contributed to (among other things) their own sense of normalcy. Materials under consideration include travel narratives by European and Middle Eastern travelers, merchants and sailors; European Crusader poems and Middle Eastern descriptions of real interactions with Crusaders; religious texts; love poetry in both traditions written to the transgressive cultural other; maps and accounts of the marvellous; and fictional stories that feature travel and "orientalism." The course concludes with Shakespeare's famous tragedy of the Moor Othello and his Venetian wife Desdemona.

*Books available at the Wellesley College Bookstore:*

H. Haddawy (trans.), *The Arabian nights.*
Sir John Mandeville, *The travels of Sir John Mandeville.*
Nizami, *The haft paykar*, trans. J.S. Meisami.
*The poem of the Cid*, trans. R. Hamilton and J. Perry.
Marco Polo, *The travels of Marco Polo*, trans. R. Latham.
Edward Said, *Orientalism.*
W. Shakespeare, *Othello.*
*The Song of Roland*, trans. G. Burgess.

All materials listed in the syllabus are available in the Reserve Room at the Margaret Clapp Library.

*Requirements:*

(1) Regular attendance and participation in class discussions; attendance at lectures by outside speakers, as marked in the syllabus. Attendance and participation count for 10% of the class grade.

(2) Participation in discussions on electronic bulletin ENG-315. Each week one or two students will be responsible for posting comments on the week's reading by Thursday; these comments will be worth 10% of the grade. In addition, all students should contribute something to the bulletin each week. Participation in these discussions will count for 15% of the grade over the course of the semester.

(3) Students are required to write two papers for the course. The first paper, 5-10 pages in length, is due on 21 October and will be worth 25% of the grade; the second, 10-15 pages, is due on 2 December and will be worth 40% of the grade. Over the course of the semester all students should address in their papers both the Islamic and the European materials, either separately or in combination.

## II. Weekly Schedule

1. Introduction and visit to Clapp Library Special Collections
2. Orientalism
    Reading: E. Said, *Orientalism*, pp. 1-110.
3. Travel literature I: European travelers
    Reading: Marco Polo, *Travels*, pp. 33-45, 113-181, 250-312; Sir John Mandeville, *Travels*, pp. 43-54, 72-88, 104-110.
4. Travel literature II: Middle Eastern travelers
    Reading: Ibn Battuta, *Travels*, pp. 593-618 (Sind and north-western India); Sharaf al-Din Marvazi, *The natural properties of animals*, pp. 13-60 (China, the Turks, India, the Ethiopians, remote countries and islands); al-Sharif al-Idrisi, *India and the neighbouring territories*, pp. 23-74; Biruni, *Alberuni's India*, pp. 17-32, 99-104; B. Lewis (trans.), *Islam*, vol. 2, pp. 82-87, 106-123.

5. Others within the medieval Islamic world
   Reading on Jews and Christians: N. Stillman, *The Jews of Arab lands*, pp. 113-114, 119-123, 145-148, 149-151, 157-161, 167-170, 214-216; Al-Jahiz, *The life and works of Jahiz*, p. 38.
   Reading on ethnic types: Nasir al-Din Tusi, *The Nasirean ethics*, pp. 43-48; Kay Ka'us, *A mirror for princes*, pp. 99-108; Lewis, *Islam*, vol. 2, pp. 243-251.
   Reading on ethnic rivalry: Lewis, *Islam*, vol. 2, pp. 201-210.
6. Wonders and marvels
   Reading: Mandeville, *Travels*, pp. 165-190; Prester John, *The Letter and the Legend*, pp. 67-79; Qur'an, photocopy (on signs and belief/disbelief, *jinn*, eschatology); A.J. Arberry (trans.), *Muslim saints and mystics*, pp. 53-61, 62-79, 161-165; Buzurg ibn Shahriyar, *The Book of the Wonders of India*, pp. 1-111 (skim); Al-Jahiz, *The life and works of Jahiz*, pp. 142-146, 151, 157-158, 195-199; Ibn al-Marzuban, *The superority of dogs to many of those who wear clothes*, pp. 1-34 (skim).
7. Love poetry
   Reading: Jaufré Rudel, photocopy; William IX of Aquitaine, photocopy; Michael Sells, *Desert tracings*, pp. 60-66, 70-76; Ibn Hazm, *The ring of the dove*, pp. 15-64.
8. The Arabian nights
   Reading: Haddawy, *The Arabian nights*, pp. 1-29, 66-77, 114-206.
9. Chaucer I: Romance
   Reading: General Prologue, lines 1-100, 309-360, 747-821; The Squire's Tale; The Franklin's Tale; Nizami, *The haft paykar*, pp. 96-144.
   Assignment: visit to Special Collections to look at Ellesmere manuscript facsimile.
10. Chivalric romance I: Pilgrims and crusaders
    Reading: *The Song of Roland*; Usama ibn Munqidh, *An Arab-Syrian gentleman and warrior in the period of the Crusades*, pp. 63-79, 161-170, 202-218.
11. Chivalric romance II: Nationalism, commerce, and collaboration.
    Reading: *The Poem of the Cid*
12. Chaucer II: Marriage
    Reading: Chaucer, Man of Law's Tale; Boccaccio, *The Decameron*, Prologue, Day 1.3, Day 2.7, Day 2.9, Day 5.2, Day 10.9.

13. Shakespeare: The Renaissance Other
   Reading: *Othello*.

### III. Assignments

*A. First Assignment*

(1) Discuss the value of applying Edward Said's theory of "orientalism" to the Middle Ages by examining its appropriateness to one of the texts that we have read so far, including texts that originated either in Europe or the Middle East. You do not have to treat every aspect of Said's theory; in fact, you should not try to do so. Limit yourself to one or two features of his analysis – for example, his image of the "oriental" as untrustworthy and childlike, or his theory of knowledge as a way to gain power – and discuss its applicability to the text you have chosen. As a side issue, you might also consider whether Said's theory applies more or less closely to European texts or to Middle Eastern ones. Indeed, if you get interested enough in this last question, you might write your entire paper as a comparison of two texts – one European, one Middle Eastern – keeping in mind the question of how appropriate to each is Said's theory.

(2) Make maps of either a part or the whole of two voyages described in the readings so far (e.g., Marco Polo and Mandeville). Write a paper about your maps. In this paper you might dicuss what made it easy or hard, straightforward or impossible, to map a section of the journey; the ways in which your two maps differ from each other and the reasons for the differences as they express themselves in the texts; or the ways in which your maps differ from actual medieval maps (see the various histories of maps and geography listed on the reserve list) and why (of course you do not need to consider all these issues). Try to develop a theory about your maps that leads you back into the texts in question and helps you to understand the world view represented there. Include your two maps with your written analysis.

(3) Read the chapters from "The Journey of William of Rubrick" (mid-thirteenth century, before Marco Polo and Mandeville) that detail his initial experiences in the court of the Great Khan (about 30 pages, see Kathryn Lynch for references) and compare the descriptions of the Khan's court made by this Franciscan missionary to those of the merchant Marco Polo in our reading assignment. Think about why these two accounts are different, either those reasons that may relate to their historical moments or those that relate to the

individual circumstances of the authors, and why these differences matter. Which of the two is more "modern" in its outlook? Which is more "medieval"? Look both at the objective physical details and at narrative style, especially the creation of a voice, and think about how these are related to each other and to the subject of this course, "otherness."

(4) Compare Marco Polo's account of Kubilai Khan's court with the account of the Mongols by the thirteenth-century Persian writer Juvayni (*A History of the World Conqueror*, trans. J. A. Boyle – see Louise Marlow for availability and page references). What similarities and differences do you notice between the accounts of the Venetian merchant and visitor to the Mongol court and the Persian administrator whose people lived directly under Mongol rule? How can this comparison be used to advance our understanding of the "fact vs. fiction" problem we were discussing in class? Can we use these two texts to make any larger arguments about perceptions of otherness?

(5) Explore sections of either al-Hamadhani's *Maqamat* or al-Hariri's *Assemblies* and discuss the use of travel as a motif in these fictional narratives. Are there elements of exoticisation or orientalising in these stories? How might you relate these fictional treatments of travel to the "real" travel accounts of, say, Marco Polo or Ibn Battuta, or to the spurious (?) travel narratives of Mandeville and perhaps al-Sharif al-Idrisi? Do the stories seem to reflect a distinctively medieval understanding of travel, and if so how, or are they in some respects strikingly modern?

(6) Compare Ibn Fadlan's discussion af the various groups he visits (the Turks, Khazars, Bulgars and Russians). How does his treatment of the different groups reflect his ideas of otherness? If you wish, you may read this text in conjunction with Marvazi's discussion of the Chinese, Turks and Indians. What common features do you notice, and what contrasts? What might account for these similarities and differences, and how might such a comparison be instructive in shaping our understanding of perceptions of otherness and the role of literary genres in expressing those perceptions? See Louise Marlow for references and availability.

(7) Compare the fictional travels of Ibn Fadlan in Michael Crichton's *Eaters of the Dead* with those of the real Ibn Fadlan (see above) – or you may pick a different Middle Eastern traveller. You may consider both the text and the fictional scholarly apparatus. If you have read and studied the Anglo-Saxon poem *Beowulf* this might be an especially appropriate topic; Crichton's Ibn Fadlan encounters the situation of the Beowulf story in an environment that is

culturally "other" to him. In this topic you will not only be contrasting the European and Middle Eastern perspectives, but will be noting the inscription of modern attitudes to the culture of the past as an "other" as well. Crichton's book is available in paperback at most bookstores.

(8) You may construct your own topic individually as well, perhaps different from but modeled on some of the juxtapositions described above. Perhaps there is another modern travel narrative you would like to look at in connection with a medieval text – or perhaps you can imagine pairings of medieval texts that we have not thought of, or contrasts among the treatments of groups within a single text. If you do design a different topic, just get it approved by one of us.

These papers should be anywhere between 5 to 10 pages in length. Please indicate by number on the title page of your paper which topic you are addressing. Louise Marlow and Kathryn Lynch will both be reading and marking all papers. You should feel free to consult with either of us in the course of setting up or writing this essay.

*B. Final/Term Paper Assignment*

The first thing that we want to stress is that there is really no fixed assignment for this paper. This should be your culminating piece of work for the semester, and it is entirely appropriate that the selection of what to work on and how to focus your research and argument should be up to you. We offer the following topics as possibilities only, and ones that may get you thinking along a variety of lines that we think could result in productive work. If you do select one of the topics below, please indicate on your title page or in your heading the number of your topic.

(1) Compare the arts of love written by Ibn Hazm (*The Ring of the Dove*) and Andreas Capellanus (*The Art of Courtly Love*). Think not only about the rules themselves that each author offers, but also about the forms of the two works, their use of anecdote, poetry, and the palinodes at the ends. Do you think that a case for influence could be made? What are the problems of evidence that the comparison raises? What kinds of differences in approach to the subject matter are there in the two cases? How does such an "art" of love relate to court culture?

(2) Consider a poem of Chaucer's that we are not reading in class but that also deals with the "Orient," broadly defined. Two possibilities are the Prioress's Tale, which describes a conflict between a Christian community in

Asia and a Jewish one, or one of the legends in Chaucer's *Legends of Good Women*. Several of the women Chaucer writes about in this long poem are from the "East" – Cleopatra, Dido, Thisbe to name three who emerge from long literary and cultural traditions that would be interesting to study in connection with Chaucer's representations. If you are interested in pursuing this topic, you might see Kathryn Lynch for reading suggestions. A study of Cleopatra might also lead you to think about Shakespeare's *Antony and Cleopatra*, and the kinds of symbolic meanings that place may have in Shakespeare's play.

(3) Contextualize one of the poems that we are reading historically. You might think about the real-life prototype of the Cid, Rodrigo Diaz de Vivar; or the connection between the *Song of Roland* and the First Crusade, which was undertaken simultaneously with the probable date of that poem; or the real historical background of Venice as a cultural metropolis, which might have caused Shakespeare to pick that city as one of the important locations for Othello (for this topic, see the book on reserve by W.H. McNeill, *Venice, the Hinge of Europe*).

(4) Continue your theoretical thinking about "orientalism" by considering its relationship either to theories of nationhood or nationalism or to feminism. Gayatri Spivak's book *In Other Worlds* has some interesting reflections on the place of feminism, and especially French feminism, in a self-consciously theoretical and politically engaged internationalism. Similarly, an essay by Homi Bhabha, "DissemiNation," raises intriguing questions about inherent features of the modern nation that sit somewhat uneasily with Said's "essentializing" of the dichotomy of East/West (see Kathryn Lynch for reference). Beware, some of this theoretical reading is rather heavy going compared to Said. But these writers, if you can sift through them, do raise provocative questions – for example, how does feminist theory cause you to rethink the issues of gender and geography? Does reading another theorist cause you to rethink or qualify your judgments about Said's "orientalism"? Is "orientalism" the right word, and if not what implications does terminology have for theory? After identifying the theoretical issues you want to focus on, you should then try to return at least briefly to a medieval text to test the relative merits of Said's theory against those of an alternative theory. You can also identify a different theorist to put into dialogue with Said, or you can look at the set of short pieces in the forum on the place of the personal in scholarship in the October, 1996, *PMLA* (Kathryn Lynch passed out some short excerpts from this discussion in class).

(5) Read from the summaries and extracts of the Christian polemicist Peter the Venerable (twelfth century; in a book called *Peter the Venerable and Islam*), who claimed that Islam was a Christian heresy. Think about how thus conceiving of Islam as an "other within" rather than an "other without" alters the representation of Islam in any single European work that we have read, or in a group of works. You might consult Susan Schibanoff, "Worlds Apart: Orientalism, Antifeminism, and Heresy in Chaucer's Man of Law's Tale," *Exemplaria* 8 (1996): 59-96.

(6) After reading the *Song of Roland*, take a look at another Charlemagne romance. One we recommend is the fifteenth-century Middle English (no, hasn't been translated) *Sultan of Babylon* (in *Three Middle English Charlemagne Romances*, on reserve), an almost self-parodic late medieval romance that shows a kind of baroque excess of anti-Islamic sentiment and so makes an interesting bridge to the early modern period.

(7) Compare the narrative techniques employed in the *Thousand and One Nights* and the *Haft Paykar*. Among the topics you might consider are the role of framing in each text, the differences between open and closed frames, cyclical structures, and the interplay of didacticism and entertainment in the stories. Do your observations lead you to draw any conclusions about the role of the author in oral and literary traditions? Bear in mind that many of the stories in the *Haft Paykar* had a long life in Persian oral storytelling tradition before Nizami and others gave them lasting written form.

(8) Consider the theme of love of the cultural other in *Desert Tracings*, the *Haft Paykar*, and/or the *Thousand and One Nights*. In which of these cases is such love presented as transgressive, and what elements of context (literary and historical) might account for this? You might also consider the issues of availability, separation and consummation. How might Ibn Hazm characterize the forms of love described in the poems and stories you are discussing? Or, alternatively, you might compare love of the cultural other in one of the above "Eastern" texts with cross-cultural love and marriage in the Man of Law's Tale or in one of the tales of the *Decameron*.

(9) With reference to Amin Maalouf's *The Crusades Through Arab Eyes* consider the account of the Franks (Crusaders) given by Usama. How, in your opinion, did Usama's role of intermediary between the Franks and the inhabitants of Damascus affect his response to the Frankish presence? In what ways do Usama's memoirs reflect a mentality similar to or different from that

represented in the *Song of Roland*, and how might you account for these similarities and differences?

(10) Consider the treatment of the marvelous in the *Book of the Wonders of India* and the *Thousand and One Nights*. What constitutes the marvelous in each text? To what extent is marvelousness discussed explicitly, and with what effect? How might medieval audiences have reacted to these tales? How do the narrative techniques employed in each text work to create certain reader responses?

(11) "Meeting of Minds": Imagine a dialogue between two of the writers we have read since the first set of topics. What would these two figures have to say to each other? What might they choose to talk about? And how would their perspectives differ on some of the big issues of their time (and ours), like the Crusades or war in general, the role of women, religious doctrines (like the divinity of Christ or the image of the afterlife), moneylending, trade, marriage or miscegenation, magic (marvels, miracles), beauty, storytelling, and more (or, of course, less – you don't have to get them talking about ALL these subjects)? Carry on the dialogue for about six to eight pages; then write an analysis of the dialogue for an equal number of pages. In your analysis, explain why you chose the two figures, what was easy or hard about writing the dialogue, what you think that it reveals, what you like about it, and what you are still dissatisfied with. This exercise will really take a lot of imagination, not least because some of our "writers" are more properly "corporate authors"; that is, they are scribes who organized and wrote down literature that had been created partly by others and that was oral in its primary mode of dissemination. This discrepancy is something that you might want to discuss in the analysis section of the assignment. You might also try to work in actual quotations from the works written by your figures, though most of the writing should, of course, be your own.

Some possible pairs include: the author of the *Song of Roland* and Usama, Ibn Hazm and the author of the Cid, the author of the *Arabian Nights* and Geoffrey Chaucer. As these pairings suggest, we are thinking that you might want to work cross-culturally; you may come up with different pairs if you wish (just clear them with us), and they may in fact come from the same general cultural area (i.e., both Islamic or both European). Do not pair any of the travel writers from before the first paper, however.

This paper should be about 10-15 pages in length.

IV. SUPPLEMENTARY READING LIST

(This reading list has been partially updated to make it more useful to others who might be planning to teach in this subject area.)

Akehurst, F. R. P., and S. C. Van D'Elden (eds.). *The Stranger in Medieval Society*. Medieval Cultures, 12. Minneapolis, University of Minnesota Press, 1997.

Anderson, B. *Imagined Communities: Reflections on the Origin and Spread of Nationalism*. Rev. ed. London, Verso, 1991.

Asin Palacios, M. *Islam and the Divine Comedy*. London, Cass, 1968.

Atiya, A. S. *The Crusade in the Later Middle Ages*. London, Methuen, 1938.

'Attar, Farid al-Din/A. J. Arberry (tr.). *Muslim Saints and Mystics*. Chicago, University of Chicago Press, 1966.

al-Azmeh, A. "Barbarians in Arab Eyes." *Past and Present* 134 (1992) 3-18.

Beazley, C. R. *The Dawn of Modern Geography*. Vol. 3, *A History of Exploration and Geographical Science from the Middle of the Thirteenth Century to the Early Years of the Fifteenth Century (c. A. D. 1260-1420)*. Oxford, Clarendon Press, 1906.

Bennett, J. *The Rediscovery of Sir John Mandeville*. New York, Modern Language Association of America, 1954.

Biruni/E. C. Sachau (tr.). *Alberuni's India*. Delhi, Low Price Publications, 1989; reprint of 1910 edition.

Boccaccio, G./C. Singleton (tr.). *The Decameron*. Berkeley, University of California Press, 1982.

Brauer, R.W. *Boundaries and Frontiers in Medieval Muslim Geography*. Transactions of the American Philosophical Society, vol. 85, pt. 6, 1995.

Burgess, G. (tr.). *The Song of Roland*. London, New York, Penguin, 1990.

Buzurg ibn Shahriyar/G. S. P. Freeman-Grenville (tr.). *The Book of the Wonders of India*. London, the Hague, East-West Publications, 1981.

Campbell, K. H. *The 1001 Nights*. Cambridge, Dar Mahjar, 1985.

Campbell, M. *The Witness and the Other World: Exotic European Travel Writing, 400-1600*. Ithaca, Cornell University Press, 1988.

Caracciolo, P. *The Arabian Nights in English Literature*. New York, St. Martin's Press, 1988.

Chaucer, G. *Canterbury Tales*. Baltimore, Penguin, 1952.

———. *Love Visions*. Harmondsworth, New York, Penguin, 1983.

———. *The Riverside Chaucer*. Boston, Houghton Mifflin, 1987.

Cohen, J. J. *Of Giants: Sex, Monsters, and the Middle Ages*. Medieval Cultures, 17. Minneapolis, University of Minnesota Press, 1999.
——— (ed.). *The Postcolonial Middle Ages*. New York, St. Martin's Press, 2000.
Daftari, F. *The Assassin Legends*. London and New York, Tauris, 1994.
Daniel, N. *Islam and the West: The Making of an Image*. Edinburgh, Edinburgh University Press, 1962.
Dawson, C. (ed.). *Mission to Asia*. Medieval Academy Reprints for Teaching 8. Toronto, University of Toronto Press, 1980.
Delany, S. *The Naked Text: Chaucer's Legend of Good Women*. Berkeley, University of California Press, 1994.
Eickelman, D., and J. Piscatori (eds.). *Muslim Travellers: Pilgrimage, Migration, and the Religious Imagination*. Berkeley, University of California Press, 1990.
Firdawsi/J. W. Clinton (tr.). *The Tragedy of Sohrab and Rustam*. Seattle, University of Washington Press, 1987.
Friedman, J. B. *The Monstrous Races in Medieval Art and Thought*. Cambridge, Mass., Harvard University Press, 1981.
Furnivall, F. J. *The Stacions of Rome ... and The Pilgrims Sea-Voyage*. London, N. Trubner and Co., 1867.
Gerhardt, M. I. *The Art of Story-Telling. A Literary Study of the Thousand and One Nights*. Leiden, E. J. Brill, 1963.
Gittes, K. S. *Framing the Canterbury Tales*. New York, Greenwood Press, 1991.
Goss, U. P. (ed.). *The Meeting of Two Worlds: Cultural Exchange Between East and West During the Period of the Crusades*. Kalamazoo, Western Michigan University, 1986.
Gower, J. *Confessio Amantis*. In *The English Works of John Gower*. Ed. G. C. Macaulay. EETS, e.s. 81-82. 1900-01. Rpt. Oxford, Oxford University Press, 1979.
Haddawy, H. (tr.). *The Arabian Nights*. New York, W.W. Norton, 1990.
al-Hamadhani/W. J. Prendergast (tr.). *The Maqamat of Badi' al-Zaman al-Hamadhani*. London, Curzon Press, 1973.
Hamilton, R., and J. Perry (trs.). *The Poem of the Cid*. Harmondsworth, Penguin, 1975.
Hamori, A. *On the Art of Medieval Arabic Literature*. Princeton, Princeton University Press, 1974.

al-Hariri/T. Chenery (tr.). *The Assemblies of al-Hariri*. London, Williams and Norgate, 1867-1898.

Harley, J. B., and D. Woodward (eds.). *The History of Cartography*. Chicago, University of Chicago Press, 1987.

Harvey, P. D. A. *Medieval Maps*. Toronto, Buffalo, University of Toronto Press, 1991.

Heath, P. *Allegory and Philosophy in Avicenna (Ibn Sina)*. Philadelphia, University of Pennsylvania Press, 1992.

Higgins, I. M. *Writing East: The "Travels" of Sir John Mandeville*. Philadelphia, University of Pennsylvania Press, 1997.

Hillenbrand, C. *The Crusades: Islamic Perspectives*. New York, Routledge, 2000.

Holt, P. M. *The Age of the Crusades: The Near East from the Eleventh Century*. London, New York, Longman, 1986.

Hourani, A. *A History of the Arab Peoples*. Cambridge, Mass., Belknap Press of Harvard University Press, 1991.

———. *Islam in European Thought*. Cambridge, New York, Cambridge University Press, 1991.

Hovannisian, R. C., and G. Sabagh (eds.). *The Thousand and One Nights in Arabic Literature and Society*. Cambridge and New York, Cambridge University Press, 1997.

Howard, D. R. *Writers and Pilgrims: Medieval Pilgrimage Narratives*. Berkeley, University of California Press, 1980.

Ibn Battuta/H. A. R. Gibb (tr.). *The Travels of Ibn Battuta*, vols. 2, 3. Cambridge, Cambridge University Press, 1971.

———/S. Hamdun and N. King (trs.). *Ibn Battuta in Black Africa*. London, Collings, 1975.

Ibn Hazm/A. J. Arberry (tr.). *The Ring of the Dove*. New York, AMS Press, 1981.

Ibn al-Kalbi/Nabih Amin Faris (tr.). *Book of Idols*. Princeton, Princeton University Press, 1952.

Inden, R. *Imagining India*. Oxford, Basil Blackwell, 1990.

Ingham, P. C. *Sovereign Fantasies: Arthurian Romance and the Making of Britain*. Philadelphia, University of Pennsylvania Press, 2001.

Irwin, R. *The Arabian Nights, a Companion*. London and New York, Penguin, 1994.

Jacobus de Voragine/G. Ryan and H. Ripperger (trs.). *The Golden Legend of Jacobus de Voragine*. London, New York, Longmans, Green and Co., 1941.

al-Jahiz/C. Pellat (tr.). *The Life and Works of Jahiz*. Berkeley, University of California Press, 1969.

Kabbani, R. *Europe's Myths of Orient*. Bloomington, Indiana University Press, 1986.

Kay Ka'us ibn Iskandar/R. Levy (tr.). *A Mirror for Princes: The Qabusnama by Kay Ka'us ibn Iskandar*. London, the Cresset Press, 1951.

Kimble, G. H. *Geography in the Middle Ages*. London, Methuen, 1938.

Kritzeck, J. *Peter the Venerable and Islam*. Princeton, Princeton University Press, 1964.

Lawrence, B. *Shahrastani on the Indian Religions*. The Hague, Mouton, 1976.

Lewis, Bernard (tr.). *Islam from the Prophet Muhammad to the Capture of Constantinople*, vol. 2. New York, Walker, 1974.

———. *The Muslim Discovery of Europe*. New York, Norton, 1982.

Lupack, A. (ed.). *Three Middle English Charlemagne Romances*. Kalamazoo, Western Michigan University, 1990.

Lynch, K. (ed.). *Chaucer's Cultural Geography*. New York, Routledge, 2002.

Maalouf, A. *The Crusades in Arab Eyes*. New York, Schocken Books, 1985.

McNeill, W. H. *Venice, the Hinge of Europe, 1081-1797*. Chicago, University of Chicago Press, 1974.

Malti-Douglas, F. *Woman's Body, Woman's Word*. Princeton, Princeton University Press, 1991.

Mandeville, Sir John/C. W. R. D. Moseley (tr.). *The Travels of Sir John Mandeville*. Harmondsworth, Penguin, 1983.

Marco Polo/R. Latham (tr.). *The Travels of Marco Polo*. Harmondsworth, Penguin, 1958.

Marwazi, Sharaf al-Din/V. Minorsky (tr.). *Sharaf al-Din Tahir Marvazi on China, the Turks and India*. London, the Royal Asiatic Society, 1942.

Mehta, Gita. *Karma Cola, Marketing the Mystic East*. New York, Vintage International, 1996.

Menocal, M. R. *The Arabic Role in Medieval Literary History*. Philadelphia, University of Pennsylvania Press, 1987.

Metlitzki, D. *The Matter of Araby in Medieval England*. New Haven, Yale University Press, 1977.

Musawi, M. J. *Scheherazade in England*. Washington, D. C., Three Continents Press, 1981.

Netton, I. R. *Seek Knowledge: Thought and Travel in the House of Islam.* Richmond, U. K., Curzon Press, 1996.

Nizami/J. S. Meisami (tr.). *The Haft Paykar.* Oxford and New York, Oxford University Press, 1995.

Peters, E. *Christian Society and the Crusades, 1198-1229.* Philadelphia, University of Pennsylvania Press, 1971.

Petrus Alfonsi/E. Holmes, P. R. Quarrie (trs.). *The Disciplina Clericalis of Petrus Alfonsi.* Berkeley, University of California Press, 1977.

Prawer, J. *The World of the Crusaders.* New York, Quadrangle Books, 1972.

———. *The History of the Jews in the Latin Kingdom of Jerusalem.* Oxford, Clarendon Press, 1988.

Riley-Smith, J. *The Crusades, a Short History.* New Haven, Yale University Press, 1987.

Rodinson, M. *Europe and the Mystique of Islam.* Seattle, University of Washington Press, 1987.

Romm, J. S. *The Edges of the Earth in Ancient Thought.* Princeton, Princeton University Press, 1992.

Said, E. *Orientalism.* New York, Vintage, 1978. Reprinted and expanded, 1994.

al-Sharif al-Idrisi/S. Maqbul Ahmad. *India and the Neighbouring Territories.* Leiden, E.J. Brill, 1960.

Sells, M. (tr.). *Desert Tracings.* Middletown, Conn., Wesleyan University Press, 1989.

Shatzmiller, M. *Crusaders and Muslims in Twelfth-Century Syria.* Leiden and New York, E. J. Brill, 1993.

Slessarev, V. *Prester John: The Letter and the Legend.* Minneapolis, University of Minnesota Press, 1959.

Southern, R. W. *Western Views of Islam in the Middle Ages.* Cambridge, Harvard University Press, 1962.

Stillman, N. A. *The Jews of Arab Lands.* Philadelphia, Jewish Publication Society of America, 1979.

Stoneman, R. (ed. and tr.). *Legends of Alexander the Great.* London, J.M. Dent; Rutland, VT, C. E. Tuttle, 1994.

Tolan, J. V. *Petrus Alfonsi and his Medieval Readers.* Gainesville, University Press of Florida, 1993.

Tomasch, S., and S. Gilles (eds.). *Text and Territory: Geographical Imagination in the European Middle Ages.* Philadelphia, University of Pennsylvania Press, 1998.

Tusi, Nasir al-Din/G. M. Wickens. *The Nasirean Ethics*. London, George Allen and Unwin, 1964.
Usama ibn Munqidh/P. Hitti (tr.). *An Arab-Syrian Gentleman and Warrior in the Period of the Crusades*. New York, Columbia University Press, 1929.
Westrem, S. D. (ed.). *Discovering New Worlds: Essays on Medieval Exploration and Imagination*. New York, Garland, 1991.
Yule, H. *Cathay and the Way Thither: Being a Collection of Medieval Notices of China*. London, Hakluyt Society, 1913-16.
Zacher, C. *Curiosity and Pilgrimage. The Literature of Discovery in Fourteenth-Century England*. Baltimore, the Johns Hopkins University Press, 1976.

# 12

# Center and Periphery in the Teaching of Medieval History*

## *Teofilo F. Ruiz*

IN A RECENTLY PUBLISHED COLLECTION of medieval sources edited by the well-known historian, Warren Hollister, and three of his colleagues and former students, we gaze upon a history written and studied almost exclusively from the center (Hollister, Leedom and Meyer 1997). After more than three decades of feminist stirrings, after years of cultural and multi-cultural battles, the new social history and the *histoire des mentalités* promoted by *Annales* and *Past & Present*, Hollister, whose loss all medievalists mourn and who for many years set the standard for the study of English medieval history in this country, and his co-editors remain deeply wedded to political, institutional and intellectual history – by the latter I mean the old fashioned history of ideas. They remain committed as well to a geographical terrain which does not wander too far from Paris and London, the learned foci of twelfth-century western medieval Europe and until recently the centers of political power in contemporary Europe. In this predilection they do not stand alone. Their

---

*This essay was presented at a Fordham University conference on Teaching the Middle Ages shortly before my move to UCLA in 1998. Were I to deliver this paper now, my approach would have been very different and, after the experience of a heterogenous student body at UCLA, my emphasis on comparative history would have been greater. This would have meant not only comparison within Europe, but beyond Europe to include developments in China, India, Africa and the New World. My syllabus would have also looked different, reflecting the strong Hispanic presence in Los Angeles, and the historical resources of the area.

selections, in fact, reflect accurately the manner in which medieval history has been taught in the United States for more than a century.

What makes this collection so remarkable, however, is its dogged determination to give only token representation, very token indeed, to sources which may illuminate the lives of women, of the poor, or of areas other than England and France. We may, to paraphrase Jacques Le Goff, but in a different key, call this the other Middle Ages.

And Hollister et al. are not alone. The general textbooks, including Hollister's own textbook, from which our students learn or – if one is truly perverse, do not really learn or learn only incompletely – address materials from the geographical and social peripheries of privileged cultures only as adjuncts to their central narrative. What I mean by this is that the history of women, of marginalized social, ethnic and religious groups, of the Mediterranean lands, of Scandinavia and eastern Europe become excursus to a central narrative. The main concern of this normative history is to tell the story of those areas and people in the Middle Ages that went on to establish their hegemony over Europe and over the world in a later age. This is Whiggish history at its very best, in which the past is seen only as a prelude to an imperial present.

We are too familiar with Walter Benjamin's short and beautiful allegory on the angel of history not to realize that what we call progress, that is, the march into history of privileged western powers, is not as rosy as we once thought (Benjamin 1969, 257-58). Moreover, if we are going to be really Whiggish historians, then we should be studying the history of medieval Spain over time, because from 1494 almost to the defeat of the Spanish *tercios* at Rocroi in 1643, Spain was truly the world's first superpower. Moreover, Spain and Italy, neglected orphans at the table of history through great segments of their national past, hold more promise today as industrial nations and appear to be moving far more successfully into the next century than England, mired as it is in endless social and economic troubles.

For all I am saying, however, I am not advocating a dismissal of the canonical sources in medieval historiography. I certainly would not wish to teach from a reader or a text book that does not include excerpts from

Aquinas or Dante, or that would ignore Paris for the sake of Prague or even Madrid, or give short shrift to Martin Luther for the sake of Martin Guerre. We should have the latter without forgetting the former. How, then, are we to accomplish this and what are the obstacles in our paths?

*Teaching the peripheries from the center*

It is obvious to all of us that there is often a wide gulf between what we write and publish as scholars, that is, the research we do, the books we read, the kind of methodologies we follow and the history we teach in the classrooms. To some extent, I too am guilty of these charges. We make brave attempts to integrate our research and writing into our curriculum but often fail in doing so, or succeed only partially. In introductory courses of the Middle Ages, above all, we may feel the need not to neglect the "basics," that is to say, the master political narrative of western medieval history: the rise of Christianity, barbarian invasions, monastic reform, Investiture Controversy, Crusades, the rise of cities, the rise of feudal monarchies, the cultural revival of the twelfth century and, as a fitting and Whiggish conclusion, the genesis of the nation-state. Consciously or unconsciously, we have privileged one kind of history over another and one kind of people over other kinds. And dare I add, one class or social group over another? I do not have to remind you that for peasants in medieval Europe, probably more than ninety per cent of the population, the accomplishments of the University of Paris or the *Romance of the Rose* meant absolutely nothing and would not have any kind of impact on their descendants' lives until very recently. The transactions of kings and popes, of learned scholars paled when compared to the peasants' vital needs for rain and good crops, and their scant hope of relief from the unending brutality and horror of their daily lives. Most of the brutality and horror, one should add, was inflicted on them by powerful ecclesiastical or lay lords. Yet, we usually begin our descriptions of the social order – at least most textbooks do – with those on top.

We also – or should I say, I – fail to teach what I know and write about because I/we often lack the materials with which to teach.

Recently the University of Pennsylvania Press has published a collection of translated primary sources on Iberian history. Edited by Olivia Constable, the book contains material from Islamic, Jewish and Christian sources, seeking to provide an entry into the cultural, religious, ethnic and politic plurality of the medieval Spanish kingdoms (Constable 1997). As commendable as this enterprise is, however, we have had to wait until the eve of the new millennium for such tools to become available. No such collections are available, or at least not fully, for Scandinavia, eastern Europe, southern Italy or North Africa.

And, worse yet, we often do not trust our students in introductory courses with material that appears to us as too complex, too exotic or that demands the synthesizing of diverse historical perspectives. How much easier it is to present a narrative of comforting and familiar historical highlights that follows the well-trodden path laid out by our elders. However, we do this at our own peril and at the peril of our students. And to continue to follow along this road only exacerbates some of the problems and prejudices imbedded in our traditional histories.

*Center and periphery*

We must begin by recognizing that we are, as the French structuralists and deconstructionists have argued, prisoners of language, and by employing and accepting such concepts as center and periphery, we are already admitting to a hierarchy, not only in terms of culture and historical significance, but, far more important, in terms of power. Why should Paris be a center to a Spanish periphery? It can only be so if we look at history and the world from the perspective of Paris, but not if we are to look at medieval history from the perspective of Córdoba, which by the year 1000 was a highly civilized place, a center for higher learning, when Paris still enjoyed a rough village life. Or, let's look at the world from the perspective of eighth-century Ireland, still a lively center for Late Antique culture at a time when learning throughout most of the medieval West was almost extinguished. Our new medieval history has to set aside some of these cultural, geographical and political hierarchies and attempt an integrated vision of the Middle Ages from a variety of perspectives.

To restate the case, medieval history as presently taught throughout most of the United States is done from the perspective, often the exclusive perspective, of Paris, London and, in the specific case of papal reform and the Investiture Controversy, Rome. Notwithstanding the longstanding and accurate critique of Pirenne's classic formulation on the shift of European culture from the Mediterranean to the north, medieval historiography continues to follow Pirenne, as if more than half a century of new historical learning has not taken place. We have to stop thinking of some historical entities as centers and others as peripheries. Doing so relegates some important aspects of Europe's history to a secondary role, while privileging others.

To return to an earlier example, I think that comparing Córdoba or Baghdad in the ninth, tenth and even the fabled twelfth century to Paris, London or even a Christian city in northern Spain would come as a severe shock to students brought up on the "oriental" vision of Islam and on the hegemonic culture of the West. The comparison, however, cannot be a passing reference to Córdoba's greatness or Baghdad's magnificence which the students may conveniently forget or set aside, but rather a detailed description of that other world and a full contextualizing of medieval history. By the same token, we cannot read Janet Abu-Lughod's suggestive book, *Before European Hegemony: The World System, A.D. 1250-1350*, without realizing to what an extent the partial collapse of the Silk Road and of eastern trade affected and transformed western European life, or without thinking of the importance of Africa as a supplier of gold for the European economy until the opening of the Atlantic (Abu-Lughod 1989).

Since I do not wish to be accused of a southern bias, one should think of the role of Scandinavia's social, demographic and economic transformations in the eighth, ninth and tenth centuries and the impact of the Northmen expansion into France, England, Sicily and Russia. One cannot understand the dynamic creativity of the Normans as they settled in Normandy, England, Sicily and Kievan Rus without full reference to

Scandinavian society and culture. Yet, few of us are really capable of discussing those developments with authority, and our textbooks and sources certainly do not do so satisfactorily.

There are also various kinds of center-and-periphery hierarchies. Hegemonic cultures have their centers and their peripheries, and neglected cultures have their centers and peripheries as well. There are geographical peripheries and centers, and there are social and economic peripheries and centers. Of geographical hierarchies, think of the history of France as told almost exclusively from the perspective of Paris and remember how much we know about Britanny, Gascony or even the Languedoc. Or think of Madrid as compared to Galicia. How very different the history of Spain in the sixteenth century would read if written from the perspective of Catalonia or Mexico.

The other center/margin dynamic is social. For all the lip service we pay to social history, we seldom attempt to engage our students in the history of the lower social groups, peasants, urban workers, or in the history of marginal groups, though marginality has its alluring qualities and runs well in the classroom. A good number of recent books serve as models of what and how we could be teaching our students. That is, by placing our story into a comparative framework, they study important issues in medieval history from a diversity of social and geographical perspectives. I am thinking of William C. Jordan's study of the 1315-1317 famine. Jordan reconstructs peasant life, beliefs, animal husbandry and climatic changes as context for the attempts by royal and local authorities to deal with the onslaught of hunger. His book casts a wide net over all of northern Europe and studies the famine from a truly comparative perspective. Understanding the famine in Scandinavian realms becomes as important as understanding its impact in France (Jordan 1996).

David Nirenberg's exciting book, *Communities of Violence*, focuses on intrareligious violence between Muslims, Christian and Jews in fourteenth-century Aragon with a comparative excursus across the Pyrenees. A tour de force, Nirenberg's book brings to light the complex world of religious beliefs, sectarian antagonisms, compromise and violence. It is history written from below and from a so-called geographic periphery; yet, it is very good history, gripping, moving and a novel way of seeing and learning about the other Middle Ages (Nirenberg 1996). I think students, even in introductory courses, will be delighted with such books and will leave our classrooms with a completely different feel for the Middle Ages and, by extension, for their own world than they would from reading the description of the coronation of Charlemagne for the umpteenth time. In the same line, Robert Bartlett's wonderful *The Making of Europe* is an equally formidable reformulation of European medieval history, this time perceived from its eastern borders (Bartlett 1994).

## How to teach the new Middle Ages

I have long thought of myself as a historian of the obvious; that is, what I publish, it seems to me, articulates what everyone already knows. So it is with these recommendations and suggestions, which many of you may say to yourselves: "but I already do that," or "I do even better than that."

First, we must all work to change the books we use in the classrooms, the documents we read or to supplement these sources with new ones that offer a more nuanced understanding of the variegated history of the Middle Ages. There are signs of a growing sensitivity to such an approach. Edward Peters's *Europe in the Middle Ages* shows a willingness to include material from most parts of Europe and to set it in a comparative mold (Peters 1997). But when our expertise is lacking or the available books do not do the job, then there is always someone in our own institutions or nearby who might not be reluctant – in fact might be very glad – to lend her or his knowledge to others. What I am suggesting here is not only an inclusive and integrated teaching of the Middle Ages but also a cooperative and interdisciplinary one, a teaching whereby we have scholars in other fields or geographical areas bring to our students and to ourselves as well their particular perception and expertise. We must move from under the shadow of prescribed textbooks, because they have such tremendous impacts on our students and, of course, on ourselves. Long ago I chose to go to Princeton because I had learned about the Middle Ages and feudalism from the grand old Strayer and Munro text book. All my graduate seminars at Princeton were on Philip the Fair, and I was trained as a French institutional historian. Fortunately for me, Strayer was a nurturing and liberal master, who encouraged his students to follow other paths. His encouragement of other types of history, the influence of the Davis Center and of the École des Hautes Études have made my work look very different today from what it was twenty years ago.

Nonetheless, the influence of textbooks has proved as enduring as the methodological approaches and biases emphasized in undergraduate teaching. Recently I taught a graduate course on violence, festivals and marginality in late medieval Europe. We read many different texts in class, from Spanish, Italian, French and English primary sources to the latest monographic literature on these topics to Foucault, Geertz, literary theory et al. Two students walked out of the class, angrily contending that this was not history. If this was the history taught today, they added, they wanted nothing to do with it. After all, they just wished to work on imperial policies during the Investiture Controversy. I am not in the least a fan of postmodernism, but I am convinced that in the same manner in which we must study places other than the feudal nobility and social groups other than the clergy and the nobility, so must we also begin changing what our students read, and what we ourselves read.

In addition, we must constantly bring our students face to face, in direct contact with, the artifacts of medieval culture, both high and low. We must expose them not only to music and art, the usual slide show of Gothic cathedrals or the playing of Gregorian chants, but to an array of historical material that is diverse and down to earth. Listening to the music of the *Cantigas de Santa María*, with its rich Muslim and Jewish cadences – Mediterranean in fact – or looking at the illuminations that accompany the text of the *Cantigas* does far more for the students' understanding of multiculturalism in medieval Spain than a long lecture. Holding in their hands an eight-hundred-year-old manuscript, a medieval sword or ax, a miniature reproduction of a medieval plow leads to an understanding of material culture which cannot be learned solely by reading. Young students and not so young students are always impressed by the age of these artifacts and, even more so, by being able to hold them in their hands. We all have some small treasure at home, some item we purchased long ago (probably, as in my case) at an intolerable price for a graduate student's or young instructor's budget. But we sacrificed and bought a leaf of a manuscript, an old book, because we remembered the first thrill of working with a manuscript, the extraordinary experience of touching the very heart of history. That is precisely the feeling we must communicate to and instill in our students, if we wish to engage them fully into learning about the Middle Ages. Trust me, if your illuminated parchment or lead seal survived the Middle Ages, rapacious noblemen, rebelling peasants, rats and war, it will also survive your students' handling.

We must also take them out of the classroom. New York is a wonderful laboratory for exploring the enduring influence of medieval culture and social forms. Medieval themes are present in many aspects of our culture and material life. Beyond the great museums of the city, the Cloisters and the Met above all, there are the borrowing of Romanesque, Gothic, Islamic and Jewish architectural forms. Think of Cass Gilbert's great Woolworth building or of the great mosque on 3rd Ave and 96th street or, in the neighborhoods, the flower district, the diamond district, etc, which, like medieval towns, reproduce the agglomeration of trades in one quarter.

There is more we can do. James Powers and Lorraine Attreed discuss in *Perspectives* the use of movies in the teaching of medieval history (Attreed and Powers 1997). Among the films recommended was not just the classical "The Lion in Winter," but also a science-fiction film, "Voyager. An Odyssey in Time," depicting the brutal life of peasants in Cumbria on the eve of the Black Death. T. K. Rabb's piece in *Perspectives* is a good guide as to how to deploy these films and visual material for educational purposes (Rabb 1997). Most of all, we must begin to teach medieval history from a multigeographical, multisocial perspective. We must include the histories of people who have been neglected, perceived as adjuncts or taught only as special topics or exotic examples. And this teaching must be done not just from Paris and London, but from the borders and frontiers of medieval life; not just from the perspective of hegemonic groups but from the viewpoint of those on the margins of society as well.

## REFERENCES

Abu-Lughod, J. L. 1980. *Before European Hegemony. The World System, A.D. 1250-1350*. Oxford: Oxford University Press.

Attreed, L., and J. F. Powers. 1997. Lessons in the Dark: Teaching the Middle Ages with Film. *Perspectives* 35 (January): 11-16.

Bartlett, R. 1993. *The Making of Europe. Conquest, Colonization and Cultural Change 950-1350*. Princeton: Princeton University Press.

Benjamin, W. 1969. *Illuminations. Essays and Reflections*. Ed. Hannah Arendt. New York: Schocken.

Constable, O. R., ed. 1997. *Medieval Iberia. Readings from Christian, Muslim, and Jewish Sources*. Philadelphia: University of Pennsylvania Press.

Hollister, C. W., J. W. Leedom, M. A. Meyer, D. S. Spear. 1997. *Medieval Europe. A Short Sourcebook*. 3rd ed. New York: The McGraw-Hill Companies, Inc.

Jordan, W. C. 1996. *The Great Famine. Northern Europe in the Early Fourteenth Century*. Princeton: Princeton University Press.

Nirenberg, D. 1996. *Communities of Violence. Persecution of Minorities in the Middle Ages*. Princeton: Princeton University Press.

Peters, E. 1997. *Europe and the Middle Ages*. 3rd ed. Saddle River: Prentice-Hall.

Rabb, T. K. 1997. The Uses of Film in the Teaching of History: Results of a National Workshop. *Perspectives* 35 (March): 35-36.

APPENDIX
Sample Syllabus (UCLA: History 121D)
Crisis and Renewal: From Late Medieval to Early Modern, 1300-1525

Originally, this article included a sample syllabus for a broad survey of medieval history. In it, I sought to integrate some of the ideas that I have discussed in my essay. Since writing the piece, I have been teaching at the University of California at Los Angeles, and the experience – teaching an exceedingly diverse student body, most of them of non-western origin – has further convinced me of the need to provide a multi-perspectival approach to the teaching of history in general and to that of the Middle Ages in particular. This new syllabus describes a course which focus on the late Middle Ages. Without sacrificing some of the central themes of late medieval history: the crisis of late medieval society, the intellectual contributions of the Italian Renaissance, or neglecting to include traditional readings, it also provides extensive coverage of the Iberian peninsula, of religious minorities, and of the encounter between the Old World and the New. The Course Reader, which supplements the reading list, includes substantial portions of Chaucer's *Canterbury Tales* (for a discussion of women and social difference), all of Dante's *Inferno*, Cortés' third letter from Mexico to Charles V and Aztec accounts of the conquest of Mexico. The course makes a liberal use of movies, fiction and the numerous museums in the Los Angeles area.

A. COURSE DESCRIPTION

This course examines the crises of late medieval society (widespread famines in 1315-17, wars, plagues, popular rebellions), and the manner in which, during the fourteenth and fifteenth centuries, men and women responded to these crises by formulating new concepts of love, art, religion and political organization. The emphasis throughout is not on a sustained political narrative; my aim, rather, is to explore the structures of late medieval society and show how the society, economy and culture were transformed and refashioned by the upheavals besetting Europe at the onset of modernity. Thus, in tracing the response to economic, political and social crises, we will also chart the transition from the medieval to the modern.

*Web Site*

Through the use of a password (to be given on the first day of classes), you may access a class web site. There you will find copies of the syllabus, outlines, assignments, images and music. More importantly, you may access the readings included in the Course Reader, read them on line, download and print them.

*Requirements*

A mid-term exam (all essays), 30%. A short paper (between 8 and 10 pages) or performance (please see accompanying paper description), 30%. A final exam, 40%. The final exam is not cumulative. Class attendance and participation will be rewarded. The final exam will be offered as either a take-home or in-class exam. No web site to be used in papers or exams.

*Required Readings* (all paperbacks)

Boccaccio, Giovanni. *The Decameron*. Penguin Books.
Burckhardt, Jacob. *The Civilization of the Renaissance in Italy.* Harper.
Froissart, Jean. *The Chronicles*. Penguin Books.
Hay, Denys. *Europe in the Fourteenth and Fifteenth Centuries.* Longman.
Huizinga, Johan. *The Autumn of the Middle Ages.* Chicago.
Malory, Thomas. *Le morte d'Arthur*. Penguin Books.
There will also be a short Course Reader to be purchased at Ackerman Student Union's Bookstore.

*Strongly Suggested*

Allmand, Christopher. *The Hundred Years War: England and France at War, c. 1300-c.1450.*
Aston, T. H., and C. H. E. Philpin, eds. *The Brenner Debate: Agrarian Class Structure and Economic Development on Pre-Industrial Europe.*
Brucker, Gene. *Florentine Politics and Society, 1343-1378.*
Burke, Peter. *The Italian Renaissance. Culture and Society in Italy.*
Chaucer, Geoffrey. *The Canterbury Tales.*
de Commynes, Phillippe. *Mémoires.*
Dante. *The Divine Comedy*, vol. 1: *Inferno.*
Dobson, R. B., ed. *The Peasants' Revolt of 1381.*
Duby, Georges. *The Three Orders. Feudal Society Imagined.*

———. *Rural Economy and Country Life in the Medieval West.*

———. *The Knight, the Lady, and the Priest: The Making of Modern Marriage in Medieval France.*

Fernández-Armesto, Felipe. *Before Columbus. Exploration and Colonization from the Mediterranean to the Atlantic, 1229-1492.*

Foucault, Michel. *Discipline and Punish: The Birth of the Prison.*

Freedman, Paul H. *The Origins of Peasant Servitude in Medieval Catalonia.*

Geremek, Bronislaw, *The Margins of Society in Late Medieval Paris.*

Gies, Frances and Joseph. *Marriage and the Family in the Middle Ages.*

Ginzburg, Carlo. *Ecstasies. Deciphering the Witches' Sabbath.*

Hanawalt, Barbara, and Kathryn Reyerson, eds. *City and Spectacle in Medieval Europe.*

Hilton, R.H., and T.H. Aston. *The English Rising of 1381.*

Holmes, George. *Europe: Hierarchy and Revolt, 1320-1450.*

Jordan, William C. *The Great Famine: Northern Europe in the Early Fourteenth Century.*

Keen, Maurice. *Chivalry.*

Leff, Gordon. *Paris and Oxford Universities in the Thirteenth and Fourteenth Centuries.*

Mollat, Michel. *The Poor in the Middle Ages.*

———, and Phillippe Wolff. *The Popular Revolutions of the Late Middle Ages.*

Mullett, Michael. *Popular Culture and Popular Protest in Late Medieval and Early Modern Europe.*

Nirenberg, David. *Communities of Violence.*

Perroy, Edouard. *The Hundred Years War.*

Phillips, William D., and Carla Rahn. *The Worlds of Christopher Columbus.*

Rörig, Fritz. *The Medieval Town.*

Ruiz, Teofilo F. *Spanish Society, 1400-1600.*

———. *Crisis and Continuity.*

Ziegler, Philip. *The Black Death.*

B. WRITING ASSIGNMENT

Please note carefully. Web sites cannot be used for either papers or exams. We will monitor all assignments, and material pasted from web sites will not be accepted. You must write a paper in this class. The requirement can be fulfilled in different ways. Choose one of these options:

1. A close reading of one or two of the primary sources assigned as books (Boccaccio's *Decameron,* Froissart's *Chronicles* or from the additional bibliography) or from excerpts in the Course Reader. If you have questions about this assignment please do come to see me to explain it. Paper should be eight pages or longer.

2. A research paper. If you are interested in medieval history or literature, are proficient in foreign languages, and plan to apply to graduate school in a field related to the Middle Ages, I will consider working with you on a research paper. If you decide to attempt a research paper, you should discuss this with me no later than the second week of the term. No research paper will be allowed after the third week. A research paper should be between fifteen and twenty pages.

3. A performance. Music, dancing, theatrical representation, photography, website construction, or any other artistic or creative endeavors. Performances will be presented on the last day of classes.

4. Your paper may also be a report on a visit to three museums to see art from the fourteenth, fifteenth, and early sixteenth centuries. You must do more than just describe the paintings or sculptures. You must develop a thesis, argue a point, and do so from a comparative perspective in which you compare art work from three different museums. Eight pages or more.

5. You may also write a paper based on the reading of two works of fiction (related to the period we are describing). I will circulate a list of possible titles. Eight pages or more.

6. You may also write a paper on very specific movies. I will pass a list of movies which may be used for your paper on the first week of the term. Eight pages or more.

C. LECTURE OUTLINES

*Lecture 1. Europe in 1300*

Required readings: Hay, *Europe in the Fourteenth and Fifteenth Centuries,* chaps. 1, 2 & 3; Course Reader, Week One. Strongly suggested: Holmes, *Europe: Hierarchy and Revolt;* Jordan, *The Great Famine,* chaps. 1 & 2; *The Brenner Debate.*

The objective of this introductory lecture is to familiarize students with how historians are able to reconstruct the past, what type of sources we use and from what perspective or perspectives we examine the extant literary, iconographic and historical evidence. This first lecture will also set the geographical, linguistic, archival and historiographical contexts for the course, and will seek to reconstruct how medieval men and women imagined their society. In addition, I wish to introduce the manner in which medieval men and women saw and represented themselves on the eve of the great crises of late medieval society.

I. Introduction: towards a definition of crisis
   Historians and historical crisis: how to create a field (the new social history), literary and documentary sources, new ways of reading evidence
II. Background: Europe at the beginning of the XIVth century
   A. Geography, language, sources: the formation of linguistic and geographical borders, from local to regional to national, secular and ecclesiastic record-keeping, private records, biographies
   B. The political setting at the beginning of the XIVth Century
III. Patterns: medieval society imagined
   Social hierarchies and the crown: those who work, those who pray, those who fight

*Lecture 2. Europe in 1300: Rural Society*

   Required readings: Hay, chap. 4. Strongly suggested: Ruiz, *Crisis and Continuity*.

I. The social, political, and economic structure of western Europe in 1300: the peasantry
   A. The peasantry's life cycle: how did the peasants live in 1300? How did they cultivate the soil? What did they grow? What was their relation to the lords? To the church?
   B. Changes in productivity and agriculture: towards a new concept of property, the rise of a money economy, the village community and its transformation after 1300, the village and the peasant family
   C. The breakdown of the village community: "class" differences among the peasants, privatizing the commons

II. Lordship and peasantry in western Europe: the impact of rural change on western society
    The Brenner thesis and its critics, rural change as a cause of the late medieval crisis
III. Peasant society at the onset of the crisis: peasant lives and the village community

*Lecture 3. Europe in 1300: City Life and the Bourgeoisie*

I. The social, political, and economic structure of western Europe in 1300: the bourgeoisie
    A. The bourgeoisie on the eve of the crisis: the origins and development of urban life
    B. Cities in medieval life: industry, commerce and agriculture in European towns
II. The relation of the bourgeoisie to other groups in society
    A. Town and crown
    B. The bourgeois and the workers: the rise of a mercantile society, God's time and merchant's time
    C. The new spirituality (an urban phenomenon): the poor in late medieval society, marginality, the nobility and the cities
III. Changes in mentality
    A. Charity and welfare: a new attitude towards poverty (voluntary and involuntary poverty)
    B. The intellectual life of towns: the universities
    C. Civic life and art: the Italian experiment

*Lecture 4. Church, State and Learning*

    Required readings: Hay, chaps. 4, 5 & 6. Strongly suggested: Holmes, chaps. 2 & 4.

I. The church in 1300
    A. The king and church: the Sicilian Vespers (1282), Anagni (1303)
    B. Mendicants, inquisition, and heresy
II. The state and the rise of the nation
    Thaumaturgical kingship, sacred kingship (France), non-sacred kingship (Castile), the king and his agents

III. Learning in 1300
  A. The universities (philosophy and theology): the medieval synthesis (Aquinas), the modern way (Ockham), questioning Aristotle
  B. The end of the medieval spring

*Lecture 5. Famine and War*

Required readings: begin to read Froissart's *Chronicles;* Course Reader, Week Two. Strongly suggested: Jordan (complete); Holmes, chap.1.

I. The famines of 1315-21
  A. The problem of hunger: the impact of hunger on European society, hunger and politics, demographic change (Malthusian pressure or structural crisis?), hunger and religion, hunger and crime
  B. The question of cannibalism: towards an anthropology of medieval history, myths and realities
  C. Dealing with the crisis: the failure of medieval government, the failure of prayer
  D. The end of famine: the road to recovery
II. War: the Hundred Years War
  A. The beginning of the Hundred Years War: from dynastic to global war, feudal or national?, suzerainty and sovereignty
  B. France and England in 1337: political conditions, economic and social conditions, dynastic issues

*Lecture 6. The Four Horsemen of the Apocalypse: War (continued)*

Required readings: Hay, chap. 6; Froissart (continue); Introduction to Boccaccio's *Decameron*; Course Reader, Week Three; begin to read Malory's *Le morte d'Arthur*. Strongly suggested: Allmand, *The Hundred Years War*; Ziegler, *The Black Death* (complete).

I. The Hundred Years War: its social, political and economic impact on European society
  The disasters of the war, Froissart's account, warfare and social change, new weapons and military technology (the long bow, gunpowder, canons, siege technology)
II. Chivalry and literature: fantasy and reality
  The revival of romance, the cruelty of the war

III. The English in France
   A. Crécy, Poitiers, Agincourt: king of Paris, king of Bourges
   B. The recovery: Jeanne d'Arc
IV. From feudal monarchies to nations
   A. The making of France and England
   B. The end of the conflict: the road towards modernity (Tudor and Valois)

*Lecture 7. The Four Horsemen of the Apocalypse: The Black Death*

I. Pestilence: the coming of the Black Death to Europe
   A. The Black Death: origins and etiology
   B. The impact of the plague: how and where the plague spread, mortality figures (how many people died?)
   C. Case studies: samples from western Europe
II. Social and cultural responses to the plague
   A. The plague and apocalyptic movements: the flagellants
   B. The plague, the Jews and the lepers
   C. New spirituality, new devotions: the church and the aftermath of the plague
III. Politics and economy after the Black Death
   The rise of "new" men, wage and price controls, towards new restrictions on the peasantry, the world of those who survived, the return of the plague

*Lecture 8. The Four Horsemen of the Apocalypse: Popular Rebellions*

Required readings: Hay, chaps. 3 & 4; Froissart, *Chronicles*; Course Reader, Week Four. Strongly suggested: Mollat & Wolff, *The Popular Revolutions of the Late Middle Ages*; Hilton and Aston, *The English Rising of 1381*.

I. Popular revolts in late medieval Europe
   A. Towards an understanding of revolution: falling feudal rents, rising taxes (a scramble for money)
   B. Fraticelli agitation: the question of property
II. Peasant uprisings: the cry of the countryside
   A. The "common people," the "lean folks": 1323-28, rebellion of the Karls; 1356-58, the *Jacquerie*
   B. 1381, the English Peasant Revolt: Wat Tyler, John Ball
   C. Catalonia: the war of the *remenças*, 1462-85

III. Urban revolutions: bourgeois and proletarian
   A. Blue Nails, the cry of the proletariat: Cola di Rienzi (1313-1354); Étienne Marcel and urban revolt in Paris; 1378, the rise of the *Ciompi*
   B. Demagogues and others: Salvestro de Medici
   C. Proto-capitalists in a changing world: rich and poor (the growth of social distinction)
   D. Discourses of difference and otherness
IV. The final outcome
   The victory of those on top, representations of the victims

*Lecture 9. The Answers of Late Medieval Society: Politics*

Required readings: Hay, chaps. 5, 6, 7 & 8; Burckhardt, *The Civilization of the Renaissance*, Part I; Course Reader, Week Four. Strongly suggested: Holmes, chaps. 4, 6 & 7.

I. Politics, ideas and the nation
   A. The ideological context: the recovery of Aristotle, the naturalness of the state, the contributions of Aquinas, Dante's *De Monarchia*
   B. Marsilio de Padua's *The Defender of Peace*: formulating concepts of sovereignty, church and king
   C. Bartolus (*quod omnes tangit*)
II. Taxation and the makings of the state
   The new structures of government, the "Defense of the Realm," "*Pro patria mori*"
III. The Avignon papacy
   The Babylonian captivity, the conciliar movement
IV. The Italian answer
   The state as a work of art; tyrants, republicans and oligarch; patronage (legitimization by art)
V. A positive balance: the value of work

*Lecture 10. The Answer of Late Medieval Society: Politics*

Required readings: Hay, chap. 6; Course Reader, Week Five. Strongly suggested: Ruiz, *Crisis and Continuity;* Ruiz, *Spanish Society*, chaps. 1-4. Freedman, *The Origins of Peasant Servitude*.

I. A case study: Castile at the end of the fifteenth century
   A. Castile and Spain in the late Middle Ages: the civil war, alienation of the royal domain
   B. Society and economy before the Catholic Monarchs: the Mesta, feudal rents, income from the Jews, *montazgo y portazgo*
II. The reign of Ferdinand and Isabella
   A. The restoration of order: the Santa Hermandad
   B. Economic recovery
   C. Dealing with the aristocracy: the return of the military orders, restoration of the royal domain, the nobility as servants of the state, an uneasy compromise, the making of a bureaucracy
   D. The conquest of Granada and national unity
   E. Spain in Europe
   F. The discovery of the New World

*Lecture 11. The Answer of Late Medieval Society: Culture and Mentality I*

Required readings: Hay, chap. 13; Course Reader, Week Six; Burckhardt, Parts II, III & IV; Boccaccio, *Decameron*. Strongly suggested: Holmes, chap. 8; Burke, *The Italian Renaissance* (complete).

I. The world of Dante: learning in the late Middle Ages
   The universities, the seven liberal arts, letters and arms
II. The coming of the Renaissance
   A. The Renaissance in Italy: origins, lay education, study of the humanities, rhetoric and the classics
   B. Petrarch, the birth of humanism: the sonnet, Cicero's and Augustine's shadows
III. Art and reality in Renaissance Italy
   A. Giotto and his world: frescos in the Arena chapel (Padua), saints' lives in the Bardi and Peruzzi chapels of the church of Santa Croce (Florence)
   B. Realism vs. symbolism and allegory
IV. The new humanism
   Lorenzo Valla and philology, Pico della Mirandola ("Oration on the Dignity of Man")

*Lecture 12. The Answer of Late Medieval Society: Culture and Mentality II*

Required readings: Hay, chaps. 12 & 13; Burckhardt, Parts IV & VI; begin to read Huizinga, *The Autumn of the Middle Ages*; begin to read Malory, *Le morte d'Arthur*.

I. Art and literature
   A. Two cultures: Italy and the north
   B. The "waning of the Middle Ages"
   C. Huizinga's vision: art and death in northern Europe, the violent tenor of life
   D. Morbidity and religion
   E. The revival of courtly love: towards a new vision of love, misogyny in *Le Morte d'Arthur*

II. The secularization of medieval society
   A. The secularization of politics: the rise of the state, towards Machiavelli
   B. The secularization of art: pagan motifs in Renaissance art, the centrality of the human figure
   C. The secularization of economics: the birth of capitalism
   D. The secularization of learning: science (the revival of skepticism), printing and reading

*Lecture 13. The Answer of Late Medieval Society: Love, Sexuality, Marriage and Misogyny I*

Required readings: Boccaccio, *Decameron;* Huizinga, chaps. 8, 9 & 10; Malory, *Le morte d'Arthur*; Course Reader, Week Seven.

I. Love, marriage, family and misogyny in late medieval Europe
   A. Courtly love: the courtly tradition, the courtly tradition condemned, the courtly tradition remade
   B. The church's position on love, sexuality and marriage: celibacy and the body, ecclesiastical ideas on marriage

II. The transformation of love
   A. The naturalness of love in Boccaccio's *Decameron*: the return of the repressed, love and anti-clerical stories, the Black Death and new concepts of sexuality

B. Love and marriage: medieval attacks on marriage, love as an escape, the subversiveness of sexuality
C. Mystic love
III. The world of Chaucer
   A. *Amor vincit omnia*
   B. The power of love in "The Knight's Tale"
   C. Sexuality, marriage and love in "The Miller's Tale"
   D. Marriage in "The wife of Bath's Tale" and in "The Franklin's Tale": rape and punishment, women on top, women as objects, marriage as a union of equals

*Lecture 14. The Answer of Late Medieval Society: Love, Sexuality, Marriage and Misogyny II*

Required readings: Hay, chap. 12; Course Reader, Week Seven.

I. Western attitudes towards women
   A. The making of misogyny: classical roots, the books of Genesis as normative texts, patristic literature, the awful revolution (spirit and flesh)
   B. The history of women in the central Middle Ages: from courtly love to witch craze
II. The origins of the witch craze
   A. Religion, science, magic
   B. Fear in the west: the rise of the state, economic change, the end of the village community
   C. The question of gender
   D. The question of Satan
   E. The *Malleus Maleficarum*: *Summa desiderantes affectibus* (1484), mountain vs. plain, the christianization of Europe, survival of agrarian cults
III. Representations of evil
   Child murder, cannibalism, sexual orgies, myths and realities

*Lecture 15. Religion and Marginality: A Case Study*

Required readings: Course Reader, Week Eight. Strongly suggested: Geremek, *The Margins of Society*.

I. Marginality
   Towards a definition of the marginal, marginality in the Middle Ages and in the Early Modern Period, towards a typology of marginality
II. Inventing otherness, revisited
   Recent critics of "persecuting societies": David Nirenberg's *Communities of Violence*; woman as other; gender and age
III. Jews, *Conversos*, Muslims and Christians
   A. Jewish life in the Peninsula: the events of 1391; conversion, assimilation and resistance, anti-*converso* riots
   B. The guardians of orthodoxy: representations of self, representations of others
   C. The inquisition: the inquisition and royal policy, dealing with the *conversos*, the edict of expulsion

*Lecture 16. The Answer of Late Medieval Society: Royal Entries, Festivals, Carnival and the Theatre of Power. The Blending of High and Popular Culture*

   Required readings: Huizinga, chaps. 4, 5 & 6; Burckhardt, Parts V & VI; Course Reader, Week Eight. Strongly suggested: Mikhail Bakhtin, *Rabelais and His World.*

I. Chivalry
   The military ethos of society, arms and letters, a Castilian case study (the myth of the Reconquest, a society organized for war), the idea of fame (Jorge Manrique)
II. Royal entries
   A. King and city, king and people, city and countryside, liminality
   B. A Castilian case study: the entry of Fernando de Antequera (1410), princely entries (Briviesca), royal entries (Jaen, 1460s)
III. Festivals and power
   A. Calendrical and non-calendrical festivities, festivals as theaters and sites of power, discourses of hegemony, color symbolism
   B. A Castilian case study: Valladolid (May 1428); Jaén and the constable Don Miguel Lucas de Iranzo
IV. Carnival
   A. Carnival as subversion, carnival as a site for hegemonic discourses, the nature of power
   B. A Castilian case study: carnivals in Jaén, carnival as revolution

*Lecture 17. Books of Chivalry and Knights-Errant*

Required readings: Malory (finish reading *La morte d'Arthur*); finish reading Froissart; Course Reader, Week Nine.

I. Fiction and reality
II. Deeds of chivalry
III. *Pas d'armes*
IV. A Castilian case study
   *El Victorial*, Suero de Quiñones, the impact of *Amadís de Gaula*, self-fashioning and representation
V. Books of chivalry in the New World: Bernal Díaz del Castillo

*Lecture 18. The End of the Middle Ages and the Beginnings of Modernity*

Required readings: Hay, chaps. 14 & 15; complete reading Burckhardt and Huizinga; Course Reader, Week Ten. Strongly suggested: Phillips, *The Worlds of Christopher Columbus;* Fernández-Armesto, *Before Columbus.*

I. The birth of a new age
   The Ottoman Turks, the fall of Constantinople (1453), the exile of Greek classical scholars (Marsilio Ficino and the Platonic Academy, the reception of skepticism and Epicurean philosophy)
II. The coming of mysteries
   The reception of Hermes Trismegistus, the search for the Deep Past, the end of the Italian experiment, 1494 (Italy invaded by the barbarians), the Sack of Rome
III. The Renaissance in the north: Erasmus

*Lecture 19. The Expansion of Western Europe*

I. Military, economic and religious rivalry between Christendom and Islam
   The kingdom of Prester John, the Portuguese capture of Ceuta (1415), the opening of the Atlantic (the Canary Islands), the spice trade
II. New technological developments
   A. Knowledge of geography and astronomy: Pierre d'Ailly's *Imago Mundi*, maps and sea charts, sailing by the Pole Star, astrolabes and sailing south of the Equator, Abraham Zacuto's *O regimento do astrolabo*

B. Ship building in the Atlantic: the world of Henry the Navigator, the *caravela redonda*, broadside cannon fire
C. The Portuguese in Africa
D. Vasco da Gama and the voyage to India

*Lecture 20. The Encounter of the Old World and the New*

Required reading: Course Reader, Week Eleven.

I. From Europe to the valley of Mexico
   The decline of the Mediterranean, the rise of an Atlantic civilization, the impact of America on European culture, gold and silver; sugar, slavery and capitalism
II. The encounter in the valley of Mexico
   Cortés and Moctezuma, "unnatural cruelty," the conquest of women (representation and power)
III. A new order in Europe: Charles V and the rise of Imperial Spain
IV. Summation

# CONTRIBUTORS

Carmela Vircillo Franklin (Ph.D., Classics, Harvard University, 1977), Associate Professor of Classics, Columbia University.

Albrecht Classen ( (Ph.D., University of Virginia, 1986), Professor of German Studies, University of Arizona.

Jennifer R. Goodman (Ph.D., English, Harvard University, 1981), Professor of English, Texas A & M University.

Richard F. Gyug (Ph.D., Center for Medieval Studies, University of Toronto, 1984), Associate Professor of History, Fordham University

Linda G. Jones (Ph.D, University of California at Santa Barbara, 2003), Deputy Director of the Barcelona (Spain) Study Center of the University of California Education Abroad Program.

Kathryn L. Lynch (M.A., Ph.D., University of Virginia, 1978, 1982), Katherine Lee Bates and Sophie Chantal Hart Professor of English, Department of English, Wellesley College.

Louise Marlow (Ph.D., Near Eastern Studies, Princeton University, 1987), Department of Religion, Wellesley College.

Sally McKee (Ph.D., Centre for Medieval Studies, University of Toronto, 1992), Associate Professor of History, University of California at Davis

Teofilo F. Ruiz (Ph.D., Princeton University, 1974), Professor of History, University of California at Los Angeles.

James D. Ryan (Ph.D., History, New York University, 1972), Resident Professor, Department of History, Bronx Community College, City University of New York.

Alan M. Stahl (Ph.D., University of Pennsylvania, 1977), Director, Michael of Rhodes Project, Dibner Institute for the History of Science and Technology at M.I.T.

Evelyn Birge Vitz (Ph.D., Yale University, 1968), Professor of French, New York University.

# Index

'Abbasid Caliphate, 120
'Abd al-Wahhāb al-Sha'rani, Sufi mystic, autobiographical writing,107, 131
Abu Hamid al-Ghazali, autobiographical writing, 107, 109-110, 112, 120-122, 130, 132; and Sufism, 121, 132; at the Nizamiyya Institute, 120, 122;
*Iḥyā' 'ulūm al-dīn* (*The Revival of the Religious Sciences*), 120
Abu-Lughod, Janet, 251
Acre, fall of, 87, 88
Afonso II, King of Portugal, 22
Ahmad ibn 'Ajiba, Moroccan Sufi, autobiographical writing, 107, 110, 112, 126-130, 132, 133
Alfonso X, *Cantigas de Santa María*, 254; *Siete Partidas*, 177
Almalyq, 30, 32, 33; bishopric, 29, 34; Carlino of *Grassis*, bishop, 29; Richard of Burgundy, Franciscan bishop, 32
Ambrose, 7, 10; *De paradiso*, 8, 9
Andreas Capellanus, *The Art of Courtly Love*, 237
Anglo-Norman, see language *and* literature
Athanasius, *Life of St. Anthony*, 110
Augustine of Hippo, 7, 10, 11, 14, 107, 109, 115, 121, 130, 131, 133; *Confessions*, 108, 110, 112-114; *Contra Faustum*, 14, 15; *De ciuitate Dei*, 11, 13; *De Genesi contra Manichaeos*, 8, 9
authority of a book, 206, 207
autobiographical writings, *see* 'Abd al-Wahhāb al-Sha'rani, Abu Hamid al-Ghazali, Ahmad ibn 'Ajiba, Augustine of Hippo, Galen, Guibert of Nogent, Ibn al-'Arabi, Ibn Sina, James I of Aragon, pseudo-Aristotle, al-Razi, Samau'al al-Maghribi, Saul/Paul, al-Suyuti
Aztec accounts of the conquest of Mexico, 257

Bartlett, Robert (*The Making of Europe*), 253
Bede, 3, 5, 6, 7, 10-12, 13-16; *Libri quatuor in principium Genesis*, 7, 11, 13, 15
Benedict Biscop, abbot of Wearmouth-Jarrow, 5
Benediktbeuern *Ludus de nativitate*, 166, 167, 169, 171
*Beowulf,* 218, 220, 236
Berard of Carbio, Franciscan preacher in Iberia, 22, 23;
Bernard of Clairvaux, 165
Béroul, jongleur, 206, 207
Bertrandon de la Brocquière, European traveler, 97
Bhabha, Homi ("DissemiNation"), 238
Bible, 3; apocrypha (James, Nicodemus, pseudo-Matthew), 61; Canticle of Habbaccuc, 6, 7; Codex Amiatinus, 4-6, 14; Codex Grandior, 3-5; Hebrew, 3, 5, 9, 14, 15; Hexaemeron, 8; pandect, 3-6; Pentateuch, 3; Septuagint, 3, 5, 9, 15; Vetus latina, 3-5, 7-15; Vulgate, 4, 5, 7-16
biblical exegesis, 6-15; of Gregory and Cassian, 7
al-Biruni, Middle Eastern traveler, 229
Black Death: status of women in

Dubrovnik after, 75; economic decline after, 144
Boccaccio, Giovanni, 85, 220, 230, 239, 260
*Book of the Wonders of India*, 220, 240
Bosnians, 76; queen of, 72, 73, 75
Buondelmonti, Cristoforo, 44, 45; *Descriptio insulae Cretae*, 44-49, 54; drawings of Constantinople, 45
Burzôê, autobibliographical writing, 108

Caesarius of Heisterbach, *Dialogus Miraculorum*, 174
Cassiodorus, 3-5; *Institutiones*, 4, 5
Ceolfrith, abbot of Wearmouth-Jarrow, 3-6
Chaghatai Khanate, Mongol state in Central Asia, 19, 20, 27, 29, 30, 31, 35; Ali Sultan, khan, 33; Bukhara, trading center, 30, 31; Buzan khan, 31; Cangshi khan, 31-33; Chaghatai khan, 30, 31; confederation of Turks, Uighurs, Qara-Khitais and Persians, 30; Du'a khan, 31; Eljigidai khan, 31; Mongholistan, eastern Chaghatai, 34; Tarmashirin khan ('Ala al-Din), 31; Tashkent, trading center, 30; *see* Almalyq, Samarqand, Urgench
*chansons de geste*, 89, 93, 196, 197, 201, 206
Chaucer, Geoffrey (*The Canterbury Tales*), 214, 215, 218, 220, 221, 230, 237, 238, 240, 257; orientalism of, 215; place of Islam in, 215
China (Cathay), 20, 26-29, 31; Franciscan convents, 29; Khan-baliq, 27; Yüan dynasty, 30, 34
Chingiz Khan, 29, 30; *yasa* (Chingiz' law), 30
Chrétien de Troyes, 192, 203, 206; *Erec et Enide*, 200, 201; *Yvain*, 203
chronicles, *see* historians and histories

church councils: Lateran IV, 176, 177; Lyons I, 25; Lyons II, 26; Orléans III, 176; Whitby, 5
church rites: eastern, 42; Glagolitic, 76; Greek and Latin, 44; Easter vigil Mass, adult baptisms, 175
colonial society, 43; and regimes, 44, 48, 49; colonialism, 218
conversion of the Jews, as an apocalyptic sign, 173; *see "Jeu d'Adam"*
conversion narratives, Christian and Muslim, 105-134; 'Abdallah b. Salam, 109; Anselmo Turmeda, 109; Clovis, 111; Constantine's conversion, 110; differences, 105, 107, 130, 132, 133; independent origins, 106, 108; similarities, 129, 131; *see* dreams and visions
Cortés, Hernán, Third Letter from Mexico to Charles V, 257
course titles: "Arthurian Legends," 222; "Crisis and Renewal: From Late Medieval to Early Modern," 257-271; "Images of the Other in the European and Islamic Middle Ages," 213, 232-246; "Orientalism in Medieval Literature," 216
court clerks, *see* minstrels and clerks
courts, royal or noble, 22, 25, 32, 34, 92-94, 97, 182, 189-192, 198, 200, 201, 205-207; court culture, 237; courtliness (*cortoisie*), 202; courtly love, 89, 90
Crete (Venetian), 39-47, 49, 50, 52, 56; Calergi family, 49-51; Candia, 45, 51; captured by the Ottoman Turks, 41; feudatories, 42; free Latins, 44; Greek peasantry, 49-52; Greek-Cretan nobility, 42, 48, 49, 51, 52; intermarriage, 50, 51; Latin-Cretans, 48; Latin-Greek hostility, 39, 40; Rethimno (district), 39; revolts of Greek-Cretans, 39, 49;

Sifi Gavala and Rovithi, outlawed Greek-Cretan rebels, 39, 40, 50; Tadeo Giustiniani, Venetian representative, 39, 50; Venetian government, 42, 48

Crichton, Michael (*Eaters of the Dead*), 236, 237

crusades, 21, 87-89, 218, 240; Arabic views of, 227, 239; Christian militancy, 20, 21; crusader attitudes, 20, 85, 86; crusader poems, 232; First, 20, 238; Fourth, 41; Fifth, 22; crusade epics, *see* Johann von Würzburg, *Reinfried von Braunschweig*, Ulrich von dem Türlin, Wolfram von Eschenbach

curriculum, 231; at Wellesley College, 213, 216, 217; globalizing, 217, 223, 225; liberal arts, 226; multicultural, 230

Dante Alighieri, 249, 257
Datini archives, 147
demographic and economic depression of the early Renaissance, 144
*Deux Bourdeurs Ribauds*, 197-199
Dominicans, *see* mendicant orders
dreams and visions, 105-134; dream commentaries by Vincent of Beauvais and Albertus Magnus, 109; hadith on, 111; and liminal experiences, 112, 116, 125, 131; Muslim interpreters of dreams ('Abd al-Ghani al-Nabulsi, Abu Sa'id al-Wa'iz, al-Dinawari, Ibn Abi Dunya, Ibn Shahin, Ibn Sirin, Ja'far al-Sadiq), 118; oneiromancy, 118; of the Prophet Muhammad, 111, 117; Sufi traditions, 119

Dubrovnik (Ragusa), 59, 62-69, 74-76; Dominicus, archbishop, 63; Ludovicus Beccatelli, archbishop, 68; cathedral, 62, 67; church of S. Maria de Castello, 65; church of S. Vitus, 63, 67-69; convent of S. Maria, 64; cult of Blaise, 60; earthquake of 1667, 64; monastery of S. Simeon, 60, 63-65, 67, 70-73, 75-77, 79, 80; monastery of SS. Simeon and Jude, 71; patriciate, 59, 60, 74-76, 80; role of the city in religious matters, 78; role of women, 74, 75, 80; Senate, 73, 79; Vitalis, archbishop, 70, 78, 79; *see* historians and histories *for Annales ragusini anonymi*, Junius Restić, Miletius, Nicolò di Ragnina, and Philippus de Diversis

east/west relations: between Europe and the Islamic world, 87, 213, 227; Christian relations toward religions of conquered lands, 21; cultural contacts, 221; in Geoffrey of Monmouth, 222; Islamic prohibitions against Christian evangelization, 20; Muslim tolerance, 97; *see* crusades *and* European attitudes

Elizabeth Kotromanić, queen of Hungary, 62
Ethiopia, Christian community, 28
ethnic identity, 40-44, 49-55; official, 43; popular, 43; *see* otherness
European attitudes, 98; changes after the fall of Acre, 87; exoticisation, 227; fascination with the foreign world, 99; indifference toward religion, 96, 97; intolerance, 85, 86; tolerance, 85-87, 89, 90-97, 99; toward non-Christians in conquered lands, 21; toward outsiders, 85, 93; toward skin color, 86; *see* otherness

al-Farabi, Arabic philosopher, 109
*Flamenca*, Occitan romance, 203-206
Florence, 142, 143; gold florin, 142
*Fortunatus*, German chapbook, 97-99

Francis of Assisi, 22, 23; preaching in Egypt, 22; Franciscans, *see* mendicant orders
French, *see* language *and* literature
Froissart, Jean, *The Chronicles*, 260

Galen, autobiographical and autobibliographical writing, 108, 109
Genoa, 140, 142, 143; Genoese, 41
Geoffrey of Monmouth, east/west distinctions in story of Britain's foundation, 222
Georgius de Croxis, bishop of Trebinje and Makaraska, 64
German, *see* literature
Germanic expansion against Bohemians and Slavs, 21
al-Ghazali, *see* Abu Hamid al-Ghazali
Great Bullion Famine, 143-145
Gregory of Tours, *History of the Franks*, 54
Guibert of Nogent, autobiographial writing, 107, 110-112, 114-116, 130, 132-134; spiritual anxieties, 116; tales of the devil tormenting sinners, 116; temptations, 115

al-Hamadhani, *Maqamat*, 236
al-Hariri, *Assemblies*, 236
Hermann of Cologne, anti-Jewish polemic,123
*Herzog Ernst*, goliardic epic, 86, 87, 94, 96, 97, 99; late medieval popularity, 95
*histoire des mentalités*, 247
historians and histories: *Annales ragusini anonymi*, 65-72, 74-76, 78; Bartholomew of Pisa, 33; Chronicle of the 24 Generals, 33; *Illyrici sacri* (Farlati and Coleti), 65, 66, 68, 70, 71, 73, 74, 76, 77, 79; Junius Restić, 66, 68, 70, 73, 74, 76, 78, 79; Miletius, 62; Morosini, 150; Nicolò di Ragnina, 64, 66-70, 72, 74-76, 78; Nicolò Trevisan, 149; Philippus de Diversis, 70, 73; Ragusan chroniclers, 76-78; Ughelli, 79; Whiggish history, 248, 249
Hollister, Warren, 247, 248

Ibn 'Ajiba, *see* Ahmad ibn 'Ajiba
Ibn al-'Arabi, *al-Futūḥāt al-makkiyya* (spiritual autobiography), 120, 131
Ibn Battuta, Middle Eastern traveler, 219, 229, 236
Ibn Fadlan, Middle Eastern traveler, 227, 236
Ibn Hazm, *The Ring of the Dove*, 214, 237, 239, 240
Ibn Ishaq, *The Life of Muhammad*, 109, 118, 128
Ibn al-Marzuban, 219
Ibn Sina (Avicenna), autobiographical writing, 108, 109
Ilkhanate, Mongol dynasty in Persia, 25-28, 30; Abaqa, ilkhan, 26; Abu Sa'id, ilkhan, 28; Arghun, ilkhan, 26, 28; Ghazan, ilkhan, 28; Hülegü, founder and ilkhan, 25, 26; Öljeitü, ilkhan, 28; *see* Sultaniyya
India, 20, 28; Christian communities, 28; *see* Quilon
Ishaq (Isaac) ibn 'Imran, Arabic philosopher, 109
Isidore of Seville, commentary on Genesis, 7
Islam, 20, 22, 28, 30-32; Qur'an, 20, 31, 219; Saracens, 23; *shari'a*, 20, 30; Isma'ili Shi'ism, 121; *see* Sufi mystics

James I of Aragon, 176; *Llibre dels Feys (Book of Deeds)*, 109
Jerome, 5, 7, 11; *Hebraicae quaestiones in libro Geneseos*, 11, 13, 14
Jerusalem, 26, 61-63, 65, 67, 69, 70

*Jeu d'Adam*, Anglo-Norman play, 161-184; character *quidam de sinagoga*, 161, 165-171, 173-175, 177-180, 183; intended for conversion of the Jews, 162, 163, 174-176, 181, 183, 184; Jewish themes in Adam and Cain scenes, 163-165; linking Jew and Christian, 179; meaning for Christian audience, 179, 181; multiple audiences, 183; Procession of Prophets, 163, 165, 166

Jewish-Christian relations: Christian appropriation of Hebrew Scripture, 180; Christian Holy Week prohibitions, 176; disputation literature of the mid-twelfth century (Judah ha-Levi, Peter the Venerable, Peter Abelard), 176; Hermann of Cologne, anti-Jewish polemic, 123; Jewish reaction to Ascension procession, 168; proximity of Jewish and Christian communities in England and France, 177, 178; Rigord's criticism of social contacts, 177; theme of *sinagoga*, 166; see "*Jeu d'Adam*"

Joachim of Fiore, 24

Johann von Würzburg, *Wilhelm von Österreich*, 95

John the Archcantor, 5

John Mandeville, 214, 229, 235, 236

John of Marignolli, papal envoy to the Mongol empire, 34

John of Montecorvino, papal envoy to the Mongol empire, 26; archbishop of Khan-baliq, 27, 31, 34

John of Plano Carpini, O.F.M., papal ambassador to Mongol empire, 25

Jordan Catalan, *Mirabilia descripta*, 28; bishop of Quilon, 28

Jordan, William C., 252

Joseph Kimhi, *Book of the Covenant*, 163, 179

Juvayni, *A History of the World Conqueror*, 236

Khan-baliq, 31; archbishopric, 32; John of Montecorvino, archbishop, 27, 31, 34; Nicholas, archbishop, 31, 32; see Mongol empire

language, 51, 121; Anglo-Norman, 181; Arabic, 119, 125; English, 181; French, 181, 182; Greek, 42, 46; Latin, 46; linking Jew and Christian, 182; Occitan, 199, 203; Old Ragusan, 76; Romance and Slavic bilingualism, 60; Slavic, 76

Le Goff, Jacques, 248

literature: Anglo-Norman, 161-184; Arthurian, 87; different genres in east and west, 219; exordia topos, 99; French, 89, 182, 189-208; German, 85-100; Persian, 239; Saracen Princess topos, 89, 90, 94, 96

*Ludus de Antichristo*, 166, 169, 173

Maimonides, Moses (Moses ben Rabbi Maimon), 85; *Responsa*, 167

Mamluks, 25, 26, 28

Marco Polo, 26, 86, 214, 219, 229, 235, 236

Marvazi, Middle Eastern traveler, 229

*Meditations on the Life of Christ*, 61

Mellinkoff, Ruth (*The Mark of Cain*), 165

mendicant orders, 22, 29; convents in Qipchaq, Georgia, Greater Armenia, Persia, Mesopotamia, and China, 29; Dominicans, 20-22, 24-26, 31; Dominican *Societas peregrinantium*, 28; Francis of Alexandria, missionary at Almalyq, 33; Franciscans, 20-25, 27, 32, 34; Pascal of Victoria, Franciscan missionary; 32, 33; proselytizing, 176;

see Francis of Assisi
Middle Eastern studies, 223-226; Oriental Studies, 224
millenarian expectations, 21
minstrels, 190; repertory, 191; role in development of romance, 189-208
minstrels and clerks, 189; as story-tellers, 192; at court, 189; clerks as "resident intellectuals," 190; education of clerks, 190; interaction between, 191, 192, 206, 207; patrons and patronage of, 190-192, 202; role in development of romance, 189-208; role in performance, 193; similar interests and ambitions, 189
missions and evangelization, Christian, 19-27, 29-35, 218; subordinated to military or secular interests, 21; see mendicant orders and Almalyq, Khanbaliq, Quilon, Samarqand, Sultaniyya, Urgench (missionary bishoprics)
Mongholistan, see Chaghatai Khanate
Mongol empire, 21, 25, 27, 28, 30, 31, 34, 218; battle of Ayn Jalut, 25; court, 236; Güyük, khan, 25; Öngut Körguz, conversion to Christianity, 87; Qubilai (Kubilai), the Great Khan, 26, 235, 236; Timür Öljeitü, successor to Qubilai, 26; see also Chaghatai Khanate, China, Chingiz Khan, Ilkhanate, Qipchaq
multiculturalism, 87, 213, 231; in the curriculum, 230, 254; in medieval Spain, 254
Nasir al-Din Tusi, *The Nasirean Ethics*, 219
national identity and nationalism, 218; debates about, 52-55; generalists vs localists, 54; modernists vs perennialists, 53
Nestorians, in Chaghatai Khanate, 30
Nirenberg, David (*Communities of Violence*), 252
Nizami, *Haft paykar*, 230, 239

orientalism, 215, 232, 235, 238
otherness, the "other," 227, 230, 232, 237, 239; see ethnic identity and European attitudes

*Pearl*-poet, 220
Pegolotti, *Description of Countries*, 32
Persia, 20, 25, 27-30; Franciscan convent in, 29
Peter the Chanter, 172, 193, 194
Peter the Venerable, 239; *Adversus iudeorum inveteratam duritiem*, 163, 165, 176, 180; letter to Louis VII, 164
Peters, Edward (*Europe in the Middle Ages*), 253
Petrarch, 48, 49
Petrus Alfonsi, *Disciplina clericalis*, 214
Pierre de Saint-Cloud, *Roman de Renart*, 194, 195
Pirenne, Henri, 251
*Poem of the Cid*, 214, 238, 240
popes and papacy, 21-23, 25, 27; Benedict XII (*Laeti rumores Deo*), 32; Clement V, 27, 32; Gregory the Great, 6, 7; Gregory IX (*Cum hora undecima*), 23, 24; Gregory X, 26; Innocent IV, 23, 25; John XXII (*Redemptor noster*), 28, 31; Leo X, 64; Nicholas IV (*Gaudemus in domino*), 24, 26, 28
Presentation in the Temple, 60, 61, 64
Prester John, 99
Priest Conrad, *Rolandslied*, 89
pseudo-Aristotle, autobiographical and autobibliographical writing, 108, 109
pseudo-Augustine, *Contra Judaeos, paganos et Arianos, Sermo de symbolo*, 162, 168

# INDEX

Qipchaq, the Khanate of the Golden Horde, 26, 28; Franciscan convent in, 29; Möngke-Temür, khan, 26; Sarai, 32
Quilon (India), bishopric, 28

Ragusa, *see* Dubrovnik
Raimon Vidal, *Abril issi'e*, 199
Raoul de Houdenc, *Roman des eles*, 202
al-Razi, autobiographical writing, 108
*Reinfried von Braunschweig*, crusade epic, 88, 90, 95
relics: *panniculus* of Christ, 60, 64-71, 73-76, 78; S. Blaise, 79
Renaut de Beaujeu, *Le bel inconnu*, 201
*Roman de Renart*, 194-196, 199
romance, romances, 189-208, 214; birth of, 192; clerks as authors, 192; court phenomenon, 192, 199; *conteurs*, 201; of Charlemagne, 239; perceived as books, 193; performance of, 193-200, 203, 205; reputation of the Middle East and Africa in, 214; *see* minstrels *and* minstrels and clerks
Rome, *romanitas*, 3-5, 19

Said, Edward (*Orientalism*), 216, 218, 224, 225, 229, 230, 235
St. Victor, abbey of, 163
Samarqand, 30, 31; bishopric, 29, 31; Thomas Mancasola, Dominican bishop, 31
Samau'al al-Maghribi, autobiographical writing, 107-110, 112, 122, 124, 130-133; anti-Jewish polemic, 123; *Ifhām al-Yahūd*, 122, 123
Saul/Paul, autobiographical writing, 111
Shakespeare, 232; *Othello*, 214, 219, 232; *Antony and Cleopatra*, 238
al-Sharif al-Idrisi, Middle Eastern traveler, 229, 236
Silk Route, 29, 30

Simeon the Prophet, 70, 72, 74; cult in Aachen, Dubrovnik, Saint-Denis, Venice and Zadar, 61-63
*Song of Roland*, 214, 219, 238-240
sources, notarial, 43, 49-51; official and literary, 42, 43, 54; wills, 43, 44
Spivak, Gayatri (*In Other Worlds*), 238
Sufi mystics, 107, 121, 124, 133; dreams and visions, 119; Sidi Talha, 127, 128; spiritual progression, 111; *see* 'Abd al-Wahhāb al-Sha'rani, Abu Hamid al-Ghazali, Ahmad ibn 'Ajiba
*Sultan of Babylon* (Charlemagne romance), 239
Sultaniyya, archbishopric, 27, 28, 32; Franco of Perugia, archbishop, 28
al-Suyuti, autobiographical writing, 110

teaching, 213-271; integrating research, 249; Islamic literature, need for more background, 230; master political narrative of elites, 249; multiculturalism, 254; multi-perspectival approach, 257; restrictive concepts of center and periphery, 247, 250, 252, 253; sample syllabuses, 232-246, 257-271; textbooks and source books, 248, 250, 253, 254; world systems, 251; *see* course titles *and* curriculum
team-teaching, 213-231; difficulties, 219, 220, 227, 228, 230; European perspective, 215; European and Islamic Middle Ages, 226; genre questions, 229; interdisciplinarity, 213, 219, 221, 230; Islamic perspective, 227, 228; literary treatments of otherness, 227
Thomas Mancasola, Dominican envoy to Chaghatai Khanate, 31
*Thousand and One Nights* (*Arabian Nights*), 214, 215, 220, 230, 239, 240
Tomaso Mocenigo, doge, deathbed ora-

tion, 143-145, 152
travel literature, European and Middle Eastern, 229, 232; al-Biruni, 229; Ibn Battuta, 219, 229, 236; John Mandeville, 214, 229, 235, 236; Marco Polo, 26, 86, 214, 219, 229, 235, 235; Marvazi, 229; al-Sharif al-Idrisi, 229, 236
Turner, Victor, 112

Ulrich von dem Türlin, *Willehalm*, 89, 90, 91, 92, 93, 94; work dedicated to Ottokar II, 90
Urgench, 32; bishopric, 29
Usamah Ibn-Munqidh, account of the Crusade, 221, 239, 240

Venice, 48, 59, 61, 68, 140-144, 150, 152; commerce, 139, 144, 147, 150, 151; convoys to Alexandria, Beirut and the Black Sea, 145-150; export of Levantine luxuries to Tuscany and Lombardy, 145; Genoese War (1351-1355), 146; gold ducat, 140, 141, 143; imperial embargo against, 151; mint, 139, 140-142, 144, 145; reorganization of the mint, 139, 141, 142; shortage of gold and silver, 151; shortage of gold bullion, 141; silver coinage, 139-141, 143; War of Chioggia, 140, 146, 149
Vivarium, 3, 4

Wearmouth-Jarrow, monastery, 3-7
William of Adam, O.P., *De modo Saracenos extirpandi*, 28
William of Rubruck, Franciscan missionary, 25, 235
Wolfram von Eschenbach, 86, 87, 89, 90, 94; *Parzival*, 86, 88; *Willehalm*, 86, 88, 92, 93
Yüan dynasty, *see* China
Zadar, 62, 76; monastery of S. Maria, 62

www.ingramcontent.com/pod-product-compliance
Lightning Source LLC
Chambersburg PA
CBHW051420290426
44109CB00016B/1372